LITURGY, PRAYER AND SPIRITUALITY

KEVIN W. IRWIN

PAULIST PRESS
New York/Ramsey

ACKNOWLEDGMENTS

Excerpts from *Documents of Vatican II* reprinted with permission of America Press. © 1966. Quotations of the *Didache* and the *Apology of Justin* are from the translation of Lucien Deiss, *Springtime of the Liturgy*, translated by Matthew O'Connell, published by The Liturgical Press, copyrighted by The Order of St. Benedict, Inc., Collegeville, Minnesota. Excerpts from *Music in Catholic Worship* (Revised Edition) copyright 1983 United States Catholic Conference, *Liturgical Music Today* copyright 1982 United States Catholic Conference, and *Environment and Art in Catholic Worship* copyright 1978 United States Catholic Conference are used with permission of the copyright owner. All rights reserved. Scripture texts from the *New American Bible*, copyright © 1970, by the Confraternity of Christian Doctrine, Washington, D.C., are used by permission of copyright owner. All rights reserved. English translation of the Canticle of Zechariah and Canticle of Simeon used by permission of the International Consultation on English Texts. Excerpts from "Little Gidding" in *Four Quartets* by T. S. Eliot are reprinted by permission of Harcourt Brace Jovanovich, Inc.; copyright 1943 by T. S. Eliot, renewed 1971 by Esme Valerie Eliot, and by permission of Faber and Faber, London. Excerpts from the English translation of *Roman Calendar* © 1970, International Committee on English in the Liturgy, Inc. (ICEL); excerpts from the English translation of *Rite of Funerals* © 1970, ICEL; excerpts from the English translation of *The Roman Missal* © 1973, ICEL; excerpts from the English translation of *The Liturgy of the Hours* © 1974, ICEL; excerpts from the English translation of *Rite of Christian Initiation of Adults* © 1974, 1978, ICEL; excerpts from the English translation of *Rite of Penance* © 1974, ICEL; excerpts from the English translation of *Ordination of Deacons, Priests, and Bishops* © 1975, ICEL; excerpts from the English translation of *Institution of Readers and Acolytes; Admission to Candidacy for Ordination as Deacons and Priests*, © 1976, ICEL; excerpts from the English translation of the "Introduction" from the *Lectionary for Mass* (second *editio typica*), © 1981, ICEL; excerpts from the English translation of *Pastoral Care of the Sick: Rites of Anointing and Viaticum* © 1982, ICEL; excerpts from the English translation of *Documents on the Liturgy, 1963–1979: Conciliar, Papal, and Curial Texts* © 1982, ICEL. All rights reserved. Excerpts from *The Psalms: A New Translation* used by permission of Paulist Press and The Grail, England. Excerpts from " 'Thanksgiving for the Light': Toward A Theology of Vespers," *Diakona* 13 (1978). Used by the permission of the publisher.

CONTENTS

INTRODUCTION   1

I. RELATING LITURGY, PRAYER AND SPIRITUALITY

Chapter One
LITURGICAL PRAYER AND
LITURGICAL SPIRITUALITY   7

Chapter Two
LITURGY: COMMUNAL RESPONSE TO GOD   25

Chapter Three
HUMAN LIFE AND CHRISTIAN WORSHIP   42

II. ELEMENTS OF LITURGICAL PRAYER

Chapter Four
CORPORATE WORK DONE IN FAITH   65

Chapter Five
PROCLAMATION OF THE WORD OF GOD   99

Chapter Six
PARTICIPATION IN MEMORY AND HOPE   127

Chapter Seven
A PATTERNED EXPERIENCE OF PRAYER   159

Chapter Eight
LITURGICAL TIME: FEASTS AND SEASONS   186

Chapter Nine
TRINITARIAN PRAYER   222

III. IMPLICATIONS FOR LITURGICAL SPIRITUALITY

Chapter Ten
LITURGY: AN EXPERIENCE OF PRAYER   249

Chapter Eleven
LITURGY AND THE LIFE OF FAITH   277

Chapter Twelve
LITURGY AND MISSION   302

BIBLIOGRAPHY   329

INTRODUCTION

The purpose of this work is to aid Roman Catholics in discovering the richness inherent in celebrating the Church's liturgy. This work aims to help all involved in worship to appreciate the elements that comprise the common prayer called *liturgy* and to explore the implications which celebrating liturgy has for living the Christian life.

Part One of the book focuses on the important distinctions which should be kept in mind concerning liturgy, prayer and spirituality. Clearly, liturgy is not correlative with one's spiritual life, but at the same time it has always been cherished as an essential part of Christian prayer and spirituality. Liturgy as a response to God who always searches for us is established and the relationship between human life and Christian liturgy is described. Liturgy is not so much a separation from the world in which we live as it is the place where our lives of faith receive focus and shape. Liturgy helps us discover how God manifests and discloses his ever mysterious presence to us in all of life.

Part Two of the book delineates what are the "elements" of the liturgy that are found in all sacramental and liturgical celebrations. The fact that liturgy is essentially communitarian is used as a foundation for understanding the importance of the proclamation of the word of God at liturgy (especially in the present reform). That the liturgy offers and provides us with a share in the very life of God through Christ's paschal mystery forms a pivotal chapter for *participation* is at the heart of the uniqueness of liturgical prayer. That the liturgy involves a patterned experience of prayer, that it occurs in a rhythm of a yearly cycle we call "feasts and seasons," and involves calling on God as three persons with a variety of names, images and likenesses is discussed as essential components of liturgical prayer.

Part Three deals with the implications which liturgy has for contemporary spirituality. Certainly in the present reform the quality of liturgical celebration is important in order to express and celebrate well the mysteries inherent in it. This is treated along with some suggestions about planning and celebrating. That the liturgy relates to our whole lives is reiterated in the section on liturgy and the life of faith. How liturgy relates to and can enliven personal prayer is noted, along with a review of how the present rites of the Church bring out this life relation very clearly. That the liturgy leads beyond the act of worship to a spirituality that necessarily involves mission is explored in the concluding chapter.

Throughout, reference is made to the texts and rites of the contemporary Catholic liturgy to disclose the richness that is inherent in the revised liturgy but which is sometimes ignored or untapped. It is hoped that this work will help all who celebrate liturgy to come to a deeper appreciation of what is involved in liturgy—the experience of the Church at prayer.

Much of this work grew out of lectures delivered at Fordham University from 1980–82 in a course entitled "Liturgical Spirituality" in the Graduate School of Religion and Religious Education. I am indebted to many students for questions, observations and criticisms that made me rethink ideas which (hopefully) are presented here with more nuance and precision. Part of this work was developed into a position paper on the relationship between liturgy and spirituality for a working group of the North American Academy of Liturgy. I am especially grateful to those colleagues whose careful and insightful comments and suggestions made at the 1982 meeting of the Academy have been incorporated into the completed work. In addition, I wish to acknowledge the fruitful interchange on this same topic in which I was involved in May 1982 at a symposium sponsored by the Office of Divine Worship, Archdiocese of Chicago. I owe special thanks to Rev. Daniel Coughlin for inviting me to present a position paper for this gathering and to the participants for their observations on the importance of this topic for the progress of the liturgical renewal in our day.

On a more pastoral level I want to acknowledge those who asked me to present lectures on liturgy, prayer and spirituality in renewal programs for religious and clergy. In particular I wish to acknowledge the English-speaking tertian programs of the Congregation of Christian Brothers and the Ursuline Sisters of the Roman Union, held annually in Rome. While teaching at Fordham I have also been involved in pastoral work in the archdiocese of New York. Among the various groups which have influenced my thoughts on the important place that liturgy has for our spiritual lives are the parishioners of Immaculate Heart of Mary Church, Scarsdale, N.Y., where I have been in residence. I am most grateful to them for keeping me honest, not to say very realistic about the possibilities of celebrating liturgy in a varied and active congregation.

Finally, a word about the community to whom I dedicate this book. From an initial visit to St. Anselm's Abbey in June 1981 to the present this community has impressed me with the simplicity and sincerity with which it celebrates the sacred mysteries and lives the Christian life. The first chapters of this book were written while visiting there, and the final editing is being completed during my present visit to the monastery. I am deeply indebted to these men for their unassuming yet poignant reminder that this life is all about "the search for God."

> The concern must be whether the novice truly seeks God and whether he shows eagerness for the Work of God, for obedience and for trials. The novice should be clearly told all the hardships and difficulties that will lead him to God. (*Rule of St. Benedict*, chap. 58)

May the words written in this book help the monk in all of us to continue that search, and may they be an offering to this particular monastic community that has enriched and challenged my perception of what it means to search for God, and has reminded me again and again that in the end that is all that really matters. As I write these final words from St. Anselm's I cannot help but think that the date and feast we celebrate today is truly providential.

Conversion of St. Paul
January 25, 1983

Part One:

RELATING LITURGY, PRAYER AND SPIRITUALITY

Chapter One
LITURGICAL PRAYER
AND LITURGICAL SPIRITUALITY

In order to clarify the relationship between liturgy and spirituality it is important to establish some understanding of both "spirituality" and "liturgy." This involves stepping back from the experience to determine the foundation of all activities that constitute the life of a Christian, especially those actions that may be termed "spiritual" or liturgical." This foundation is faith. Our first concern is to explore what we mean by faith, how spirituality reflects the lived faith of the Christian, and the place liturgy holds in Christian spirituality. These initial considerations lead to exploring what is meant by liturgical spirituality and how the liturgy relates to other forms of prayer.

FAITH

It is axiomatic in liturgical and sacramental theology to assert that sacraments are sacraments of faith and that without faith there can be no sacrament.[1] Hence, faith becomes the most appropriate starting point for any consideration of liturgy and sacrament. In the Judaeo-Christian tradition, revelation enjoys a most privileged position in that it reveals and recounts the history of God's dealings with his chosen people (both Israel and the "new Israel," the people of Christ) and their journey to him. The starting point for initiating and solidifying the relationship between God and his chosen ones is his call and their response. The story of God's call to Abraham and Abraham's ready response stands as a significant paradigm in both the Old and New Testaments for the kinds of confident dependence on

God which should mark the lives of those who profess to be believers.

For Abraham, life was lived on God's terms and perseverance in faith led to the fulfillment of God's promises—"descendants as countless as the stars of the sky and the sands of the seashore; your descendants shall take possession of the gates of their enemies, and in your descendants all the nations of the earth shall find blessing—all this because you obeyed my command" (Gen 22:17-18). For Abraham, everything depended on faith, a confident dependence and trust in God. Everything Abraham received was given by God—but the condition was that he trust in God's revelation and promise to him. Abraham lived in faith, a faith that led to a relationship of grateful acceptance of what God had in store for him and his descendants. Any notions of self-justification or earning God's favor by the mere observance of the law would now cede to priority and pride of place given to trusting in God's promises. Gifts from God were precisely that, gifts freely given because of the attitude and obedience of Abraham. For us, the issues are the same. When everything depends on faith, then everything is understood as a grace from God (Rom 4:16). The response of an individual or a community involved in such a relationship with God is humble acceptance, grateful praise, and heartfelt thanks—the attitudes which mark the prayer of the Christian at worship.

It is no wonder that Abraham stands at the head of Israel's forefathers as an important model of enduring trust in God, a God who is named in the Old Testament the God of "Abraham, Isaac and Jacob." Abraham's importance extends to the New Testament where St. Paul maintains that what justified Abraham was not his observance of the law, as important as the law was for an observant Jew. Rather, the promises made to Abraham and his descendants were made in view of the justice that comes from faith (Rom 4:13). Paul uses the example of Abraham as a model for later generations: "For our faith will be credited to us also if we believe in him who raised Jesus our Lord from the dead" (Rom 4:23). For Abraham, faith meant being confident that he would be "the father of many nations" (Rom 4:18; Gen 15:5-6) despite physical improbability due to his age and the barrenness of his wife Sarah. St. Paul emphasizes this when he states that "though it seemed Abraham's hope could not be fulfilled, he hoped and he believed" (Rom 4:18). And as if that were not enough of a test and trial, Abraham had to trust so firmly in God's word that he had to subject himself to an even more incredible test—he had to be willing to give up his son Isaac in sacrifice (Gen 22:1–19). For Abraham, obedience, dependence and trust were names for the faith God required of him; and each of these terms signified attitudes that were total and unqualified, or, in the poet's turn of phrase: "Quick now, here, now, always—A condition of complete simplicity/ (Costing nothing less than everything)."[2] At the Easter Vigil it is the story of Abraham's willing sacrifice of Isaac that is proclaimed as a "type" and model of obedience to the Father that also characterized Jesus' self-offering. Such obedient faith should also mark those baptized on this night and all the baptized whose very baptism is predicated on faith and trust in God. Abraham's single-minded and single-hearted dedication is also recalled in Christian worship when we pray: "Look with favor on these offerings and accept them as once you accepted the gifts of your servant Abel, the sacrifice of Abraham, our father in faith, and the bread and wine offered by your priest Melchisedech" (Roman Canon).

In the New Testament, Jesus' invitation to believe in him comes right after the mission-inaugurating event of his baptism in the Jordan by John the Baptist. Hopes, promises, and foreshadowings are summed up and completed now for the promised Messiah had indeed come: "This is the time of fulfillment. The reign of God is at hand! Reform your lives and believe in the good news" (Mk 1:15). The absolute condition for discipleship for Jesus' first followers was to follow him in faith. For all succeeding generations of the Church, this absolute condition remains—to believe in the Gospel and to trust in Jesus as Lord. For miracles to be worked, faith and trust in Jesus had to come first (Mk 5:21–43). After his resurrection and before his ascension Jesus commanded his disciples to baptize all nations and to teach them all he had taught (Mt 28:19), thus to spread his message and to continue his invitation to believe in him. In

the earliest Christian community the requirement for initiation
was "to reform and be baptized" (Acts 2:38) with the understanding that both required faith-filled acceptance of the Gospel
(Acts 2:41).

That the Christian life is patterned after the call by God and
the response in faith by his chosen people is concretized liturgically in our annual observance of Lent and Easter. The imposition of ashes at the beginning of Lent may be accompanied with
the formula "turn away from sin and be faithful to the Gospel,"
(referring to Mk 1:15) and one of the prayers used during the
liturgy of the word at the Easter Vigil (following the reading of
Exodus 14:15–15:1, the account of the Exodus) reads:

> Father,
> even today we see the wonders
> of the miracles you worked long ago.
> You once saved a single nation from slavery,
> and now you offer that salvation to all through baptism.
> May the peoples of the world become true sons of Abraham
> and prove worthy of the heritage of Israel.

The life of faith for the Christian is life lived in a gifted relationship with God based on his constant call, which call invites our
ever-deepening response. Like Abraham, our faith is the foundation of justification, not the works that we do. It is in *response*
to God's invitation to a relationship in faith and love that we
offer prayer, worship and our very lives in service. For Israel it
was God's constant fidelity (for example to Abraham and his
descendants) that motivated the psalmist's acclamation:

> O praise the Lord, all you nations,
>   acclaim him, all you peoples!
> Strong is his love for us;
>   he is faithful for ever.   (Ps 117)

It is on God's fidelity and invitation that we rely when we
profess our faith in him. And it is on God's fidelity that we rely
and to his invitation that we respond when we gather for the
prayer we call "liturgy."

THE JOURNEY OF FAITH

While the kind of faith exhibited by Abraham provides a model for the faith of believers of all generations, the very fact that it was unwavering and resolute can make such an attitude in life seem too ideal and unrealizable. Clearly, faith on our part is necessary for liturgy and sacraments to make sense. But it should be recalled that perfect faith of undoubted commitment to the Lord is not what is required. In fact, were we "perfect" and of "full stature in Christ" there would be no need for the strength, support, and challenge to faith which are all part of the experience of liturgy.

That doubts and wavering commitments plague us should not surprise us, especially when we reflect on other scriptural models and examples of faith. One such example that fits into the editorial plan of the evangelist Matthew concerns the lack of faith the disciples evidenced at the stilling of the storm (Mt 8:23–27). Here the disciples acknowledge who Jesus is by affirming that he is "Lord" ("Lord, save us! We are lost"—v. 25), and they beg him to protect them from the storm-tossed sea. Before calming the waters Jesus first rebukes them by saying "How little faith you have" (v. 26). The editorial point at issue here for Matthew is to instruct and to console contemporary congregations who experience doubts and fears in believing in Jesus. After all, if some of the disciples, the privileged eye-witnesses to Jesus' power and works, had to rely on their Lord for courage and support because their faith wavered and was weak, later generations should not be surprised when they experience similar doubts of faith.[3]

Other, more particular examples of doubts, even denials of faith, come from important New Testament figures. It was Peter, the "rock" of faith (Mt 16:18) who denied knowing the Lord (Mt 26:69–75); yet it was he who ultimately led the infant Church and converted many to profess faith in Jesus as Messiah (Acts 2:22). St. Paul, the most famous apostle and preacher to the Gentiles, first persecuted the community he later cherished (Gal 2:1–21). In her own way the Virgin Mary, the model of faith, received the angel's message that she was to bear the child Jesus with the question: "How can this be since I do not know man?" (Lk 1:34). After the resurrection it was a lack of faith that earned Thomas the nickname "doubting" for all posterity (Jn 20:24–25). But even (or especially) Thomas' example stands as most significant, for he who doubted gave up his unbelief and acknowledged the risen Jesus as Lord (Jn 20:28).

In some ways these models of faith function more clearly for us who seek to come to know the meaning of faith in our day. In fact, growth and development in faith are almost expected and required in the Christian life and in Christian liturgy. For this task Peter, Paul, Thomas and Mary function as consoling yet challenging examples of those who ultimately trusted and put their lives at the service of God.

Besides these examples from the New Testament about growth in faith, the liturgical life of the Church itself offers insight and support. By its very nature the liturgy is a repeated, ritual action. The covenant of baptism is renewed weekly at the Sunday Eucharist and the commitment we make in baptism is ratified each year at Easter with the rite of the renewal of baptismal promises. This liturgical example of the progressive side of living in faith reflects the common experience we all have that the Christian life involves a process of growing in the faith first professed at baptism and repeatedly confessed and acknowledged in the liturgy. The promises represented by baptism are not made once-for-all or all-at-once. They are made again and again in our hearts and at the Church's experience of common faith profession, the liturgy.

Faith for the Christian is life lived in relationship with God, a relationship granted us by his invitation and love. The foundation of this intimacy and relationship is the ever-constant call of God. We stand before him at liturgy as believers who want to grow in faith, the "faithful" who seek to deepen trust in him. In fact, the challenge to deepen faith is the challenge which prevents faith from becoming dry, sterile or academic. To struggle with faith, says the poet, may well reveal unknown (or at least untapped) resources: "There lives more faith in honest doubt, believe me, than in half the creeds."[4] Or in the words of St. Paul: "We are afflicted in every way possible, but we are not crushed; full of doubts, we never despair. We are persecuted but never abandoned; we are struck down but never destroyed" (2 Cor 4:8–9). Through all this "we walk by faith, not by sight" (2 Cor 5:7) even as we pray that God will strengthen us in faith and love as his pilgrim Church on earth (third eucharistic prayer). Liturgy and sacraments are for the faithful, but their very repetition is a source of strength and a means of growth in the faith professed. The foundation of this faith is God's call; our attitude in faith is our (individual and collective) response to this call.

SPIRITUALITY AND LITURGY

For our purposes, spirituality may be described as the experience of our relationship with God in faith and the ways in which we live out our faith. Spirituality involves our coming to know God, our response to God, and the prayer and work we perform in faith. For Christians, spirituality occurs in and among the community of the Church, the community formed by hearing and responding to the same call and invitation from God.

Christian spirituality involves others in the tradition of the Church or in our present experience who seek to live in relationship with this same God. Because of this variety of people and historical periods there are a variety of "spiritualities" that have existed in the Church and that influence contemporary communities of faith. Sometimes we refer to this variety as "schools" of spirituality, such as the Carmelite, Jesuit, Benedictine or Dominican "school." In our contemporary experience the variety inherent in Christian spirituality is also seen in various "movements" such as charismatic renewal, cursillo, or marriage encounter. Whatever the school or movement considered, what is clear is that Christian spirituality involves the ready response to the word of God in prayer and action, in practices performed with others in common and those performed while alone. But in fidelity to the Lord's call to a people, Christian spirituality is communal and community-oriented; it is not self-contained, self-serving, or only self-concerned. In fact, one of the goals of Christian spirituality is an integration of the many facets of the life of an individual believer in communion with others and in relationship with God.

Taken in this wide sense, spirituality involves the composite of actions, prayers, ascetical practices, and deeds of witness in which Christians engage by way of responding to God in faith. It may be said that the language of faith is prayer, and the external expression of faith is action. While prayer (especially liturgical prayer) is an important focus for Christian spirituality, it is not co-terminous with it. What occurs in moments of prayer enlivens and deepens a believer's response to God's call, and it deepens faith. But that experience of prayer necessarily shapes how one views the world, how one acts in the world, and the way one witnesses to the enduring power of the word of God in the world.[5]

The contribution made by the many varied schools of spirituality is that these reflect particular ways of ordering our response to God in faith. A particular school of spirituality may emphasize individual meditation over communal prayer, or another may emphasize the demands of the apostolate, thus making spirituality reflect the apostolic needs of the time.[6] Developing a spirituality derived from the liturgy need not mean abandoning the insight gained from a school or tradition of spirituality. Rather the contribution of the liturgy to all these movements or approaches and its importance when evaluating appropriate means toward living a spiritual life is that it is the prayer shared by the whole Church, by all Christians. The liturgy is not reserved for a particular group or relegated to one school or approach to spirituality. The liturgy is the privileged experience of the Church's prayer and is an important basis and foundation for spirituality. In fact, the liturgy has repeatedly been called the *Church's* spirituality[7] because it touches the lives of all Christians. This is not to suggest that all liturgical rites and ceremonies affect all people in the same way or that all liturgical ceremonies have the same weight and importance attached to them in all the communities that celebrate them. But it is to suggest that every Christian is influenced, in however minimal or maximal a way, by the liturgy. A monastic community, for example, will celebrate the liturgy of the hours in common as well as the Eucharist on a more regular basis than the people who do not live in such a community. And, conversely, people who gather once weekly for Sunday Eucharist are themselves influenced by the liturgy although their experience of common liturgical prayer is less frequent than those who gather several times a day for liturgy. Yet both can share in a spirituality that is derived from the liturgy and can be called "liturgical." That the liturgy was to be restored to a privileged position in Christian spirituality is clear from the often repeated text from the Constitution on the Sacred Liturgy: the liturgy "is the summit toward which the activity of the Church is directed; at the same time it is the fountain from which all its power flows" (no. 10). Yet, it is important to make a distinction between the experience of the liturgy, that is, liturgical prayer, and what may be termed a liturgical spirituality.

What occurs at the liturgy is a series of actions, prayers, proclamations, and symbolic gestures which comprise the Christian community's response in faith to all that has been accomplished in Christ. At moments of liturgical prayer we experience a fundamentally incarnational view of the Christian life derived from the person of Jesus. We take natural things (water, light) and things that are the product of human labor (bread, wine, oil) and we use them in our common worship. These things are taken out of their "natural" environment and are placed in a liturgical experience in such a way that their meaning is transformed. But in being natural symbols they remain important examples of the universe, now graced and redeemed in Christ.[8] Hence at the liturgy we pray:

[Father] . . . Through all eternity you live in unapproachable
    light.
Source of life and goodness, you have created all things, to fill
    your creatures with every blessing.
                                            (Eucharistic Prayer IV)

Father, you are holy indeed,
and all creation rightly gives you praise.

All life, all holiness comes from you
through your Son, Jesus Christ our Lord,
by the working of the Holy Spirit.

(Eucharistic Prayer III)

The focus of attention in the liturgy is the combination of the use of the goods of creation prayed over and blessed, the proclaimed word of salvation and redemption in Christ, and the response in faith of the gathered community. By sharing in the sacred word of revelation and the signs and symbols of creation now transformed at the liturgy by the words and prayer of blessing, the community shares again and again in God's infinite and abiding love for all peoples. This is what comprises liturgical prayer. Liturgical spirituality, however, is something much wider, and yet it finds its focus and direction from the experience of liturgical prayer. In fact, the development of a liturgical spirituality is a necessary correlative of sharing in the experience of liturgy.

The liturgy serves well as an integrating force between prayer and life where what is celebrated in the cult is intended to be lived out in the rest of life. What makes liturgical spirituality wider than the experience of doing liturgy itself is the fact that the actions and prayers of the liturgy are intended to be more than self-contained and self-concerned activities. Liturgical spirituality, as derived from the experience of liturgy, offers a way of looking at all of creation, at all the events of our lives, and at all of humanity through the perspective of the paschal mystery of Jesus—which is the center of Christian worship ("Christ has died, Christ is risen, Christ will come again"). The fundamentally incarnational view of life that is so evident in liturgy is extended beyond the cult to how one prays, reflects, and acts outside the experience of liturgy.

So, for example, it is important to realize and reflect on what the Church celebrates when it celebrates the liturgy, and then to see how this liturgical celebration influences how we look at life. At Christmas what we celebrate in essence is the mystery of the incarnation—"the word became flesh and made his dwelling among us" (Jn 1:14). As the Church celebrates this mystery in the liturgy it explores and points to the implications of this mystery and the abiding presence of God in us. What is celebrated at Christmas is not only the mystery that Christ took on human form but that our humanity has been and is forever graced by, with and in Christ. Hence at Christmas, the real emphasis moves from details about Jesus' birth to reflection on (and celebration of) what it means for us to be divinized in Christ. From the perspective of developing a liturgical spirituality, the challenge is to see how the celebration of the liturgy (of the hours and the Eucharist) at Christmas puts us in contact with the presence of God revealed in the mystery of the incarnation and orients how we relate to each other and to all creation now graced in Christ. The beauty of creation, the wonder of human life, and how we live the life of grace outside the liturgical setting become points for reflection and action (matter for "spirituality") in the community of the Church. Spirituality, therefore, derives from the liturgy, and liturgical spirituality means more than just sharing in liturgical rites. How we, who have been graced by the incarnation, live as brothers and sisters who share this relationship in Christ would be one of the challenges provided by spirituality derived from the liturgical celebration of Christmas.

FORMATIVE NATURE OF LITURGICAL PRAYER

Since the liturgy is the Church's (official) prayer it stands in a privileged position in the development of spirituality. Not only does it foster ways of acting as responses to prayer, it should also influence the way one prays outside the liturgy. Sometimes we see a conflict and gap between liturgy and personal contemplative prayer. Thomas Merton remarks that this separation is more of a modern, "pseudo-problem" because the early and medieval Christian tradition did not know of this difficulty. "Liturgy by its very nature tends to prolong itself in individual contemplative prayer, and mental prayer in its turn disposes us for and seeks fulfillment in liturgical worship."[9] In fact, the texts used at liturgy provide material for reflection on the mysteries of our faith as they are celebrated liturgically. They also help clarify what is the Church's understanding of a particular feast or season celebrated. As Nathan Mitchell has observed:

> Personal prayer explodes into the speech of public praise and sacramental action, while the speech of worship erupts into the "still point" of silence where, as T. S. Eliot says, "there is only the dance." The prayer of the heart structures the experience of worship, while worship shapes the content of personal prayer.[10]

But it should be remembered that the juncture and medium through which liturgical forms and texts are primarily communicated, experienced and celebrated is the event of liturgy itself. Hence an understanding and appreciation of the elements that comprise the experience of liturgy can serve to foster an awareness of what is involved in liturgy, what kind of personal prayer can be derived from it and how one's conduct and life's choices should be shaped because of it. There is a delicate balance required, therefore, between liturgy as a unique and privileged experience of God in common prayer and as a means for ordering one's spirituality. On the one hand, there is a danger of using the texts of the liturgy for other purposes, such as meditative prayer and action in the world in such a way that the texts of the liturgy become an ideology or program for action separate from the celebration of the liturgy itself. On the other hand there is the ever-present danger of abusing Christian worship in fully celebrated liturgies by not exploring the life-relation and implications which such rites should have for daily living. The liturgy is neither an ideology for action nor a self-contained cultic action. When it becomes either to the detriment or eclipse of its true nature, then it is out of focus. Striking something of a balance between poles such as these will be easier when liturgy is allowed to be itself—a privileged focus for the prayer of the church. The liturgy exists in and for the Church and it is an assumed part of the Church's life. If allowed to exist and be celebrated in and for itself it cannot but influence a spirituality that can be termed "liturgical." Where ideology would tend to argue a position and offer actions as a consequence, liturgy is never so neat that it can be summarized into such a package. Allowing the liturgy the space to breathe and be itself can help it from becoming oriented toward such a pre-determined ideology. Similarly, when probed for its implications and full meaning, it will also become obvious that an appropriate response in life is required by and derived from the celebration of the liturgy.

An assumption and desired goal of much of the liturgical revision in the contemporary experience of the Christian churches is the reuniting of liturgy with the devotional life of Christians. The Constitution on the Sacred Liturgy states:

> Popular devotions of the Christian people are warmly commended, provided they accord with the laws and norms of the Church. . . . These devotions should also be drawn up that they harmonize with the liturgical seasons, accord with the sacred liturgy, are in some fashion derived from it, and lead the people to it, since the liturgy by its very nature far surpasses any of them (no. 13).

That there should be a harmony between the experience of liturgical prayer and the rest of one's spirituality is one level of integration; this text underscores that there should be a harmony between liturgy and personal prayer, and this is a goal toward which one should strive. Despite the efforts of liturgical pioneers and the authoritative encouragement toward this end, such a unification still remains a goal for many.[11] The books of Pius Parsch and Aemiliana Lohr, among others, were commentaries on the liturgy whose intent was to develop an appreciation and an awareness of what occurred at the liturgy. This was to have its effect on one's personal appropriation of the liturgy. Allowing the laity to read English translations of the liturgy in hand missals was another example of providing means for understanding and appreciating what was taking place in liturgy.

These attempts at developing a liturgical sense in personal devotions and prayers were, however, based on a kind of liturgy that was fixed, and which left congregations very passive. In the recent revisions of the liturgy since Vatican II, with emphasis on option and variety, clearly another kind of approach toward making the liturgy exert an influence on other aspects of spirituality is called for. In addition, the rather recent encouragement of "active participation" gives this task greater urgency and import. The use of the vernacular in worship, the number and variety of roles exercised in liturgy, and the awareness that more is involved than saying and doing the right thing at liturgy[12] provide a new context for the task of reuniting liturgical and personal prayer. No longer is it comprehension or following along that is to be fostered. Now it is planning and celebrating liturgy in such a way that the active participation of all and a communal experience of worship is fostered.

Where formerly the understanding of the given liturgical texts (in Latin) was of paramount importance in making the liturgy a source of spiritual enrichment for people (hence the use of missals by the laity), all too often this was responsible for making the liturgy seem to be a word-dominated experience for the laity while the clergy performed actions and spoke words. More recently, the clear proclamation of texts (in the vernacular) and the effective use of symbols and engagement in ritual actions by the whole assembly have been emphasized, and it is all of these together which comprise the liturgical experience of prayer.[13]

While the reuniting of liturgy and personal prayer is most desirable and many strides have been made in this direction, nevertheless it must also be admitted that all too often the experience of contemporary congregations is that personal and liturgical piety are not in harmony.[14] What makes this task all the more problematic is that the recent liturgical reforms are themselves in the process of evolution and development. For example, the emphasis given to the Easter Vigil, the high point of the Church's liturgical year, had often centered on the diaconal proclamation of the *Exsultet,* as can be seen in pre-conciliar commentaries on the liturgy.[15] And yet, the recently revised Rite of Christian Initiation for Adults gives this vigil a different cast and focus, for now it is the restoration of baptism-confirmation-Eucharist as initiatory—the experience of the sacraments themselves—that receives great emphasis at Easter. While the *Exsultet* is still proclaimed, the whole thrust and cast of this liturgy is toward initiation, with Lent as the final time of preparation for initiating new members at the Vigil and the annual renewal of what initiation implies for the already baptized. Part of the task in liturgical catechesis and celebration is to help reorient communities around traditional symbols and recently restored rituals, whose significance is meant to be tapped for the celebration of liturgy and for other devotions and personal prayer. In addition to this, the liturgical revisions called for at the Council invite an on-going process in liturgical implementation that respects cultural diversity within the Roman rite. Even if this agenda of liturgical acculturation has not been explored very fully as of yet, it nonetheless remains part of the agenda for on-going liturgical revision and adaptation.[16]

In the light of this state of implementation and acculturation, the opportunity is provided for developing *bases* for liturgical prayer, as opposed to one model of liturgy for all communities. Delineating what these bases are (or "elements" as noted in Part Two of this book) offers the possibility of providing the sub-structure of that which grounds both liturgical prayer and liturgical spirituality. Since these bases ground liturgical prayer, they also offer insight into how the liturgy can help to form and mold other experiences of personal prayer. While these bases are seen to be foundational, they are also understood expansively, that is, it is assumed that these would be experienced liturgically in many, varied, and evolving worship situations. This respects the variety of communities in which we celebrate liturgy, and it respects the on-going nature of liturgical revision and implementation.

The essential foundation of liturgy and spirituality is *faith,* a confident trust that God's call to us will be responded to with the same disarming resoluteness that marked Abraham's response. In the midst of doubt and failure in achieving this level of commitment, we derive hope and consolation from other champions of faith (Peter, Paul, Thomas and Mary) whose faith profession was born of both doubt and trust, and even prior infidelity. The repetition of the liturgy with its many and varied forms underscores the fact that the rites themselves are to serve the ever-deepening growth in faith of believers. In response to God's call and initiative we celebrate liturgy and we seek to live out our spirituality in the communion of the Church, a mixed community of the worthy and the less worthy, the confident and the doubtful, the virtuous and the sinful. We pray in solemn liturgical assemblies and in the privacy of our rooms in secret that we, the pilgrim Church on earth, may become the elect in the kingdom of heaven. We pray that we might reach the perfection and full life willed by God for us in Christ. We do this by being faithful to the Church's prayer in liturgy, with all that liturgical celebration implies, and by being faithful to the implications which the liturgy can have for our spiritual lives. In faith we profess the confident and trustful prayer of Zechariah, uttered at the birth and circumcision of John the Baptist:

> Blessed be the Lord, the God of Israel;
> he has come to his people and set them free.
> He promised to show mercy to our fathers
> and to remember his holy covenant.
> This was the oath he swore to our father Abraham:
> to set us free from the hands of our enemies,
> free to worship him without fear,
> holy and righteous in his sight
>   all the days of our life.   (Lk 1:68, 72–75)

Liturgical spirituality involves both communal worship in faith and trust as well as life lived in holiness and justice before our God.

NOTES

1. The question of the faith expression of parents who present children for infant baptism and the "requirements" for sacraments

serve to concretize this issue in the contemporary Church. See Francis J. Buckley, "The Right to the Sacraments of Initiation," *Catholic Mind* 77 (June 1979) 17–37; Juan Luis Segundo. "A New Crisis for the Sacraments," in *The Sacraments Today,* trans. John Drury (Maryknoll: Orbis Books, 1974) pp. 3–20; Paul Vanbergen, "The Baptism of Infants of 'non satis credentes' Parents," *Studia Liturgica* 12 (1977) 4–9. For an approach to sacramental administration in parish life based on the Rite of Christian Initiation of Adults, see "To Speak of Sacraments and Faith Renewal," Rochester Diocesan Guidelines, reprinted in *Origins* 10 (April 9, 1981) 673–688.

2. T. S. Eliot, "Little Gidding," *Four Quartets,* in *The Complete Poems and Plays* (New York: Harcourt, Brace and World, 1952) p. 145.

3. See Günther Bornkamm, "The Stilling of the Storm in Matthew," in G. Bornkamm, G. Barth and H. J. Held, eds., *Tradition and Interpretation in Matthew,* trans. Percy Scott (Philadelphia: Westminster Press, 1963) pp. 52–57.

4. A. Tennyson, *In Memoriam,* Pt. XCVI, Stanza 3.

5. This is developed more fully in Part Three of the book.

6. See Gabriel Braso, *Liturgy and Spirituality,* trans. Leonard J. Doyle (Collegeville: The Liturgical Press, 1960) pp. 3–55.

7. Louis Bouyer makes the following statement: "The liturgy, to our way of thinking, is that system of prayers and rites traditionally canonized by the church as her own prayer and worship." (From *Liturgical Piety* [Notre Dame: University of Notre Dame Press, 1955] p. 1.)

8. On the "naturalness" of symbols see, for example, David Power, "Symbolism in Worship: A Survey," *The Way* 13 (October 1973) 310–325; 14 (January 1974) 57–66; 15 (January 1975) 55–64; 15 (April 1975) 137–146.

9. Thomas Merton, *Contemplative Prayer* (New York: Herder and Herder, 1969) p. 55.

10. Nathan Mitchell, "Useless Prayer," in *Christians at Prayer* (Notre Dame: University of Notre Dame Press, 1977) p. 19. See also N. Mitchell, "Prayer: The Ecology of Worship," *Musart* 26/4 (Summer 1974) 9–14.

11. See G. Braso, *Liturgy and Spirituality,* pp. 19–24; L. Bouyer, *Liturgical Piety,* and L. Bouyer, *The Spirituality of the New Testament and the Fathers* (New York: Seabury, 1963).

12. See *Constitution on the Sacred Liturgy,* no. 11.

13. See *Symbol: The Language of Liturgy* (Washington: Federation of Diocesan Liturgical Commissions, 1982). This collection of essays was

24 LITURGY, PRAYER AND SPIRITUALITY

edited and published in preparation for the October 1982 convention
of the FDLC on Symbol.

14. See Robert Duggan, "Liturgical Spirituality and Liturgical Reform," *Spiritual Life* 27 (Spring 1981) 46–53.

15. See, among others, Pius Parsch, *The Church's Year of Grace*
(Collegeville: The Liturgical Press, 1964, second edition) Vol. Two, pp.
340–343, 350–352. Compare Adrien Nocent, *The Liturgical Year* (Collegeville: The Liturgical Press, 1977) Vol. Three, pp. 126–145, where
these pages deal with sacramental initiation; the author discusses the
Exsultet on pp. 111–113.

16. On the question of liturgical indigenization, see Anscar J.
Chupungco, *Cultural Adaptation of the Liturgy* (New York/Ramsey: Paulist Press, 1982).

Chapter Two
LITURGY: COMMUNAL
RESPONSE TO GOD

From the outset it is important to set a proper perspective on liturgy, prayer and spirituality (in fact on all aspects of the Christian life) by exploring the dynamic of our search for God and God's prior and unceasing search for us in the gifted relationship of faith. It is the purpose of this chapter to reflect on this central dynamic in the life of faith as it is revealed in the covenant relationship between God and his people. The priority of God's initiative will serve to illustrate that the foundation of all that we do at worship and of all that comprises spirituality for us is God's prior and constant search for us. The place of the liturgy as the means of experiencing the mystery of God until we come to know him in the kingdom will be emphasized. But again, our reflection emphasizes that liturgical prayer is essentially our communal response to all that God has done for us in calling us to himself in Christ and in sanctifying us through the power of the Holy Spirit.

Christian worship provides us with a clear illustration of searching for and being sought by God, for in the act of worship we both speak to God and listen to his word, we join in the self-offering of Christ and receive holy gifts signifying his presence with us, we sing in joyful acclamation to the Lord our God and find ourselves confounded and humbled at the forgiveness and love granted us by the Lord we worship. Worship involves doing, acting, and symbolizing on our part, but this doing is based on what God has done and does in our lives, how God has acted and acts in our world, and which symbols God has used and uses to communicate his love for us. Christian worship is our response to the profound mystery of God's seeking us so that we might share the very life of God in the community of the Church. "For worship, after all, is not primarily something that we do. It is response to what God has already done and is still doing. It is because God has first of all made us in his own image that we find implanted in us the desire to worship him and to grow in likeness to him."[1] What Christian worship does is to give shape and form to our search for God by inviting us into his very presence to be remade again and again into his image and likeness.

But our own experience and the words of the psalmist remind us that the search for God will continue throughout our mortal lives until we come to see God face to face: "There is one thing I ask of the Lord, for this I long, to live in the house of the Lord, all the days of my life, to savor the sweetness of the Lord, to behold his temple" (Ps 27:4). What Christians share in and savor, between the incarnation of the Son of God and his second coming, is the privileged expression and experience of God's love for us—Christian liturgy. In the words of the traditional psalm used at morning prayer: "O God, you are my God, for you I long; for you my soul is thirsting. My body pines for you like a dry weary land without water" (Ps 63:2).

THE COVENANT RELATIONSHIP

What is foundational in worship is God's call and invitation, demonstrated in both the Old and New Testaments by the term "covenant." In the Hebrew Scriptures Israel's search for God is always matched (overshadowed, really) by God's search for and covenant relationship with his chosen people. The God who called Abraham, Isaac, Jacob, and Moses is the God who continually called Israel to be a chosen people, and invited them to experience in succeeding generations the deeds and acts of salvation he performed for these forefathers in history. Liturgy was the moment of encounter and experience of this ever-sustaining salvation. Israel's prayer book, the Psalms, is filled

with the acclamations of praise and thanks to God as their
response to all he had done for them:

> O give thanks to the Lord for he is good,
> for his love endures forever.
> Give thanks to the God of gods,
> for his love endures forever.
> Give thanks to the Lord of lords
> for his love endures forever;
> who alone has wrought marvelous works,
> for his love endures for ever.   (Ps 136:1–4)

The recounting of God's deeds for Israel was done in the cult,
and the response of the covenanted people was in joy and
thanks, for in faith they knew that his mercy would endure for all
ages.

But covenant-religion looked to the future as well as to the
past. The covenanted people of Israel prayed for the coming of
the promised Messiah who would grace the lineage of David and
give life to all who would call on him in faith. The chosenness of
Israel would now expand to include all men and women who
professed faith in the Messiah, the one promised through all
ages. God's covenant mercy and the virtues which should mark a
covenanted people[2] are recalled daily in Zechariah's canticle at
morning prayer in the liturgy of the hours:

> Blessed be the Lord, the God of Israel;
>   he has come to his people and set them free.
> He has raised up for us a mighty savior
>   born of the house of his servant David.
> Through his holy prophets he promised of old
>   that he would save us from our enemies,
>   from the hands of all who hate us.
> He promised to show mercy to our fathers
>   and to remember his holy covenant.
> This was the oath he swore to our father Abraham:
>   to set us free from the hands of our enemies,

> free to worship him without fear,
> holy and righteous in his sight
> all the days of our life.   (Lk 1:68–75)

The unmerited and unearned selection of Israel by God as bearers of his promise and sharers in the covenant required a response on their part. The price to be paid for entering into this privileged, gifted relationship was surrender to him as the only God, to his will as their way of life, and to his word as the law of their lives. The scene from the Book of Exodus with Moses acting as intermediary, announcing the covenant and requiring a response from the people is paradigmatic for Israel. After Moses "set before the people all that the Lord had ordered him to tell them, the people all answered together, 'Everything the Lord has said we will do' " (Ex 19:7–8). From now on they were to live life on God's terms and surrender to him all that stood in the way of worshiping him alone and honoring his holy name.

The communal renewal of this covenant relationship took place for Israel at their liturgy: at home, in the synagogue, or at the temple. Whether in the familiarity of a sabbath meal at home, or as a response to being instructed on the revealed word in the synagogue, or during the ritual of offering sacrifice in the temple, these cultic rites were the setting for the renewal of the covenant. The liturgy served as the setting for Israel's on-going recommitment to the terms of the covenant with their God. These liturgical rites and gatherings (both simple and solemn) were especially important when the people forsook the covenant and in infidelity against Yahweh went awhoring after other gods. They would be reminded of the covenant God forged with them and the importance of their faith-filled and willing response to him.

The invitatory psalm that begins the liturgy of the hours reminds us of our response to the covenant, our hearing and being faithful to the revealed word of the Lord:

> Come, then, let us bow down and worship
> bending the knee before the Lord, our maker.

> For he is our God and we are his people,
>   the flock he shepherds.
> Today, listen to the voice of the Lord:
> Do not grow stubborn, as your fathers did
>   in the wilderness
> when at Meriba and Massah
>   they challenged me and provoked me,
> Although they had seen all my works.
>
> (Ps 95:6–9, ICEL Translation)

The history of Israel in the Old Testament is a sober reminder that being among the chosen of God does not guarantee being faithful to the Lord who calls. In fact, it is often the case that Israel preferred to search for other gods rather than the God of the covenant. As the eucharistic prayer reminds us, even when the chosen disobeyed, and their relationship with God was broken, God did not abandon them; instead he offered a covenant "again and again" and through the prophets' warnings taught them to hope for salvation (fourth eucharistic prayer). In the eucharistic prayers prepared for the holy year of renewal and reconciliation (1975) and which are still used in our liturgy of the Eucharist, this is made all the more poignant:

> You never cease to call us
> to a new and more abundant life.
> God of love and mercy,
> you are always ready to forgive. . . .
> Time and time again
> we broke your covenant,
> but you did not abandon us.
>
> (Eucharistic Prayer, for Masses of Reconciliation I)

What is particularly illustrative about the vicissitudes of the covenant relationship is God's overarching and overwhelming initiative, searching for his people, especially when they had been unfaithful. This hope-filled (if sobering) example of God's dealing with his chosen people should serve as a constant reminder of God's acceptance of us as we are (not as we might imagine ourselves to be)[3] and of how much we need to rely on his mercy and love as we search for him in our lives. The history of Israel in the Old Testament demonstrates that the foundation of the covenant relationship is God's enduring love. In all that we do by way of response to God, especially in our common prayer, this emphasis should always be remembered. As we pray in the third eucharistic prayer:

> From age to age you gather a people to yourself,
> so that from east to west
> a perfect offering may be made
> to the glory of your name.

> Father, hear the prayers of the family you have gathered
>   here before you.

THE NEW COVENANT

That the notion of covenant is important for an understanding of the person and message of Jesus is clear from the New Testament. After his birth Jesus had to abide by the prescriptions of the law (Lk 2:22–35) and during his life he observed the covenant-renewal rituals with his fellow Jews (Lk 2:41–50). Most significantly, the sacrifice he endured for our salvation is commemorated in the liturgy of the Eucharist as "the blood of the new and everlasting covenant." The covenant in Jesus is termed "new" because Jesus transcends the limitations of the old law and supersedes its prescriptions. The hoped-for Messiah fulfills the promises and hopes of Old Testament covenant-religion as is graphically demonstrated in Simeon's canticle (used at night prayer):

> Lord, now let your servant go in peace;
>   your word has been fulfilled:
> my own eyes have seen the salvation
>   which you have prepared in the sight of every people:
> a light to reveal you to the nations
>   and the glory of your people Israel.   (Lk 2:29–32)

The particularity and exclusive election of Israel has been transcended in the new covenant in Christ. The sacrifice and blood rituals of the temple have come to an end in his one, perfect sacrifice (see the Letter to the Hebrews). Therefore his blood was shed for *all,* for the forgiveness of sins. The responsibility of those who share in the covenant-renewal of the Eucharist is to share the good news of salvation with all peoples, and to fulfill the missionary command of Jesus to the ends of the earth (Mt 28:18-20).

To the shock and consternation of the scribes and Pharisees, the practitioners of the old law and the arbiters of the old covenant, Jesus is pictured in the New Testament at table with "tax collectors and sinners" (Lk 15:1-2). It is in this setting of familiarity and relationship that he relates the astounding parables of the lost sheep, the lost coin, and the prodigal son—all examples about God's love now offered to all people, especially to those in obvious need. This love is so overwhelming that it seeks the one lost sheep instead of being satisfied with ninety-nine who never stray (Lk 15:3-7), it searches for and celebrates the recovery of the one lost coin, instead of investing the firmly-possessed nine coins (Lk 15:8-10), and it welcomes back the son who squandered his inheritance on loose living and superficial pleasure (Lk 15:11-32). This last is all the more poignant for the scribes and Pharisees because the "logical" son (representing their positions?) objects to the father's display of kindness and forgiveness. He had kept the rules and seemingly wants what he earned. The vital center of covenant-religion can be missed when, as in the case of this elder son, rules, observances and logical action get in the way of the heart of the matter—God's enduring and abiding love. In Jesus it is often the case that old rules are transgressed in order to demonstrate the wideness of God's mercy; and in him logical actions are replaced with passionate ones (such as the cleansing of the temple area) to demonstrate the purity which should characterize religion and religious practices.

Jesus also breaks with social and religious custom by accepting water from the Samaritan woman (Jn 4:4-24). The author reminds us that Jews have nothing to do with Samaritans (v 9); hence a conversation between a Jewish male and a Samaritan

woman becomes all the more significant. The site of this exchange is significant, the place of Jacob's well (v 6), for what was
revered in the history of Israel as a sacred place would now give
way to many more sacred places and gatherings of Christians for
worship "when authentic worshipers will worship the Father in
Spirit and truth" (v 23). The Samaritan example is carried even
further in Luke's Gospel when in answer to the question "Who
is my neighbor?" Jesus tells the story of the good Samaritan (Lk
10:25-37). This passage ends with the admission that the com-
passionate Samaritan was neighbor to the one in need—in glar-
ing contrast to the priest of the old covenant who "saw him and
went on" because of the prescribed laws of ritual purity.

Like the old covenant, the new covenant through and in
Christ requires a response. This response of faith and action
would now be based on the paradoxical values of the Gospel
and would require an ever-deepening trust in the good news
Jesus came to preach. "To the poor he proclaimed the good
news of salvation, to prisoners freedom, and to those in sorrow,
joy" (fourth eucharistic prayer). This mission is recounted and
recalled in the daily proclamation of the canticle of the Blessed
Virgin Mary at evening prayer:

> He has come to the help of his servant Israel
> for he has remembered his promise of mercy,
> the promise he made to our forefathers,
> to Abraham and his children forever.   (Lk 1:54–55)

The relationship forged in the new covenant requires a complete surrender to seeing things God's way and to viewing real
life through the prism of his death and resurrection. Gospel-
inspired faith requires that we view death not as the end of life
but as the beginning of life eternal with God. It requires renunciation of this world's values and goods as the emptying and
displacement needed in order to receive God's mercy and love,
and it requires admitting weakness in our lives so that we can
grow strong in his grace and peace. The price is a high one, of
seeing things God's way and of affirming that real values are the
paradoxical ones proclaimed in the Gospel.

He has shown the strength of his arm,
he has scattered the proud in their conceit:
He has cast down the mighty from their thrones,
and has lifted up the lowly.
He has filled the hungry with good things,
and the rich he has sent away empty.   (Lk 1:51–53)

Hence, it is appropriate that we pray for the grace to live life on God's terms, despite the apparent successes we enjoy from this life: "Father, help us to seek the values that will bring us lasting joy in this changing world" (opening prayer, 21st Sunday in Ordinary Time).

Christian liturgy is the privileged expression and experience of the new covenant forged in Jesus. It is at liturgy that our searching for God is given shape and form as we hear again and again his good news and we share in his very life once more. The positive images of Christ as shepherd, healer, and reconciler as reflected in the recently revised liturgical rites are particularly appropriate in our day when a sense of meaninglessness in life, a sense of alienation from others and institutions, and a sense of isolation and loneliness are so much a part of many people's lives. Helpless to effect a real change in the paralysis that can result from such estrangement or loss of hope, we can find strength and direction from the liturgy:

> In the sacrament of penance the Father receives the repentant children who come back to him, Christ places the lost sheep on his shoulders and brings them back to the sheepfold, and the Holy Spirit resanctifies those who are the temple of God or dwells more fully in them. The expression of all this is the sharing in the Lord's table, begun again or made more ardent; such a return of children from afar brings great rejoicing at the banquet of God's Church.[4]

These clear references to Luke 15 reiterate that in the Church's common prayer, here the sacrament of penance (or reconciliation), communities rely first and foremost on God's search for them especially in their need. Christian liturgy is not for the perfect or the fully converted. It is for those who search for God, who need the images and likenesses of his incarnate love, and who rely on the power of the Spirit to make them holy.

> When we were lost
> and could not find the way to you,
> you loved us more than ever:
> Jesus, your Son, innocent and without sin,
> gave himself into our hands
> and was nailed to a cross.
> Yet before he stretched out his arms between heaven
>   and earth
> in the everlasting sign of your covenant,
> he desired to celebrate the Paschal feast
>   in the company of his disciples.
> (Eucharistic Prayer for Masses of Reconciliation I)

It is hardly coincidental that Jesus chose the paschal setting of the old covenant—the annual commemoration of Israel's deliverance from the bondage of slavery in Egypt and their being led to the land of promise as a covenanted people—to establish the rituals of the new covenant, centered in his soon to be accomplished death and resurrection. This most important moment of the cultic life of Israel is now to be fulfilled in the coming death and resurrection of the promised Messiah. Henceforth "passover" would mean more than a past event for Israel set in chronological time and geographical place. From now on Christians would "pass over" in Christ from death to life, alienation to reconciliation, sin to forgiveness, darkness to light, from this world to the world that will never end. Such would be effected among communities which respond to his enduring love, concretely expressed in the life, death and resurrection of Jesus. Once more, it is God's search for us that is the foundation of the actions we perform in liturgy:

> God our Father,
> we had wandered far from you,
> but through your Son you have brought us back.
> You gave him up to death
> so that we might turn again to you

and find our way to one another.
Therefore we celebrate the reconciliation
Christ gained for us.
> (Eucharistic Prayer for Masses of Reconciliation II)

The rites and celebrations that comprise Christian liturgy find here their origin, source and inspiration.

THE MYSTERY OF GOD

While we rely on God's initiative in seeking us throughout our lives of faith, especially when we gather for liturgy, and we speak of God's abiding presence in the gathered community, in word and in rite, we must also acknowledge the elusive quality of God's being present for and with his people. In liturgy and in prayer we rely on the assured presence of God to us, and yet we experience a lingering sense of our still being distant from God; even as we experience and try to comprehend God's love, we experience a certain dumbfoundedness as we present ourselves before him. This occurs even as we gather in the name of the Lord Jesus, at his gracious invitation. Jesus came to put a face on God and to reveal in parable, story and metaphor who God is; these images and examples are meant to lead us to experience the very mystery of God. Hence, it is important to remain aware of the otherness of God.

> To put it bluntly, it is idolatrous to think that we ever grasped God, that we comprehended him either as an objective fact "out there" or as an exalted ideal "in here." In all such cases we are trying to take God into our possession. But this is just impossible (as well as being blasphemous). God transcends anything we can grasp or contain, and when we think we have him, the truth is that he has slipped through our grasp and we are left clinging to some pitiable idol of our own making. We can never know God by seeking to grasp and manipulate him, but only by letting him grasp us.[5]

The notion expressed here is as foundational as the scene of Moses seeing the burning but unconsumed bush and fearing to look at God (Ex 3:1–6), as personally humbling as the awestruck response of Peter, James and John to the transfiguration of Christ (Mk 9:2–8) and as classical in theological circles as Rudolph Otto's *The Idea of the Holy*[6] (*mysterium tremendum et fascinans*). Such a notion of the otherness of God is important when speaking about Christian liturgy, for it prevents us from making God into our (usually manageable and neat) images and likenesses of who he should be. It is not that we cannot come to know God, but being aware of the powerful mystery of God reminds us that the way to know God is to submit to the revealed word and to respond to his revealed presence at liturgy, in prayer, and in the conduct of our lives. Our destiny as believers is to be drawn into his infinite and enduring love, expressed even now in worship. The preface to the fourth eucharistic prayer reflects something of this awesome mystery of God by stating:

> Father in heaven,
> it is right that we should give you thanks and glory:
> you alone are God, living and true.
> Through all eternity you live in unapproachable light.
> Source of life and goodness, you have created all things,
> to fill your creatures with every blessing
> and lead all men to the joyful vision of your light.

Our response to this prayer is to use the traditional preface acclamation (Is 6:2–3; Mt 21:9):

> Holy, holy, holy Lord, God of power and might,
> heaven and earth are full of your glory.
>   Hosanna in the highest.
> Blessed is he who comes in the name of the Lord.
>   Hosanna in the highest.

It is in the light of the mystery of God who offers us a covenant relationship and who inspires our response to this covenant in worship that we continue to reflect on our journey to God and our searching for him. In the words of St. Augustine: "You have made us for yourself, O Lord, and our heart is restless until it rests in thee." Or, in the words of the psalmist:

> Like the deer that yearns
> for running streams,
> so my soul is yearning
> for you, my God.
> My soul is thirsting for God,
> the God of my life;
> when can I enter and see
> the face of God?   (Ps 42:1–3)

One of the foundations of liturgical prayer is that it is a response done in faith by the community of believers who acknowledge the otherness of the revealed God and who experience this otherness yet revealed presence in common prayer. The proclamation of the revealed word and the continual affirmation of what God has done and does for us in his Son through the power of the Spirit we call "holy" is essential for Christian liturgy. It is the very holiness of God, the very otherness of our Lord and Savior, that grounds Christian prayer and the Christian life. The liturgy is a means by which we as a people respond to the initiative of God, savor and ponder his revelation to us, and so become holy as he is holy. It is all done on his terms (the terms of surrender and response required by the covenant) at his initiative and by his grace. Because we shall never know God completely or understand totally his infinite love for us, the Christian life requires ceaseless exploration and profound reflection on the mystery of God. In the words of the poet:

> With the drawing of this Love and the voice of this Calling
> We shall not cease from exploration
> And the end of all our exploring
> Will be to arrive where we started
> And know the place for the first time.[7]

The ceaseless journey and search for God is done in grateful response to the God who ceaselessly searches for us and calls us again and again into his very life.

UNTIL THE KINGDOM COMES

The center of Christian liturgy is the worship of God, made known and revealed through Jesus, whose mission was to establish the "new and everlasting covenant." The means we use to recall and remember this covenant are the rites and ceremonies that comprise the event and experience of worship. But these forms, prayers and ceremonies are themselves meant to pale and ultimately to fade away because they are meant to be a means to an end, not the end themselves.

Christian prayer and worship are meant to lead us to experience God; they are not substitutes for meeting the living God. Our human lives in faith are on a journey toward the goal of all life—God himself. Doing God's will ("thy will be done" for which we pray so often) is the only thing that really matters here and now; and we seek to do just that until the coming of the kingdom at the end of time ("thy kingdom come"). Hence, liturgy shares the same fate as the rest of our personal prayer and ascetical practices (which together comprise our "spirituality")—liturgy too is meant to fade and pass away when we meet God in the kingdom. Since the heart of worship is the God worshiped, there must of necessity be something awkward about our liturgical gatherings; they are meant to fade away when the Lord is revealed in all his glory. Liturgy, therefore, is a privileged time to share now in the grace and peace of the kingdom; but it is provisional, for it looks to the fullness of life with God in the kingdom. Liturgical prayer is privileged yet provisional. As formative of our lives as believers the liturgy is significant, for it reveals the word and will of God repeatedly; but this allegiance and action fades when compared with eternal life lived with God. It is appropriate, therefore, that we should join in the text of the hymn that reminds us:

> So, Lord, at length when sacraments shall cease
> May we be one with all your Church above,
> One with your saints in one unending peace,
> One with your saints in one unbounded love.[8]

In liturgy we continually pray for the coming of the kingdom, for the day when the Lord's presence will be fully revealed, and that we might be among the elect who are called to the eschatological banquet in the kingdom. The texts of the eucharistic liturgy themselves speak about "looking forward to his coming in glory" (fourth eucharistic prayer) and of our situation now "as we wait in joyful hope for the coming of our Savior, Jesus Christ."

Christian liturgy, therefore, looks beyond itself to the fulfillment of all our searching for God and his continual search for us. We confidently pray:

> Your gift of the Spirit,
> who raised Jesus from the dead,
> is the foretaste and promise
> of the paschal feast of heaven.

(Sunday Preface VI)

The privileged yet provisional nature of the liturgy should be recalled, especially when the present eucharistic banquet is compared with the eternal banquet of the kingdom. Just as all Christian liturgy and all our present experience of God are the result of God's search for us, so the final banquet will one day be provided by God. Our being called to the kingdom is at his invitation:

> On this mountain the LORD of hosts
>   will provide for all peoples
> A feast of rich food and choice wines,
>   juicy, rich food and pure choice wines.
> On that day it will be said:
>   "Behold our God, to whom we looked to save us!
>   This is the LORD for whom we looked;
>   let us rejoice and be glad that he has saved us!"

(Is 25:6, 9)[9]

The end result of Christian liturgy, prayer, spirituality (indeed all Christian life) is that we become fully assimilated into

the mystery of God. This will never be accomplished fully in our
human lives, but it is the hope and promise set before us in the
liturgy as celebrated and as lived by believing Christians. Ultimately the liturgy as covenant-renewal is meant to transcend the
covenant and to lead us to the full revelation of the mystery of
God in the kingdom forever. The act of liturgy is the means we
now have of responding to God, the God who ever seeks to save
us. Participation in liturgy involves a lifetime process of coming
to know who God is and of ever rediscovering the many images
and likenesses of God. These images and likenesses are proclaimed, spoken and shared in the liturgy. What is done in the
act of worship is done in response to his love and calling. The
end of it all is to come to know him, who is first and last, because
he first loved us and still loves us, his people. What we do in
liturgical prayer and all that we do in this life is done in grateful
response to him. In our search for God it is consoling yet
sobering to reflect on the fact that our searching is preceded
and sustained by God's search for us. In the words of St.
Bernard:

> If a great good is not to be twisted into a great evil, it is of
> paramount importance for every one among you who seek
> God to understand that he anticipates you, and that you are
> being sought before you sought him. The soul seeks the
> word, but it was first sought by the Word.[10]

NOTES

1. John Macquarrie, *Paths in Spirituality,* (New York: Harper and
Row, 1972) p. 15.
2. For this terminology and an exegesis of this canticle see,
Raymond Brown, *The Birth of the Messiah* (New York: Doubleday, 1977)
pp. 367–374.
3. For a popular, reflective treatment of God's acceptance of us,
and our response to this acceptance, see Peter G. van Breemen, *As
Bread That Is Broken* (Denville: Dimension Books, 1974) pp. 9–16, and
Certain as the Dawn (Denville: Dimension Books, 1980).
4. *General Instruction, Rite of Penance,* no. 6 The references in the
original text are to Lk 15:7, 10, 32, the parables noted and discussed
above.

5. John Macquarrie, *Paths in Spirituality*, p. 55.

6. Rudolph Otto, *The Idea of the Holy* (New York: Oxford University Press, 1977, reprinted).

7. T.S. Eliot, "Little Gidding," *Four Quartets*, in *The Complete Poems and Plays*, p. 145.

8. Taken from "At That First Eucharist," in *The Catholic Liturgy Book* (Baltimore: Helicon, 1975) hymn no. 359.

9. This text is used as the first reading at Mass on Wednesday of the First Week of Advent, the more eschatological part of this season. See Part Two, Chapter Eight, section on "The Incarnation Celebrations."

10. Quoted in *Asking the Fathers*, The Art of Meditation and Prayer (Wilton: Morehouse-Barlow, 1973) p. 32.

Chapter Three
HUMAN LIFE
AND CHRISTIAN WORSHIP

It was noted above that Christian liturgy rests on a fundamentally incarnational view of reality[1] in that we take things from ordinary human experience and use them in ways that express the presence of God in the liturgy, in rites of word and sacrament. It is the purpose of this chapter to explore more fully what we mean by the important juncture of human experience and Christian worship. This consideration requires that we step back from the forms of the liturgy to explore what we mean by the Christian life and how our human lives are the locus for leading the spiritual life. This leads to a reflection on what may be termed "incarnational spirituality" which in turn leads to delineating a theological and spiritual foundation for the place of liturgy and sacraments in such an incarnational approach to spirituality. All of this will lead to some reflections on the ever present (and sometimes very elusive) task of integrating liturgy and life.

THE CHRISTIAN LIFE

A perennial problem for those who wish to lead the spiritual life concerns the task of integrating the many aspects of our lives. As believers we seek to live the Christian life in a world of many non-Christian attitudes, and sometimes we contrast what is compatible with the Christian faith with what is merely "human." The distinction between what is human and what is religious can sometimes become a dichotomy both in theory and practice for us. As a result we find that we are torn between "two different worlds." Further, when the helpful distinction between the sacred and the secular becomes a dichotomy a distinct advantage is given to the sacred because we perceive that it is the sacred that draws us nearer to God and removes us from the "secular" world. Another distinction separates the soul from the body. Yet when these become totally separated, spirituality can become the process of making our souls (only) more and more God-like. Finally, the distinction between what is eternal and what is temporal can harden and become concretized in an approach to spirituality that allows us to forsake the real needs of the time and place in which we live our lives for what is timeless and (comparatively) ethereal.

What happens to Christian spirituality when these distinctions harden and become dichotomies (as helpful as they are and as significant as they can be for reflecting on the reality of the spiritual life) is that spirituality can become the means whereby believers become more and more religious by contact with the sacred, and their souls seek for what is eternal alone. Such an approach leaves out the fundamental fact of our own experience, that our lives are lived in the secular spheres of this world. We know well that our lives are thoroughly human, and that it is through our bodies that we perceive and experience reality. We are not disincarnate spirits. It is as enfleshed human beings that we live on this earth; the temporal sphere is the setting for all the activities of our lives. To make such hard and fast separations out of what, in fact, are really parts of each other, religious-human, sacred-secular, soul-body, eternal-temporal, is to establish a wrong foundation for what is Christian spirituality. The concern here is to look again at what are helpful and necessary distinctions, but to underscore that these distinctions should not be interpreted as neat separations or divisions. What we lead are lives, very human and sometimes very fragile human lives, and it is as fully human persons that we lead Christian spiritual lives.

Karl Rahner considers this question of neat separations and distinctions, and judges such a clear-cut separation the "old model" and a basically unsound approach to liturgy and sacraments.[2] He suggests that in this approach to spirituality one moves to and fro, from this secular world into a sphere of the sacred, for it is assumed that it is only in the sacral sphere that one can achieve any real encounter with God. Christians, according to this view, meet God in sacred rites and times of prayer, and it is at these moments that God makes moral demands on them and at the same time sanctifies them and bestows grace to strengthen them. In this approach God touches humans from the outside and graces them so that they may return to the secular world.[3] What is clearly missing in this "old model," and oftentimes in our own lives, is an integrated approach to the Christian life which derives from the fundamental unity of our human lives: lives in which both the sacred and the secular, the religious and the human, the eternal and the temporal, and (more personally) our souls and our bodies are parts of one whole, a totality we call life. In terms of a Christian spirituality that is integrated and that seeks to unify the divergent parts of our lives, we are to respond to God as present and active in our world, and in the events of our lives, and precisely in these moments of life to draw all the nearer to him and to each other in the holiness and power of the Holy Spirit. One way of looking at spirituality is to conceive of it as the way we respond to the Spirit of God in our prayer, in our actions, and in the deeds of witness we perform. All of this takes place in the texture and fabric of our human lives. While the life we live has parts that can be distinguished and separated, one of the tasks and purposes of Christian spirituality is to integrate them as parts of one whole—the Christian spiritual life. The perennial task is to seek and accomplish an integration among the many and divergent aspects of what is essentially one reality—the Christian life.

That this has been a perennial problem for Christianity is reflected in the statement from the *Pastoral Constitution on the Church in the Modern World:*

> Nor . . . are they any less wide of the mark who think that religion consists in acts of worship alone and in the discharge of certain moral obligations, and who imagine they can plunge themselves into earthly affairs in such a way as to imply that these are altogether divorced from the religious

life. This split between the faith which many profess and their daily lives deserves to be counted among the more serious errors of our age. Long since, the prophets of the Old Testament fought vehemently against this scandal and even more did Jesus Christ himself. . . . Therefore, let there be no false opposition between professional and social activities on the one part, and religious life on the other. (no. 43)

Worship and the rest of life are seen here to be correlatives and parts of one whole. The approach to spirituality advanced in this book seeks to be faithful to this integral approach in that it explores those things which comprise the experience of liturgy itself, the context of life in which they are experienced, and the implications which these ritual actions have for the rest of life. In the words of the Orthodox theologian Alexander Schmemann:

The Orthodox may have failed much too often to see the real implications of their "sacramentalism," but its fundamental meaning is certainly not that of escaping into a timeless "spirituality" far from the world of "action."[4]

While one of the tasks in Christian spirituality involves integrating the many facets of life (and for our purposes of determining a right understanding of the place of liturgy within human life) it is important to underscore that this task leads also to a renewed understanding of what holiness means. To be holy for the Christian is to experience the otherness of God in the here and now, and the setting for this experience is nothing other than our human lives. In Christian spirituality we are to allow God to take hold of all the events, choices, and experiences of our lives. It is not to separate holiness and worldliness; it is to make our worldly experiences and lives more and more reflections of the life of God in grace and love. To do this requires that we break down what Rahner has called the "old model" to see how the incarnation of Christ offers us a "new model" for understanding spirituality and for living the Christian life. In Rahner's old model sacraments are perceived as "religious rites which bypass the dimensions of 'real reality' or 'real life.' "[5] According to this view it is up to the individual to take sacraments and grace back into the world and to live in the world now personally graced by sacred ceremonies. Formulating a new model and way of approaching spirituality is made easier when those who share in liturgy and Christian prayer are conscious from the outset of being drawn into God's life and grace through Christ as experienced and made real in all of life.[6]

What is involved here is setting a new context for understanding what holiness really means. To become holy as based and grounded in the incarnation of Christ is to become more and more aware of what the life of God and life with God really means in everyday life, and of how all of reality is actually and truly graced because of the incarnation. "What holiness does is not to deliver us from the ordinary facts of human existence, but to transform our very ordinary existence from *within that ordinary existence.*"[7] To grow in holiness involves experiencing and viewing all of reality as graced in Christ and as redeemed by his life, death and resurrection. Hence, to become holy does not mean that we are supposed to escape time, place or the rest of reality.

From an incarnational perspective, spirituality does not mean juxtaposing the religious and human life, or the sacred on the secular, infusing the temporal with the eternal, or separating our bodies from our souls. Rather, it is to see all the facets of life (as well as these important distinctions) as reconciled and unified in the incarnation, in Christ. The life we lead is one life; allowing Christ's life and love to permeate each facet of life is what is involved in Christian spirituality.

INCARNATIONAL SPIRITUALITY

In the First Letter of John we read:

Beloved,
let us love one another
because love is of God;
everyone who loves is begotten of God
and has knowledge of God.

God's love was revealed in our midst in this way:
he sent his only Son to the world
that we might have life through him.

We have seen for ourselves, and can testify,
that the Father has sent the Son as savior of the world.
Our love is brought to perfection in this,
that we should have confidence on the day of judgment;
for our relation to this world is just like his.   (1 Jn 4:7, 9, 14, 17)

In many ways this text concretizes the implications of the mystery of the incarnation for us because it speaks about our being united to each other and to God because of love, a love made real (incarnate) in Christ. Christians believe that the incarnation of Christ stands at the center of history, as the beginning of the new era, the "year of our Lord." A fundamentally incarnational view of spirituality derived from this and other New Testament texts is based on the fact that what we call grace (and the divine life) is present everywhere where individuals do not close themselves to God.[8] The unity of the human and the divine (one of the aspects of the task involved in Christian spirituality) has been accomplished in Christ, and it is this irrevocable union of humanity and divinity in Christ that makes Christian spirituality that process of living out the implications of this mystery in our own lives.

In his humanity, Jesus came to be the image of the invisible God, and through his humanity to reveal to us who God is. In the incarnation, Jesus reveals the extraordinary love of God for us as lived out in the very ordinary circumstances of his human life. And it is precisely in living life in the ordinary that all that is of God was made credible for believers of that time and place and for believers of all ages. Because Jesus was the Son of God and yet embraced and shared our very human life, we can say that all of humanity has been transformed in him for those who believe. Human life is given new depth and dimension because of the event of Jesus' incarnation.

Because we are human beings who bear the image of God in our human lives (by baptism), for us Christian spirituality may be said to be oriented to making us more human—more and more the person God intends us to be. This fundamentally incarnational approach is an important foundation for Christian spirituality. We are made in the divine image so that in our lives we might bear the very life and love of God. The paradox of Christianity insists that the more we become like God, the more human, truly human, we become. And the more we transcend ourselves in faith, action, and prayer, the more we are remade again and again in the image of God. As the Eastern Fathers remind us, God took on human flesh so that we in our humanity might become divine.[9]

Christian spirituality is misconstrued and misdirected if we seek to let our bodies and souls separate where the soul lives with God and the body is consigned to the earth. Further, the soul is the source of life and activity in a person, and as whole persons (body and soul) we are remade in God's divine image. The complete and full union of the human and the divine, an accomplished fact in Christ in the mystery of the incarnation, is the task to be achieved by Christians. By becoming fully human, Christ "is both the sign of our destiny and the source of the only means of fulfillment. This conviction is expressed in the simple and bold formula that Jesus Christ our Lord, God's word, 'on account of his measureless love became what we are that he might make us in the end what he is.' "[10]

The issue here is the acknowledgement that we grow toward fullness in Christ, and that our lives come to reflect who God is. We cast aside false conceptions of self, inclinations toward evil and sin in order to allow God to dwell fully within us. By saying "no" to false images of ourselves and to those things, people or events that keep us from developing spiritually, we say "yes" to the Lord who made us, and who seeks to remake us again and again into fully developed human persons. The importance of our created humanity as graced irrevocably in the incarnation is stressed especially in the prayers used in the liturgy of the Christmas season. At the Mass at midnight we pray:

Lord,
accept our gifts on this joyful feast of our salvation.

By our communion with God made man,
may we become more like him
who joins our lives to yours. (Prayer over the gifts)

The lifelong task of Christians to grow in the life of God is noted
especially when we pray at the end of the Christmas Eucharist at
midnight:

God our Father,
we rejoice in the birth of our Savior.
May we share his life completely
by living as he taught. (Prayer after Communion)

The Christmas preface reiterates this as the humanity/divinity
interchange, and makes this mystery part of the declared mo-
tives for praise and thanks at the Eucharist:

Christ is your Son before all ages,
yet now he is born in time.
He has come to lift up all things to himself,
to restore unity to creation,
and to lead mankind from exile into your heavenly kingdom.
(Preface, Christmas II)

Christian spirituality involves that process of being ever assimilated into the mystery of God so that the intended unity of all
creation might be accomplished in Christ.

It is on the basis of this fundamentally incarnational view of
life and of spirituality that Rahner has developed his important
insight about grace. Grace is present

not as a special phenomenon, as one particular process *apart
from* the rest of human life. Rather it is quite simply the
ultimate depths and the radical dimension of all that which
the spiritual creature experiences, achieves and suffers in all
those areas in which it achieves its own fullness.[11]

Because of the incarnation, all human life is life lived in Christ
for those who believe and profess faith in him. The way we come

to experience the mystery of redemption is through, with and in Christ, the original manifestation of God's very being. The setting for this encounter is the very world in which we live.

This is to suggest that grace is not only available in sacred rites (Rahner's "old model"); grace is present where and when human life is lived authentically, where human beings are open to the reality of life and the love of Christ as experienced in all of life. Our humanity needs redemption because of the nature we inherit from Adam; but in the second Adam, Christ, humanity has been restored and redeemed. This is what takes place in the lives of believers both in and outside of the liturgy. In faith we know that the old order has passed away, and the sin we call original has been undone in the event of Christ's incarnation, which we call "the beginning of our redemption" (Christmas Vigil Mass, prayer over the gifts). Because of the incarnation "human nature *has been redeemed* and grace in Christ *is* always available to it."[12]

Just as the life of Jesus of Nazareth was ordinary in every way, and yet through this very ordinariness he accomplished redemption for us all because he obediently accepted his Father's will, so in an incarnational spirituality we are invited to live our ordinary human lives and to share our lives and loves with each other in such a way that we acknowledge and experience even here and now the life of God mediated once to us through Christ's humanity and as experienced now in our human lives.

What is involved in an incarnational approach to spirituality, therefore, is the acknowledgement that in Christ all of created life and all humanity has been transformed in and by him. We are reminded of this as we pray the New Testament canticles about Christ in evening prayer, especially the text from Ephesians:

> God has given us the wisdom
> to understand fully the mystery,
> the plan he was pleased
> to decree in Christ.
> A plan to be carried out
> in Christ, in the fullness of time,

to bring all things into one in him,
in the heavens and on the earth.   (Eph 1:9–10)

And as we pray in the eucharistic prayer:

In you we live and move and have our being,
Each day you show us a Father's love;
your Holy Spirit, dwelling within us,
gives us on earth the hope of unending joy.
                      (Preface, Sundays in Ordinary Time VI)

LITURGY AND SACRAMENTS

The way we come to experience the mystery of redemption
is in and through Christ, the original manifestation of God's
very being. Christ, in his humanity, has manifested to the world
the love of God, and precisely in this humanity allows us to
share in the life of God. Christ is therefore mediator, or, as
contemporary sacramental theologians use the term, Christ is
the original sacrament. Christ's " 'humanness' is *the* sign, *the*
symbol, *the* sacrament of God's self-communication to us; all
other signs, symbols and sacraments are secondary to the humanness of Jesus."[13] As the original sacrament of the Father,
Christ is intended to be the way for us to experience the actual-
ity of redemption. Christ is the sacrament of God for us.

The Church, as the community of those who share the life
of God in Christ, continues the mission of Christ in manifesting
(and discovering) the Father's life and love in space and time,
particularly in places and events far removed from the earthly
life of Jesus. This makes the Church the community of those
especially responsible for manifesting the life of God in Christ in
our world. In this sense, the Church as the continuation of
Christ in the world itself becomes sacrament, the ground sacrament, the community that lives in the sacramentality granted in
and through Christ the sacrament. "The Church is a sacrament
of the Christ event; it is a sacrament of a sacrament. . . . The
Church is the basic, historical and abiding sacrament of the
original, revelatory and one salvific self-communication of a
God who so loved the world that he gave it his only Son."[14]

As a basic sacrament, the Church—that is, the people of God—lifts into some sort of focus what our world, our history, our human existence is all about: a world that God loves in spite of sin, a redeemed world, a world that God himself has entered and shared in through the incarnation.[15]

The Church accomplishes this process in the events of ordinary human living in this world created and redeemed by God and now perceived as graced irrevocably in Christ. Individual sacraments and liturgical experiences rely on this incarnational approach to reality and on Christ and the Church as basic sacraments. Created humanity, our human condition, is the very stuff of the Christian life. It is not merely a means, made holy by grace, by which we can approach God. Rather, our human condition is the way through which we come to know God. The liturgy functions as part of this total process and as important moments in the Christian lives of those who comprise the ground sacrament, the Church. Individual sacraments and particular liturgical events function as moments of disclosure of redemption in Christ. They require that we commit ourselves to a new way of looking at life, from the perspective of and irreversible fact of Christ's humanness as the medium through which we experience divine life. What sacraments do is not to impose onto reality or to infuse into us what is not available elsewhere so that we can face the rest of our lives (Rahner's "old model"). What sacraments and liturgy do is to make explicit and to disclose in a concrete way what is available to the eyes of faith—a renewed humanity accomplished in the incarnation of Christ.

This approach to liturgy and sacraments places these experiences in a context that relates them to what has traditionally been called the "spiritual life." In this approach, the liturgy becomes an experience and a moment of disclosure. It is an experience that helps order and focus all of life. And yet it is not so compartmentalized and different from the rest of our experience that it could be considered apart from it. Liturgical prayer focuses and helps to disclose the sacramental nature of reality.

In this sense, liturgical prayer serves in the on-going development of a sacramental or liturgical view of life.

The purpose of liturgy and sacraments, then, is not to
deliver an experience of God, divorced from the rest of life.
Rather it is to be an extra-ordinary experience that helps disclose the presence of grace in all of reality, especially in the
communities where two or three gather in the name of the Lord.
Liturgy and sacraments do not deliver God to those present;
rather they offer believers the opportunity to reaffirm where and
how they relate to God, not only in the liturgical rites, but in the
rest of their lives as well.

Schmemann illustrates this point well when referring to the
place of Eucharist on Sunday:

> By remaining one of the ordinary days, and yet by revealing
> itself through the Eucharist as the eighth and first day, it gave
> all days true meaning. It made the time of this world a time of
> the *end,* and it made it also the time of the *beginning.*[16]

What occurs when celebrating Sunday Eucharist is to use the
things of this world (bread, wine) as the means by which we
affirm the goodness of all creation and the enduring presence of
Christ with us in the paschal mystery actualized in this celebration. We pray:

> All things are of your making,
> all times and seasons obey your laws,
> but you chose to create man in your own image,
> setting him over the whole world in all its wonder.
> You made man the steward of creation,
> to praise you day by day for the marvels of your wisdom
>   and power . . .
> > (Preface, Sundays in Ordinary Time V)

But the tangible means through which this is accomplished are
goods taken from creation, affirming the goodness of creation
especially now as graced in the incarnation. This celebration of
Eucharist occurs within the ordinary human rhythm of days,
taking one day from the rest and setting it aside as a time and

occasion when we step back from work (and play) to give perspective to these and all our human activities. In and through
the prayer of thanksgiving at liturgy we acknowledge the true
nature of things and God as the source of all creation and
redemption. We acknowledge that these things are received
from God, and in the Eucharist we bless the God who made
them and affirm his presence in all reality. Hence, Sunday
Eucharist is not an escape from the rest of reality for us; it is,
rather, a way of putting meaning into the rest of life.[17]

The symbolism of bread and wine is illustrative of what
occurs in the liturgical experience. In taking bread and wine we
do not use things which are "natural" (such as water and light).
Instead we take things which require human planning and inge-
nuity to make. Both bread and wine require planting (wheat,
grapes), harvesting and production. Hence these symbols in
themselves become very significant, for they reveal that what is
brought to liturgy is from the rest of life; they are important
symbols of nourishment. But they are also symbols of human
work and of human life. In becoming such, however, their
natural state has to give way to processing and industry. Besides
seeds having to fall and die to produce fruit (see Jn 12:24) both
the harvested grain and grapes have to "die" once more in
human labor to become other, new realities. The dying and
rising cycle of nature is repeated in the making of the eucharistic
symbols, bread and wine. As such, we can see that at the very
basic level of what is brought to the Eucharist from life is itself
disclosive, a sign and important symbol of the cycle of nature
and the rhythm of our lives, dying and rising. Is it any wonder
that these rich symbols are used at the liturgy to become the real
sign and symbol of Christ, whose death and resurrection is
proclaimed and effected in the Eucharist.[18] But these symbols
are not objects; they are taken and shared in the setting of a
meal so that participants can experience in these signs the life of
Christ and the life of grace he offers us.

In baptism we take the mystery of life (new birth or adult
growth) and give it its direction and purpose from the point of
view of Christ's paschal mystery, his passage from life in this
world, through the experience of life's end in death, to life

eternal gained through his resurrection. In sacramental initiation we affirm the gift of life and the beauty of the human
person as created by God, and through word and sacrament
disclose the deepest meaning of life for the believer, life lived
with God. The event is not an event out of time; it is rather a
moment in time (the first sacramental moment for infants) when
the goodness of creation and the gift of redemption is affirmed
and experienced. From this event on, the life of the believer is
forever marked as a life in which God's grace is operative and
through this grace the initiated comes to see all the rest of life
from the unique perspective of faith. Just as the human experience of eating and drinking is fundamental to the experience of
Eucharist, so the human experience of birth and life is the
foundation and setting for the sacramental event. All seven
sacraments are best understood, not as isolated moments of
grace experienced, but rather as moments of disclosure of God's
presence in the world as articulated in these particular and
significant moments in life's journey. Hence, sacraments help us
see how all of reality is redeemed and how all of life should be
interpreted in the light of God's presence within it.

The recent revision of the liturgy of the hours is another
concrete example of the intersection of time with the timeless in
God, and how through these moments of prayer believers articulate what is believed before and after these meetings for prayer.
What is involved at morning and evening, for example, is consecrating the day's prayer and work to the Lord (morning prayer),
and offering thanks for those things done well during it or
asking for forgiveness for the day's misdeeds (evening prayer).[19]
The liturgy of the hours is not an escape from the pressures of
the world or a respite from the fast pace of life to spend time
with God so much as it is the traditional means through which
communities of Christians gather to express the goodness and
beauty of all creation as coming from God, and to express the
praise and thanksgiving of all creation to its author and maker.
In the words of the Taizé office:

> The prayer of the Daily Office is part of the praise of the
> whole of creation offered to its Creator. [Our] first and

ultimate vocation is to give an intelligible form to this universal praise, and the liturgy of the Church, the Daily Office in
particular, expresses this above all. . . . By the very fact of its
existence, creation praises its maker, but this praise needs a
spiritual expression. . . . The Daily Office gives a biblical and
universal form to this prayer offered by every Christian in the
name of the whole creation.[20]

Just as we can affirm that sacraments are congruous with the
human condition, and "they are mysteries because they embody
the mysterious presence of God active in human situations and
are signs of it,"[21] so we can say that the prayer of Christians at
the liturgy of the hours discloses the deepest meaning of created
reality and gives form and articulation to the praise which is
continually offered to God by created (and redeemed) reality.

From the perspective of an incarnational approach to spirituality, liturgy and sacraments function as important means
whereby communities of Christians secure and reaffirm their
identity and that of all created reality in Christ. The rites and
symbols that comprise the liturgy become the means through
which communities gain perspective on their lives in Christ, and
reaffirm the value of all of creation now redeemed in Christ. Yet,
while the liturgy has this privileged position in terms of created
reality, it also offers a challenge to communities who gather for
common prayer. This concerns the implications which this approach to liturgy and sacraments has for living out the Christian
life.

LITURGY AND LIFE

In the light of the incarnational approach to spirituality we
can say that Jesus came into the world not to set up special
categories of what is religious and what is not. In fact, as we
have seen, one of the purposes of his taking on human flesh was
to unite in himself the sacred and the secular, the religious and
the human, the eternal and the temporal. From a spiritual point
of view this translates to mean that Jesus came to give a new
perspective to the human life that we lead; Jesus came to vivify

the ordinary and to help us see that it is in the very ordinary events of life that he dwells with us. In Christ there is a perfect convergence and congruence between these polarities in life. What liturgy is meant to do is to help us achieve a similar convergence and congruence in the activities which we assign to religious observance and to the rest of the activities of our lives. Cult and life are parts of each other with cult as an important part of life because it discloses the real meaning and depth of meaning in life.

For example, the revised rite of anointing and pastoral care of the sick envisions a communal celebration offering and interceding for healing, hope and encouragement for those weary with the burden of old age or infirm with the burden of illness. What occurs in the celebration of this sacramental rite is taking infirm and suffering humanity and offering it to the Lord of all creation. The point of the ritual is really to disclose the real meaning of illness and sickness in our lives, and to present an horizon of hope and a perspective of well-being for those anointed. But the fullest dimensions of this rite are not disclosed in the liturgical experience in isolation. Rather, as the general instruction to the rite states:

> Moreover, the role of the sick in the Church is to be a reminder to others of the essential or higher things. By their witness the sick show that our mortal life must be redeemed through the mystery of Christ's death and resurrection.[22]

Hence, what is celebrated in faith in sign and symbol in anointing is that in faith we believe that this world will pass away and that physical health is not the most desired good of all. What is envisioned in this sacramental celebration is the realization that in Christ all has been restored and renewed, and that those who share now in physical suffering themselves are united with him in a particular moment of his own passion and death. What is proclaimed and realized in faith in the ritual of anointing is that sickness and suffering are redemptive when seen from the perspective of Jesus' own suffering and redemptive death. Since the sick and the suffering share even now in the life of Christ in a particular way they themselves become sign and symbol for us of what it means to live in this world. Paradoxically, the weak and infirm reveal to us what real life is all about. The question for believers consists in whether and to what extent they see their lives enriched and focused by the anointing of fellow Christians whose very sufferings reveal depth and dimension to the whole of human life. The very infirmity of the aged and the suffering of the sick thus become sacramental as these real-life situations help disclose what the life of faith is all about—life lived in God's hands as we live in this passing world. From an incarnational perspective it can be asserted that the limits imposed on persons dealing with sickness and death are transformed and given new meaning because of the limits experienced by Jesus himself whose free acceptance of the deepest of human limits, death, led to our being freed from the death-limit in human life. In faith we know that after the pattern of life established in Christ, the limitations imposed on us in this life will pass away to reveal life eternal with God forever.

Another significant aspect of this revised ritual that exemplifies what is involved in the communal life shared by Christians is seen in the very fact that the rite is now called the "Pastoral Care of the Sick." It is not so much a question of the ritual of anointing itself in isolation from the rest of the life experience of the sick. Rather (and in accord with the view of liturgy expressed here) it is more a question of how this rite fits into the life-context of caring for the sick, and of how the sick offer others the opportunity to serve in a way that befits the vocation of the Christian. The responsibility Christians have for each other is not only that the right ritual is performed at the right times; it is that we bear each other's burdens and carry each other's crosses outside the special moments we call sacraments and liturgy. If we come to view all of reality from the perspective of the incarnation, then we see each other as brothers and sisters in the Lord. This suggests that the bond forged in baptism as unity in Christ is lived out and made real in situations of charity and love.

What is envisioned is a congruence and convergence in our lives both at sacraments and in the rest of life that imitates Jesus' own compassion and concern for the sick. This is what gives Christian liturgy its fullest expression and extension. As moments of disclosure and discovery, Christian sacraments help us to perceive the hand of God at work in all of life and to appreciate what being in Christ requires of us in response to his life. Sacraments remind us, who are members of the Church, the body of Christ, that we are part of each other in a relationship which was begun at baptism and which continues through the rest of our lives. We worship in community and we are reminded of our responsibilities to each other when we join in common prayer. When we come together for liturgy and sacraments it is these very celebrations that remind us that we do not live in isolation. As members of each other in Christ our responsibilities extend beyond the liturgy to all of life.

To celebrate sacraments is to commit ourselves time and again to the implications which this human life lived in Christ places upon us. As the Liturgy Constitution puts it:

> The liturgy is thus the outstanding means by which the faithful can express in their lives, and manifest to others, the mystery of Christ and the real nature of the true Church. It is of the essence of the Church that it be both human and divine, visible and yet invisibly expressed, eager to act and yet devoted to contemplation, present in this world and yet not at home in it. . . . Day by day the liturgy builds up those within the Church into the Lord's holy temple, into a spiritual dwelling for God (cf Eph 2:21–22)—an enterprise which will continue until Christ's full stature is achieved (cf Eph 4:13). (no. 2)

This implies that those who participate in liturgy and sacraments understand that liturgy derives from and leads back to human life. Christian liturgy makes sense when we see the rituals employed as derived from the whole of our lives, especially as those lives are redeemed and sanctified in the incarnation of Christ. As we pray at the eucharistic liturgy:

> So great was your love
> that you gave us your Son as our redeemer.

You sent him as one like ourselves,
though free from sin,
that you might see and love in us
what you see and love in Christ.
Your gifts of grace, lost by disobedience,
are now restored by the obedience of your Son.
                    (Preface, Sundays in Ordinary Time VII)

More specifically with regard to the lack of harmony and reconciliation in our world it is important to reflect on the words of
the eucharistic prayer for reconciliation:

In the midst of conflict and division,
we know it is you
who turn our minds to thoughts of peace.
Your Spirit changes our hearts:
enemies begin to speak to one another,
those who were estranged join hands in friendship,
and nations seek the way of peace together.

Your Spirit is at work
when understanding puts an end to strife,
when hatred is quenched by mercy,
and vengeance gives way to forgiveness.
                (Eucharistic Prayer for Masses of Reconciliation II)

This reveals what is meant by incarnational spirituality—for it
means that our very human lives are the place where the life of
the Spirit is lived out ("spirituality"), and because of our faith in
Christ we realize that it is in our human lives that God touches
us with grace in Christ ("incarnational"). The more we allow
our human lives to be transformed in Christ the more we will
realize that it is in the very ordinary moments of life that God
continues to reveal to us the depths of his love and mercy.
Because of the incarnation we believe that our very ordinary
lives are truly extraordinarily graced in Christ; and because of
the incarnational approach to spirituality we know that our task
is to make this extraordinarily powerful love of Christ credible
in our world. Ordinary life is indeed made extraordinary by the

incarnation; and it is up to Christians to make this extraordinary mystery credible by the kind of lives they lead. Christian ritual is made all the richer when we realize that it derives from the rest of our lives, and that it leads us back to the situations of our human lives, lives forever graced in Christ.

NOTES

1. See Part One, Chapter One, section on "Spirituality and Liturgy."

2. See Karl Rahner, "Considerations on the Active Role of the Person in the Sacramental Event," in *Theological Investigations* Vol. XIV, trans. David Bourke (New York: Seabury, 1976) pp. 162–165.

3. *Ibid.,* p. 162.

4. Alexander Schmemann, *For the Life of the World* (London: Darton, Longman and Todd, 1966) p. 24.

5. K. Rahner, "Considerations," p. 163.

6. *Ibid.,* p. 165.

7. Joseph Powers, *Spirit and Sacrament.* The Humanizing Experience (New York: Seabury, 1973) p. 128.

8. K. Rahner, "Considerations," p. 166.

9. See, for example, the texts collected in Louis Richard, *The Mystery of the Redemption* (Baltimore: Helicon Press, 1965) pp. 141–149.

10. From Irenaeus, cited in Aelred Squire, *Asking the Fathers,* p. 23.

11. K. Rahner, "Considerations," p. 167.

12. Michael J. Taylor, "Introduction," *The Sacraments,* Readings in Contemporary Sacramental Theology (Staten Island: Alba House, 1981) pp. ix–x.

13. Kenan Osborne, "Methodology and the Christian Sacraments," *Worship* 48 (November 1974) 538.

14. *Ibid.,* 542.

15. *Ibid.,* 543.

16. A Schmemann, *For the Life of the World,* p. 63.

17. *Ibid.,* p. 65.

18. See Philippe Rouillard, "From Human Meal to Christian Worship," *Worship* 52 (September 1978) 428–432.

19. See *General Instruction, Liturgy of the Hours,* nos. 38–39.

20. *The Taizé Office* (London: The Faith Press, 1966) p. 9.

21. J. D. Crichton, *Christian Celebration: The Sacraments* (London: G. Chapman, 1974) p. 13. See also, by the same author, "The Sacraments and Human Life," in M. J. Taylor, ed., *The Sacraments*, pp. 31–37. The author relies heavily on the important work of Henri-Denis, *Les sacrements ont-ils un avenir?* (Paris, 1971). See, also by Denis, *Des sacrements et des hommes* (Lyon, 1975).

22. *General Instruction, Rite of Anointing and Pastoral Care of the Sick*, no. 3.

Part Two:

ELEMENTS OF LITURGICAL PRAYER

Chapter Four
CORPORATE WORK DONE IN FAITH

In beginning to delineate and describe the elements of liturgical prayer it is important to begin with the context within which all liturgical prayer takes place, the gathered community of faith. It was noted above[1] that the language of the faith relationship of the covenanted people in the Testaments Old and New is prayer and that it is liturgical prayer especially that is the context for carrying on and sustaining the dialogue between God and his people. While it is axiomatic to say that Christian liturgical prayer is essentially communal, it is really more precise to maintain that liturgical prayer is that which is experienced and accomplished in a community which acts and works in communion with each other as the body of Christ. This foundation is more accurately described as a "work" done by the gathered community as a response in faith to the God who has called and who continues to call them in the gifted relationship of faith and love.[2]. It is the purpose of this chapter to explore the reality that all liturgical prayer is essentially prayer done in faith by the community whose identity and very life derives from the call of God.[3] Liturgical prayer is "corporate" in the sense that it is experienced in the community of the Church (with all its gifts and ministries), it is a "work" in the sense that it is experienced and accomplished by means of the active involvement of the entire community, and it is "done in faith" in the sense that the rationale and basis for any liturgical prayer is the fact that it is based on the faith shared, expressed and professed in common by the community gathered in the name of the Lord.

65

GOD'S PRESENCE TO A REDEEMED COMMUNITY

That the gathering of the community in faith was essential and foundational for the piety and common prayer of Judaism at the time of Jesus is seen in the fact that whether it was in the temple liturgies of sacrifice or in the synagogue assemblies of the word or in the sabbath meals at home, these experiences of liturgical prayer were shared in common. The God who called Abraham, Isaac, Jacob, Moses and all the chosen people was the God experienced ever anew at liturgical gatherings in Israel. The God of the covenant (the "God of Abraham, Isaac and Jacob") is a God who called (and calls) contemporary congregations the way he called the patriarchs, prophets and all succeeding generations of the chosen people—Israel. That the chosen were called to liturgical gatherings is clear, for example, in the Old Testament references to the renewal and annual commemoration of the Passover (Ex 12:1–27), in their being gathered for the hearing of the word (Neh 8:1–8) and periodic assemblies for repentance (Jl 2:12–18).[4]

That this notion of the close correlation between liturgical forms of prayer and the community gathered to pray them continues in the new people of God in the new covenant in Christ is seen in the Scriptures where the Lord promises to be present where "two or three are gathered" in his name (Mt 18:20). The custom of coming together to pray is underscored in the verse preceding this text which states: "If two of you join your voices on earth to pray for anything whatever, it shall be granted you by my Father in heaven" (Mt 18:19). Those who gather are those who have been baptized, who profess faith in the Lord, and who have been redeemed by the dying and rising of Christ. That such is a foundation for the contemporary experience of Christian liturgical prayer is seen in one of the prefaces used at Sunday Eucharist:

> Through his cross and resurrection
> he freed us from sin and death
> and called us to the glory that has made us

a chosen race, a royal priesthood,
a holy nation, a people set apart.
                              (Preface, Sundays in Ordinary Time I)

As the text of 1 Peter 2:9–10, from which the text of the preface
is derived, states: "You are . . . a people he claims for his own to
proclaim the glorious works of the One who called you from
darkness into his marvelous light." There is an intrinsic connection between being among the chosen and those who continue
to praise, remember and thank the Father for his constant call
and covenant love and forgiveness.

In the frequently cited text of the Acts of the Apostles 2:42,
which admittedly is an idealized picture of the enduring values
which should shape the Church's life,[5] there is a close correlation between the gathering together of the community and the
experience of sharing in common prayer: "And they devoted
themselves to the apostles' teaching and fellowship, to the
breaking of bread and the prayers." The situating of liturgy in
the gathered community leads to the understanding (and long-
standing assumption) that sanctification is experienced at common worship. It is these correlatives—the common life and
liturgical prayer—which mark the earliest evidences we have of
directions for Christian community prayer.

In the *Apology* of St. Justin (written around 150) the author
gives directions for the liturgy of the Lord's day. He states:

On the day named after the sun, all who live in city or
countryside assemble.
The memoirs of the apostles or the writings of the prophets
are read for us. . . .
. . . the president addresses us and exhorts us to imitate the
splendid things we have heard.
Then we all stand and pray.
. . . when we have finished praying, bread, wine, and water are
brought up. The president then prays and gives thanks according to his ability, and the people give their assent with an
'Amen!'

> ... the gifts ... are distributed, and everyone shares in them....
>
> The wealthy who are willing make contributions, each as he pleases, and the collection is deposited with the president, who aids orphans and widows.[6]

What is instructive about this text is that it reflects the coming together of the community for Eucharist, the sharing in the celebration by all present in word, gesture and in receiving the eucharistic gifts, and the concern that is evidenced for the poor of the community. The correlation of coming together for prayer, common worship, and the concern for the community (especially the poor) cited in Acts 2:42 is seen in this text from a time that is perhaps a century later. Clearly, liturgical prayer is based on the coming together, the assembly of "all who live in city or countryside."

That the Lord's day is marked with the celebration of Eucharist is cited and assumed in another early Church document, the *Didache*.[7] It states:

> Come together on the Lord's day,
> break bread and give thanks,
> having first confessed your sins
> so that your sacrifice may be pure.
> Anyone who has a quarrel with his fellow
> should not gather with you
> until he has been reconciled,
> lest your sacrifice be profaned.[8]

In specifying the kind of prayer texts to be used by the early Christian community the *Didache* refers to the hoped-for unity of the community of the Church:

> Just as the bread broken
> was first scattered on the hills,
> then was gathered and became one,
> so let your Church be gathered

from the ends of the earth into your kingdom,
for yours is glory and power through all ages.[9]

This early evidence (once again) suggests concern for the community gathered for prayer. Interestingly, it uses the underlying natural symbolism of grain made into bread as a way of speaking of intercession for the Church everywhere, that it might be gathered into the kingdom forever.

In a final example of the liturgical life of the Christian Church in this early and formative period we note the same concern for the unity of those who take part in the Eucharist and all who comprise the Church in a text of Hippolytus from the third century:

And we pray you
to send your Holy Spirit
on the offering of your holy Church,
to bring together in unity
all those who receive it.
May they be filled with the Holy Spirit
who strengthens their faith in the truth.
May we be able thus to praise and glorify you
through your Child Jesus Christ.[10]

What occurs here is the beginning of an explicit invocation in liturgical prayer for the unity of the Church as a result of the Spirit's action and continued involvement in the community. Such explicit prayers for the unity of the gathered community are called *epicleses* and are found in all the newly-composed and recently introduced eucharistic prayers in the Roman liturgy. These prayers have been hallmarks of the tradition of the eucharistic prayer, although such an explicit invocation is not found in the Roman Canon itself.[11] Liturgy is experienced in the community God calls together. The experience of liturgical prayer may be said to assume the gathering of the community and to contain prayers for those assembled as well as for the whole Church. Those who come together affirm their faith and trust in

the God of the covenant, and it is at moments of shared liturgical prayer that this relationship of faith and love is experienced
and expressed anew. As we frequently pray at our Sunday Eucharist:

> When your children sinned
> and wandered far from your friendship,
> you reunited them with yourself
> through the blood of your Son
> and the power of the Holy Spirit.
> You gather them into your Church,
> to be one as you, Father, are one
> with your Son and the Holy Spirit.
> You call them to be your people,
> to praise your wisdom in all your works.
> You make them the body of Christ
> and the dwelling-place of the Holy Spirit.
>
> (Preface, Sundays in Ordinary Time VIII)

THE CHURCH AT PRAYER—A CORPORATE WORK

Liturgy is often described as the prayer of the Church.[12] In
the earliest understanding of this description liturgy was experienced as the prayer in which the assembled community shared;
the gathered community was the foundation and setting for the
celebration of the liturgy. It was where twos and threes were
gathered that the proclaimed texts came alive, the chanted
psalms were given their fullest expression as inspired songs, and
the gestures performed made sense because the movement directed in common prayer most often involved the whole community. And yet over the course of centuries this dynamic and
active understanding of "the Church's prayer" came to be experienced less and less fully (or frequently) with the result that the
Church at prayer was not so evident. What occurred was more
explicit directions for the ministers of the liturgy (very often the
one minister, the priest) and fewer and fewer (if any!) directions
for the community which came together to pray. It is no wonder
that the liturgy came to be understood less as the Church *at*
prayer, and more as the Church's prayer in the sense of the texts

used at the liturgy. Intercession *for* the Church took prominence over praying *with,* or *among* the Church; liturgical texts themselves came to be identified with liturgy as opposed to understanding text and gesture, proclamation and singing as vital parts of the experience of worship. A more and more clear separation was made between congregations (largely passive) and those responsible for carrying out the liturgy, the clergy. These were charged with the task of interceding on behalf of the Church.[13]

Certainly in practice the gestures and actions of the liturgy remained for the clergy, but equally clear was the fact that these came to be appreciated less and less as integral parts and essential aspects of the prayer of the whole community. A solemn Mass and a private Mass, for example, had the same texts; what differentiated them was external performance and the number of ministers involved in that performance. It was a small step now for liturgy to be seen as texts for the clergy only, and whether these were "said" in a private setting (recitation of breviary alone or private Masses, for example) or were said, proclaimed and sung in Latin in large assemblies (solemn high Mass, for example) made little difference for the community present.

The difficulty here involves the fact that the essential foundation of the liturgy as an experience of communal prayer eventually dropped out of consideration in Roman Catholic practice. That the Liturgy Constitution of Vatican II was concerned to redirect attention away from individuals praying the texts and performing the rites of the liturgy (or individuals engaged in private devotions during the liturgy itself) and to restore the fundamentally corporate understanding and appreciation of the liturgy is clear.

> Liturgical services are not private functions, but are celebrations of the Church, which is the "sacrament of unity". . . . Therefore liturgical services pertain to the whole body of the Church; they manifest it and have effects upon it. . . . (no. 26)
>
> It is to be stressed that whenever rites, according to their specific nature, make provision for communal celebration

involving the presence and active participation of the faithful, this way of celebrating them is to be preferred, as far as possible, to a celebration that is individual and quasi-private. (no. 27)

This notion of the liturgy can be joined with the notion of the Church as "sacramental" (noted in Chapter Three). Since contemporary theology understands Christ as the sacrament of God the Father, and therefore the community which professes faith in Christ can be understood as sacramental, then individual Christians who share this life of faith in and among the community are, by that very participation, sharers in the life of God. Coming together for liturgy becomes not just an added extra, or a nice thing if possible; rather coming together for common prayer is the means whereby the community confirms its very life as derived from Christ and as shared with each other. Specific liturgical celebrations become the times of manifesting and expressing what this identity is all about—the life of faith in God shared in the Church. This kind of understanding of sacraments is stated clearly in the General Instruction on the Rite of Penance:

The whole Church, as a priestly people, acts in different ways in the work of reconciliation which has been entrusted to it by the Lord. Not only does the Church call sinners to repentance by preaching the word of God, but it also intercedes for them and helps penitents with maternal care and solicitude to acknowledge and admit their sins and so attain the mercy of God who alone can forgive sins. Furthermore, the Church becomes the instrument of the conversion and absolution of the penitent through the ministry entrusted by Christ to the apostles and their successors. (no. 8)

The Assembly—After centuries of eclipse liturgically, the assembly that comes together for the prayer of worship is now emphasized in the revised liturgical rites.[14] In the General Instruction of the Roman Missal, the role of those who gather to celebrate the liturgy is noted before any other ministers are mentioned: "Everyone in the eucharistic assembly has the right and duty to take his own part according to the diversity of orders and functions." (no. 58)

This text overturns centuries of eucharistic piety when congregations remained largely passive during the liturgy. It also fulfills one of the main purposes of the reform of the liturgy as is stated in the Liturgy Constitution of Vatican II:

> Mother Church earnestly desires that all the faithful be led to that full, conscious, and active participation in liturgical celebrations which is demanded by the very nature of the liturgy. Such participation by the Christian people as "a chosen race, a royal priesthood, a holy nation, a purchased people" (1 Pet 2:9; cf 2:4–5), is their right and duty by reason of their baptism.

> In the restoration and promotion of the sacred liturgy, this full and conscious participation by all the people is the aim to be considered before all else; for it is the primary and indispensable source from which the faithful are to derive the true Christian spirit. (no. 14)

The active involvement of the community is seen in the restored texts which are proclaimed and recited in the vernacular, and these prayer texts clearly speak of the whole community when they state "*we* believe in one God" or "*we* ask this through Christ our Lord." The restoration of the sign of peace to a position of emphasis underscores the fundamentally communal nature of worship. (Is it any wonder that the implementation of this gesture at the Eucharist was so hotly contested and debated? It was the single moment in the eucharistic liturgy when congregations had to acknowledge that it was their common worship as a body that was important; it was no longer to be a collection of individuals praying at the same time.)

In the important document *Environment and Art in Catholic Worship* it states:

> Because liturgical celebration is the worship action of the entire Church, it is desirable that persons representing the diversity of ages, sexes, ethnic and cultural groups in the

congregation should be involved in planning and ministering in the liturgies of the community. . . . The entire congregation is an active component. There is no audience, no passive element in the liturgical celebration. (no. 30)

This is again emphasized when this same document states that the primary demand in designing a "house for the church" is the assembly: "The norm for designing liturgical space is the assembly and its liturgies."[15]

Liturgical Roles—The same documents which speak about the importance of the assembly as the locus for the liturgical action speak equally clearly about the restoration of the variety of liturgical roles.

In liturgical celebrations, whether as a minister or as one of the faithful, each person should perform his role by doing solely and totally what the nature of things and liturgical norms require. . . .

Servers, lectors, commentators and members of the choir [among others] also exercise a genuine liturgical ministry. (Liturgy Constitution, nos. 28–29)

The following text on liturgical ministries from *Environment and Art in Catholic Worship* is particularly insightful and challenging:

Different ministries in [the] assembly do not imply "superiority" or "inferiority." Different functions are necessary in the liturgy as they are in any human, social activity. The recognition of different gifts and talents and the ordination, institution or delegation for the different services required (priest, reader, acolyte, musician, usher, etc.) is to facilitate worship. These are services to the assembly and those who perform them are servants of God who render services to the assembly. Those who perform such ministries are indeed servants of the assembly. (no. 37)

That the restoration of liturgical roles is important for the integrity of the liturgy and for the correct imaging of the Church in worship settings is a factor that should not be underestimated. The issue here concerns the collaboration of many diverse people for one act of liturgy. This means that the Church in all its diversity is represented (imaged) in the act of worship. The conventional eclipsing of liturgical roles into one, the priest (most usually), is overturned in the reformed liturgy. The Church at prayer is to be evident in the roles and ministries performed by members of the assembly gathered in the name of the Lord. An observation that may well be made about the implementation of the directives of the Council about liturgical roles concerns their relationship to the whole assembly. A criticism that has been made of liturgical ministries as implemented after the Council is that while the ministers were more usually prepared and trained for these roles and most performed well their newly rediscovered tasks at the liturgy, more often than not the rest of the assembly was neglected in terms of their necessary involvement and liturgical participation. Frequently it needs to be emphasized that those ministering at the liturgy serve the community and their functioning should not negate the involvement and participation of the assembly itself. A restored liturgy that is performance-oriented, by priest and ministers, does not get to the heart of the reform. In addition, from the perspective of a traditional understanding of ministry, those who ministered liturgically were also those who served the Christian community outside of the liturgy. That this is envisioned in the present reform of the liturgy is clear in the documentation about deacons and about special ministers of the Eucharist. These are to serve their brothers and sisters outside the liturgical assembly, thus making their liturgical role all the more rich and more true to the nature of ministry.[16]

When properly understood and properly exercised, the roles of the assembly at liturgy and of individual ministers within the liturgy help underscore the essentially communal understanding of worship. That the Church should be and become a worshiping community, an active community at prayer, is envisioned in the reform of the liturgy as we now experience it. Planning and ministering at liturgy is the task and responsibility of the whole community—the assembly primarily, in conjunction with those who exercise a special competency in celebration.

Communal Celebration of Rites—It was the intention of the Liturgy Constitution of Vatican II to restore the communal celebration of the liturgy to a central position despite centuries of practice which tolerated both communal and private liturgy as co-equal. This is made clear in the revised rites which always give pride of place to the communal celebration, for even when a quasi-private celebration may be required this is seen to be less significant as liturgical celebration.

> The assembly's celebration, that is, celebration in the midst of the faith community, by the whole community, is the normal and normative way of celebrating any sacrament or other liturgy. Even when the communal dimension is not apparent, as sometimes in communion for the sick or for prisoners, the clergy or ministers function within the context of the entire community.[17]

For example, the restoration of the liturgy of the hours to a position of prominence in the daily liturgical life of Catholics is evident in the General Instruction which speaks about the communal celebration of the hours:

> Its ecclesial celebration is best seen and especially recommended when it is performed . . . by the local Church. . . .
> Wherever possible the more important hours could be celebrated in common in the church.
> If the faithful come together and unite their hearts and voices in the Liturgy of the Hours, they manifest the Church celebrating the mystery of Christ.
> The task of those who are in sacred orders or who have a canonical mission is to direct and preside over the prayer of the community. . . . (nos. 2–23)

These statements, especially the last one, underscore the shift from the prayer of the Church stressing intercession *for* the Church to the present and preferred experience of the Church at prayer. Those who were bound to the "recitation of the

Divine Office" are here instructed to lead the people of Christ in the celebration of the hours of prayer. This particular mandate is significant because it puts a whole new cast on the clerics' obligation to the office. In fact, this is a restoration of what was the primary experience of the Church's prayer of the hours, with assembly and ministers in prayer together with those exercising liturgical roles leading the whole assembly in common prayer.[18] As the Instruction states: "Celebration in common, however, expresses more clearly the ecclesial nature of the liturgy of the hours; it makes for active participation by all, in a way suited to each one's condition. . . ." (no. 33)

Christian initiation is a clear example of how the sacamental practice of private celebrations has been overturned in the recent reform. The whole of the Rite of Christian Initiation of Adults is predicated on a communal experience of the catechumenate, particularly the community's participation in the immediate preparation of these candidates for initiation (during Lent leading to the Easter Vigil).

> The initiation of the catechumens is a gradual process that takes place within the community of the faithful. Together with the catechumens, the faithful reflect upon the value of the paschal mystery, renew their own conversion, and by their example lead the catechumens to obey the Holy Spirit more generously.[19]

This same principle of communal involvement in preparation and in the actual celebration of initiation is the same for infants as is clearly seen in the revised rite.

> The people of God, that is, the Church, made present by the local community, has an important part to play in the baptism of both children and adults.

> . . . On Sunday, baptism may be celebrated even during Mass, so that the entire community may be present and the relationship between baptism and eucharist may be clearly seen. . . .

> The Church has always understood ... that children should
> not be deprived of baptism, because they are baptized in the
> faith of the Church, a faith proclaimed for them by their
> parents and godparents, who represent both the local Church
> and the whole society of saints and believers.... [20]

While the communal celebration of the sacraments of initiation did have some precedent in the conventional practice of group baptism for infants and communal confirmations, the ritual revisions concerning the more individual and "private" sacraments of penance and anointing of the sick bring out even more clearly and directly the communal dimension of the whole sacramental and liturgical life of the Church.

Certainly the most private and personal of the sacraments has been the practice of the liturgy of penance in confession. In the General Instruction of this sacrament the intention of the Liturgy Constitution (that this rite be revised) is fulfilled when it states that the "communal celebration [of penance] shows more clearly the ecclesial nature of penance." (no. 22) The revised rite of this sacrament contains three sacramental forms, two of which are communal in nature and in celebration.[21] As the General Instruction on Penance states:

> In the sacrament of penance the faithful obtain from God's
> mercy pardon for having offended him and at the same time
> reconciliation with the Church, which they have wounded by
> their sins and which by charity, for example, and prayer seeks
> their conversion. (no. 4)

> ... Penance always therefore entails reconciliation with our
> brothers and sisters who remain harmed by our sins.

> In fact, people frequently join together to commit injustice.
> But it is also true that they help each other in doing penance;
> freed from sin by the grace of Christ, they become, with all
> persons of good will, agents of justice and peace in the world.
> (no. 5)

That the role of the Church is important in all the forms of the rite of penance (including that for individual confession and absolution) is seen in the revised formula for absolution:

> God, the father of mercies,
> through the death and resurrection of his Son
> has reconciled the world to himself
> and sent the Holy Spirit among us
> for the forgiveness of sins;
> *through the ministry of the Church*
> may God give you pardon and peace,
> and I absolve you from your sins
> in the name of the Father, and of the Son,
> and of the Holy Spirit.[22]

The revised rite for the anointing of the sick and their pastoral care indicates the significant role of the Church in this ministry and of the community gathered for the rite of anointing:

> It is thus especially fitting that all baptized Christians share in this ministry of mutual charity within the Body of Christ by doing all that they can to help the sick return to health, by showing love for the sick, and by celebrating the sacraments with them. Like the other sacraments, these too have a community aspect, which should be brought out as much as possible when they are celebrated. (no. 33)

This review of the revised rites of the liturgy of the hours and of the sacraments of initiation, penance and anointing illustrates a main concern in the liturgical revisions we now experience: that the Church as the community gathered together in faith plays an important role in liturgy and in the life setting from which liturgical rites come.

Prayer for the Local and Universal Church—To speak of the "Church at prayer" is to speak of the concrete reality of local communities and local gatherings for liturgical prayer. One of the principles involved here, however, concerns the relationship of each and every local (particular) celebration of liturgy with the Church throughout the world. No celebration of liturgy is intended for self-concerned or self-sufficient communities. Each reaches beyond the local gathering to the rest of the body represented, and this (always) includes the Church universal. There are three particular occasions in the liturgy when explicit reference is made to how each celebrating assembly relates to the wider Church, and, in turn, how the needs of the wider Church become concrete in each local celebration. The first example involves the recently restored general intercessions, whether in the sacraments (the "prayer of the faithful") or at the liturgy of the hours (particularly the intercessions at evening prayer). The structure laid out for the intercessions at Eucharist is as follows:

> In the general intercessions or prayer of the faithful, the people, exercising their priestly function, intercede for all humanity. It is appropriate that this prayer be included in all Masses celebrated with a congregation, so that petitions will be offered for the Church, for civil authorites, for those oppressed by various needs, for all people, and for the salvation of the world.[23]

The sequence of these prayers follows this outline with the addition that toward the end there may be those "for the local community." It is customary that the last petition be for the dead.[24]

The General Instruction on the liturgy of the hours relates these intercessory prayers to the whole of the hour of evening prayer by stating:

> Since the liturgy of the hours is above all the prayer of the whole Church for the whole Church, indeed for the salvation of the whole world, universal intentions should take precedence over all others, namely, for: the Church and its ministers; secular authorities; the poor, the sick, and the sorrowful;

the needs of the whole world, that is, peace and other intentions of this kind. (no. 187)

The clear direction given here (as well as in the sample formulas for the intercessions in the Sacramentary or the intercessions at evening prayer in the liturgy of the hours) is that local communities gathered for prayer should always be attentive to the needs and concerns of the Church throughout the whole world, and for the world itself. By their very nature, these prayers are meant to address the real needs and concerns of the world as well as those of the local assembly and of individuals in the assembly. Something of a balance should be struck here so that each of these aspects of the general intercessions can be evident in liturgical prayer.

Since these intercessions are by no means fixed, communities planning and celebrating liturgy can be very free to vary the needs expressed or the particular needs prayed for. A wide variety is provided in the sample formulas; these are intended to illustrate possibilities rather than stifle initiative or creativity. But it should always be recalled that one of the concerns in these prayers is for local communities to expand their understanding of what is at stake at liturgical prayer so that the needs of the whole Church are recalled and addressed. (Interestingly enough in some instances in the early Church, the role of the deacon as minister of charity was so closely connected with his role as liturgical minister that it was only natural that he would announce the intentions; he was the one responsible for the charity of the community and would therefore know for whom prayer was required from the whole community. Once again, liturgical ministry is seen to reflect the lived ministry outside the liturgy.)

Another example of prayer for the Church in the eucharistic liturgy is the *epiclesis,* the invocation of the Spirit for unity. As was noted above when referring to the early Church documentation about common prayer (specifically the prayer from Hippolytus and the *Didache*) a traditional element of the eucharistic anaphora is prayer for the gathered Church. The following are examples taken from the eucharistic prayers now in use in the Roman rite:

> May all of us who share in the body and blood of Christ
> be brought together in unity by the Holy Spirit.
> (Eucharistic Prayer II)

> Grant that we, who are nourished by his body and blood,
> may be filled with his Holy Spirit,
> and become one body, one spirit in Christ.
> (Eucharistic Prayer III)

> Lord, look upon this sacrifice which you have given to your
> Church;
> and by your Holy Spirit, gather all who share this bread and
> wine
> into the one body of Christ, a living sacrifice of praise.
> (Eucharistic Prayer IV)

> Father,
> look with love
> on those you have called
> to share in the one sacrifice of Christ.
> By the power of your Holy Spirit
> make them one body,
> healed of all division.
> (Eucharistic Prayer for Masses of Reconciliation I)

> Fill us with his Spirit
> through our sharing in this meal.
> May he take away all that divides us.
> (Eucharistic Prayer for Masses of Reconciliation II)

The traditional notion that the "Church makes the Eucharist and the Eucharist makes the Church" can be said to be exemplified here. The Church that gathers for the Eucharist is the community that intercedes at the Eucharist for the local church and for the Church universal. This is accomplished by invoking the power of the Holy Spirit.

A final example of how the liturgical community intercedes

for the whole Church (as well as those who actually join in the liturgy) involves the intercessions found in the eucharistic prayer itself. Intercessory prayer forms part of the very structure of the eucharistic anaphora in its traditional form and in its contemporary expression in the liturgy today.[25] The Roman Canon states it in this form:

> We offer [these gifts] for your holy catholic Church;
> watch over it, Lord, and guide it;
> grant it peace and unity throughout the world.
> We offer them for N. our Pope,
> for N. our bishop,
> and for all who hold and teach the catholic faith
> that comes to us from the apostles.
>
> (Roman Canon)

Interestingly, these intercessions for the whole Church (personified and exemplified in the Pope and local bishop) are placed after the epicleses in the new eucharistic prayers. They state:

> Lord, remember your Church throughout the world;
> make us grow in love,
> together with N. our Pope,
> N. our bishop, and all the clergy.
>
> (Eucharistic Prayer II)

> Strengthen in faith and love your pilgrim Church on earth;
> your servant, Pope N., our bishop N.,
> and all the bishops,
> with the clergy and the entire people your Son has gained for
>   you.
>
> (Eucharistic Prayer III)

> Lord, remember those for whom we offer this sacrifice,
> especially N. our Pope,
> N. our bishop, and bishops and clergy everywhere.
> Remember those who take part in this offering,
> those here present and all your people,
> and all who seek you with a sincere heart.
>
> (Eucharistic Prayer IV)

Keep us all
in communion of mind and heart
with N., our Pope, and N., our bishop.
Help us to work together
for the coming of your kingdom . . .
                    (Eucharistic Prayer for Masses of Reconciliation I)

May this Spirit keep us always in communion
with N., our Pope and N., our bishop,
with all the bishops and all your people.
Father, make your Church throughout the world
a sign of unity and an instrument of your peace.
                    (Eucharistic Prayer for Masses of Reconciliation II)

These texts help to illustrate the point that every act of liturgy
by a local community is itself an act of the liturgy of the whole
Church. The church at prayer is praying for and with the whole
Church throughout the world. With the restoration of the general intercessions, explicit epicleses for the unity of the Church,
and emphasis placed on the close association between the epiclesis prayer and intercessions, there is ample evidence for the
theological premise that the church at prayer is a clear manifestation of what the Church is in reality, the people of Christ
interceding through Christ to the Father for all peoples. Clearly,
in redirecting attention to the actual experience of the local
church in liturgical prayer the recently restored rites of the
liturgy also help restore intercession for and with the whole
Church to a proper place in the liturgy.

VARIETY AND COMMUNITY

A review of the evolution and history of the Western liturgy
reveals that there has always been a delicate balance established
between what the "Roman" liturgy should be like and what was
the shape of the liturgy as actually celebrated in the Western
Church. In illustrating variety within the community of the
Roman Church it is hoped that some perspective will be offered
to address the tensions that can exist in contemporary worship

situations because of variety and adaptability in worship forms caused by the plurality of peoples celebrating liturgy.

Roman and Local Liturgy—From the post-Reformation era to the reforms ushered in at Vatican II, the Roman liturgy was commonly understood to be one and the same wherever it was celebrated. In fact, the practice of celebrating the one Roman liturgy in the Latin language was a hallmark of Roman practice, which practice was said to evidence the universality of the Church. While this was commonly underscored in popular writing and understanding,[26] the fact is that even during this period there were local variations within the one liturgy. While the forms of the liturgy were rather stable and fixed at this time, some local variation was possible; in fact even when the Roman Missal and the Roman Breviaries were issued in the sixteenth century as normative for all Catholics, if a particular religious community or local church had used a prayerbook for two hundred years or more, then this local usage could be continued.[27] This toleration of local usage reflected what was common in the practice of the Western liturgy throughout the centuries.

What is conventionally called the "Roman liturgy" is actually an amalgam of many liturgical practices in places united with the Church of Rome. For example, in the period of missionary expansion of the faith and of creative ferment in the liturgy (from apostolic times through the tenth century)[28] what has come to be called the Western liturgy was experienced in a variety of ways in the area around Milan (Ambrosian liturgy), in Gaul (Gallican liturgy), in Spain (Mozarabic liturgy) and in Ireland (Celtic liturgy). While the primary elements of the liturgy remained the same in each locale (for example the liturgy of the word and of the table in the Eucharist) there were local variations within this structure. The notion of union with Rome and the primacy of Rome in matters of faith and in liturgy did not mean that always and everywhere all peoples practiced the exact same liturgical rites.[29] To profess faith in "one holy catholic and apostolic Church" was to affirm unity in the faith and prayer but not necessarily uniformity in liturgical practice. The prayer of the Church, the liturgy, not only respected the variety of the cultures where it was celebrated; the "Roman" liturgy itself also adopted some local usages and flavor for its own common prayer. That the prayerbooks used at liturgy in the Western Church were the result of a mixture of many local church and "pure" Roman usages is a matter of scholarly consensus. The kind of adaptation and acculturation in the liturgy called for by the mandate of the Second Vatican Council in the Liturgy Constitution is a return to an emphasis from this early period of the Church which is judged to be helpful and appropriate (nos. 37–40).[30] The liturgy of those who profess "one holy catholic and apostolic faith" need not be uniform; but each celebration of the local church is prayer "in union with the whole Church" (Roman Canon). Variety in the liturgy of the Roman Catholic Church based on local diversity and variety in culture is evisioned in the liturgy we presently celebrate.[31]

Kinds of Community—Besides the variation and adaptation possible because of geographical location and cultural differences there is another source of variety in the common prayer of the Church derived from the kind of people celebrating the liturgy. A classic example of this involves the evolution and present practice of the liturgy of the hours. In history there is much evidence to support the thesis that there were two forms of the liturgy of the hours commonly celebrated, the "cathedral" (or "parochial") and the "monastic." Again, while the essence and substance of the hours is maintained in each, the fact that different kinds of people gathered for them required and substantiated variety in the celebration of this daily prayer.[32] Because the monastic community could gather more frequently and could make use of psalters and liturgical books (at least more readily than those who gathered in parish churches) a greater number of psalms were used weekly. In addition, theirs was a more stark and meditative celebration of the liturgy. On the other hand the cathedral tradition of the hours is based on fewer meetings each day (emphasizing morning and evening prayer), greater ceremonial (for example, use of lights and incense more readily and frequently), fewer psalms chanted (often responsorially with the community chanting the refrain only) and emphasis on choosing psalms that reflected the particular hour of the day at which the prayer took place.

While each kind of community celebrated what can rightly be called the liturgy of the hours, the difference between parish and monastic community required differences in the prayer forms used.

In the contemporary reform of the liturgy of the hours provision is made for the variety of communities which can gather for this prayer. The "liturgy of the Church" is once again envisioned as a common prayer which reflects variety among and within local churches.

Another example of the liturgy being somewhat different and varied in history is the very liturgy celebrated in the city of Rome itself. The liturgy of the parish churches in Rome (the *tituli*) was slightly different from the liturgy celebrated when the Pope presided at common prayer. Obviously there was greater ceremonial at the papal liturgy and a greater involvement of ministers.[33] By way of contrast, the liturgy of the parishes was somewhat simpler and less elaborate. Hence, it is not only the variety between monastic life and parish life that causes variety, it is also variation caused by the occasion and celebrating community. Again, the issue of variety within the Roman rite evidenced historically leads to an important insight about the liturgy as presently celebrated.

Variety within Local Communities—One of the hallmarks of the contemporary reform of the liturgy is the variety of options possible within the revised rites. In fact, some of the tried and true distinctions within the "old" liturgy have been transcended in the approach to worship evident in the reformed rites. The "solemn" "high" and "low" Mass as distinct forms of celebrating have been ignored in favor of a much more flexible model of worship where a great variety of options is possible in liturgical prayer. Since the revised rites do not envision one set format for a given celebration of the liturgy, the contemporary liturgy calls for planning a preparation so that the variety offered is carefully reviewed and implemented pastorally. As the General Instruction on the Roman Missal states:

> The pastoral effectiveness of a celebration will be heightened
> if the texts of readings, prayers, and songs correspond as

closely as possible to the needs, religious dispositions, and aptitude of the participants. This will be achieved by an intelligent use of the broad options described in this chapter.

In planning the celebration, then, the priest should consider the general spiritual good of the assembly rather than his personal outlook. He should be mindful that the choice of texts is to be made in consultation with the ministers and others who have a function in the celebration, including the faithful in regard to the parts that more directly belong to them.

Since a variety of options is provided for the different parts of the Mass, it is necessary for the deacon, readers, psalmists, cantors, commentator, and choir to be completely sure beforehand of those texts for which they are responsible so that nothing is improvised. A harmonious planning and execution will help dispose the people spiritually to take part in the eucharist. (no. 313)

In the pastoral implementation of the revised liturgy a particularly difficult problem arises from the cultural and theological diversity within a given local community (a parish, for example). Respecting existing cultural diversity and not wanting to impose a form of worship that would be foreign to a particular community (Hispanic, black, native American, or immigrant, for example) can prove to be a difficult problem pastorally. In addressing this particular issue the document on implementing the musical aspects of the liturgy states:

The diversity of people present at a parish liturgy gives rise to a further problem. Can the same parish liturgy be an authentic expression for a grade school girl, her college-age brother, their married sister with her young family, their parents and grandparents? Can it satisfy the theologically and musically educated along with those lacking in training? Can it please those who seek a more informal style of celebration? The planning team must consider the general makeup of the total community.[34]

Some parishes, for example, try to address this issue by providing a variety of music programs for the various weekend liturgies. The music used at the evening liturgy on Saturday might well be simpler and less elaborate than the music used at a choral Eucharist on Sunday, and yet both liturgies deserve well-planned music with appropriate personnel to lead song and accompany singing with a variety of instruments. Planning liturgies for specific groups in mind, such as "family liturgies," can help focus attention on specific pastoral needs without losing the sense of the variety of the local community present and participating in the liturgy.[35] As the document on the implementation of liturgical music states:

> Often the problem of diversity can be mitigated by supplementing the parish Sunday celebration with special celebrations for smaller homogeneous groups. "The need of the faithful of a particular cultural background or of a particular age level may often be met by a music that can serve as a congenial, liturgically oriented expression of prayers." The music and other options may then be more easily suited to the particular group celebrating. Nevertheless, it would be out of harmony with the Lord's wish for unity in his Church if believers were to worship only in such homogeneous groupings. Celebration in such groups, "in which the genuine sense of community is more readily experienced, can contribute significantly to growth in awareness of the parish community, especially when all the faithful participate in the parish Mass on the Lord's day."[36]

Once again, the liturgical principle that the whole community come together, with all its variety and complexity, as seen in the tradition of Judaeo-Christian worship (especially noted above in the earliest centuries of Christian liturgical prayer) is reiterated in this contemporary document on the implementation of the revised liturgy. Being aware of diversity within the local community and dealing with this issue without marring the notion of unity in Christ amid that diversity is an obvious, yet pressing issue for the present celebration of liturgy. This review of historical precedent and the model of liturgy which we now experience, with option and variety firmly established, can aid in helping to respect and articulate the common prayer of those who comprise the local church in all its variety and complexity.[37]

COMMUNITY: CREATED OR PRESUPPOSED?

A debate which frequently surfaces when reflecting on the relationship between the liturgy and its pastoral implementation concerns the issue of to what extent the celebration of the liturgy itself creates community or presupposes community. One side of the question argues that Christians can be formed into more united communities of faith and service as a result of having celebrated the sacred mysteries. This approach emphasizes the power of the liturgy to create and sustain communities of faith. The other side of the debate argues that believers must come to the liturgy predisposed as members of communities of faith and that the function of the liturgy is to ensure and sustain the sense of unity and love already achieved. Certainly it is impossible to solve the dilemma that often occurs in pastoral practice of trying to achieve a "sense of community" among those who celebrate together by opting for one or another of these approaches. In fact, the Church on earth will always be the imperfect body of Christ, never fully formed in the image of Christ. The very repetition of the liturgy should afford ample evidence that the Church will never be perfectly converted to the Lord, and, by extension, the Christian community will never be in the position of being fully formed and complete. One of the prefaces of the liturgy of the Eucharist offers insight here:

> In this great sacrament you feed your people
> and strengthen them in holiness,
> so that the family of mankind
> may come to walk in the light of one faith,
> in one communion of love.
> We come then to this wonderful sacrament
> to be fed at your table
> and grow into the likeness of the risen Christ.
>
> (Holy Eucharist II)

All Christian liturgy, like all Christian life, leads to life with God forever in his kingdom. This eschatological aspect of the liturgy offers important insight about whether the rites themselves create or presuppose community. The more usual experience is that they do both at least partially, for all liturgy reaches beyond itself to life forever with God in his kingdom:

> Here you build your temple of living stones,
> and bring the Church to its full stature
> as the body of Christ throughout the world,
> to reach its perfection at last
> in the heavenly city of Jerusalem
> which is the vision of your peace.
>
> (Preface, Dedication of a Church I)

What is reflected here invites us to be cautious regarding the issue of forming or presupposing community. The issue is not a simple one, and it raises questions that may well and rightly challenge long-standing assumptions in pastoral practice. Certainly a lived faith and commitment to the Lord in the Christian community is required for the celebration of sacraments, but the perfectly formed Church will only be manifest when the kingdom comes. In the meantime the liturgy is a central and significant means of renewing faith in Christ and of living that faith with brothers and sisters in the family of the Church. As we pray in the communal celebration of penance:

> Almighty and merciful God,
> you have brought us together in the name of your Son
> to receive your mercy and grace in our time of need.
> Open our eyes to see the evil we have done.
> Touch our hearts and convert us to yourself.
> Where sin has divided and scattered,
> may your love make one again;
> where sin has brought weakness,
> may your power heal and strengthen;
> where sin has brought death,
> may your Spirit raise to new life.
> Give us a new heart to love you,
> so that our lives may reflect the image of your Son.
> May the world see the glory of Christ
> revealed in your Church,

and come to know
that he is the one whom you have sent,
Jesus Christ, your Son, our Lord.[38]

A HOUSE FOR THE CHURCH

In light of the revived interest in and emphasis on communal participation in liturgy, part of the present task of liturgical
implementation involves the planning, construction, and re-
modeling of fit worship spaces. Most significantly, the implementation document, *Environment and Art in Catholic Worship,*
begins with a number of important statements on the community that comes together for prayer:

> To speak of environment and artistic requirements in Catho-
> lic worship, we have to begin with ourselves—we who are the
> Church, the baptized, the initiated. (no. 27)

> Among the symbols with which liturgy deals, none is more
> important than this assembly of believers. It is common to
> use the same name to speak of the building in which those
> persons worship, but that use is misleading. In the words of
> ancient Christians, the building used for worship is called
> *domus ecclesiae,* the house of the Church. (no. 28)

Hence, the theology of the gathered community not only
forms a basis for understanding what comprises the experience
of liturgical prayer, it is the foundation for determining what are
fit places for worship.

> As common prayer and ecclesial experience, liturgy flour-
> ishes in a climate of hospitality: a situation in which people
> are comfortable with one another, either knowing or being
> introduced . . . , with mobility, in view of one another as well
> as the focus points of the rite, involved as participants and *not*
> as spectators. (no. 11)

By extension we can say that liturgical prayer itself involves
a needed sense of hospitality and welcome to the community

that comes together. The assembly acts as the body of those who invite and welcome others to common prayer. Ushers are often the first members of the assembly who can help create an atmosphere of invitation and hospitality. And the space for liturgy can carry through on these important human dimensions of welcoming and fellowship. Part of the intention behind the introductory rites is to help the gathered community become a community of faith.[39]

The anonymity and individualism that marked conventional understandings and experiences of the liturgy are overturned in favor of a liturgical atmosphere that reflects unity in common prayer. Because of the variety of worshiping communities (for example, small groups for special occasions and weekday liturgy and large groups for Sunday Eucharist) and the varying worshiping needs of the local church it is important to reflect on the statement:

> By environment we mean the larger space in which the action of the assembly takes place. . . . The environment is appropriate when it is beautiful, when it is hospitable, when it clearly invites and needs an assembly of people to complete it. Furthermore, it is appropriate when it brings people close together so that they can see and hear the entire liturgical action, when it helps people feel involved. Such an environment works with the liturgy, not against it. (no. 24)

The house for the church should serve the common prayer of the local community gathered for worship. It serves best when liturgy is truly experienced as the Church at prayer.

To speak of liturgical prayer is to speak immediately and directly about the community that comes together for this prayer. That the community should be underscored as this first element is most important, for it is in gathered communities of faith that the liturgy is experienced and appreciated. To suggest that the liturgical "community" is involved in liturgy is to suggest something of its corporate identity in Christ.

As the body gathered for liturgy the convoked assembly is where the Church experiences its identity as the people redeemed by Christ. Liturgy is then best understood as the means through which this Church expresses itself in faith as the Church at prayer. While there is no such thing as the ideal or perfect local community, the alternative way of looking at the variety within and among local communities of faith is to see it as an expression of the vitality and variety of the Church. To speak of the foundational element of liturgical prayer one must speak of the place where all liturgy is experienced, the assembly gathered in the name of the Lord.

NOTES

1. See Part One, Chapter One, section on "The Journey of Faith."
2. See Part One, Chapter Two, section on "The Covenant Relationship."
3. See Part One, Chapter One, section on "Spirituality and Liturgy."
4. The references here to Exodus and Joel are particularly illustrative because the text from Exodus is used at the Holy Thursday Evening Mass of the Lord's Supper and that of Joel is used to begin the season of Lent at the liturgy of Ash Wednesday, a *communal* season of renewal in faith culminating in the Easter triduum of which Holy Thursday evening is a part.
5. On the "idealized" nature of this text, along with the other summaries in Acts about the early Christian community (4:32–35 and 5:12–16) see Richard J. Dillon, "Acts of the Apostles," in *Jerome Biblical Commentary* (Englewood Cliffs: Prentice-Hall, 1968) 175–76. That this scriptural reference has played a part in ecclesiastical documents on the liturgy is seen in its use in the *General Instruction, Liturgy of the Hours*, no. 1. For a pastoral commentary on this text as it relates to the liturgy of the hours see J. D. Crichton, *Christian Celebration: The Prayer of the Church* (London: Geoffrey Chapman, 1976) pp. 30–33. For an insightful treat-

ment of the exhortation to prayer in secret (Mt 6) and how this relates to the liturgical prayer see Jacques Dupont, "Jesus and Liturgical Prayer," *Worship* 43 (April 1969) 198–213.

6. Text from Lucien Deiss, *Springtime of the Liturgy*, trans. Matthew O'Connell (Collegeville: The Liturgical Press, 1979) pp. 93–94.

7. There is no scholarly consensus on the dating of this document. Deiss maintains that some passages may have been written between 50–70 A.D. (roughly contemporary with the formation of the Pauline corpus) while the compilation of the Didache may have taken place in the second century, from the communities of Antioch in Syria. See *ibid.*, p. 73.

8. *Ibid.*, p. 77. The notion of reconciliation as intrinsically connected with offering common prayer is taken from Mt 5:23–24.

9. *Ibid.*, p. 75. It has been pointed out that this text (Chap. 9:4) parallels the text of Chap. 10:5 from this document: "Lord, remember your Church and deliver it from all evil; make it perfect in your love and gather it from the four winds, this sanctified Church, into your kingdom which you have prepared for it, for power and glory are yours through all ages!" That this is a pattern of blessing prayer for early Christians is clear; whether this text is from or was to be used as a Eucharist is matter for scholarly debate.

10. *Ibid.*, p. 131.

11. See Cipriano Vagaggini, *The Canon of the Mass and Liturgical Reform*, trans. Peter Coughlan (Staten Island: Alba House, 1967) pp. 98, 100–101.

12. See, among others, Louis Bouyer, *Liturgical Piety*, p. 1.

13. See Frederick R. McManus, "Prayer and the Obligation to Pray," in John Gallen, ed., *Christians at Prayer* (Notre Dame: University of Notre Dame Press, 1977) pp. 137–154.

14. A comparison of the present Order of Mass (as found in the Sacramentary) with the Tridentine Missal, for example, will show to what extent the liturgy was seen to be carried on by the clergy alone.

15. *Environment and Art in Catholic Worship* (Washington: Bishops' Committee on the Liturgy, 1978) no. 42, and nos. 40–43.

16. With regard to those who preside at liturgy in the first four centuries and their relationship to the community outside the liturgy, see Herve-Marie Legrand, "The Presidency of the Eucharist According to the Ancient Tradition," *Worship* 53 (September 1979) 413–438. For a popular treatment of the question of liturgical ministry and service outside the liturgical assembly see Robert W. Hovda, *There Are Different Ministries* (Washington: The Liturgical Conference, 1978, revised edi-

tion). See, Part Three, Chapter Eleven," section on "Liturgical and Church Ministry."

17. *Environment and Art in Catholic Worship,* no. 31.

18. See Frederick McManus, "Prayer and the Obligation to Pray," and Pierre Salmon, "History of the Obligation of Reciting the Office," in *The Breviary Through The Centuries,* trans. Sr. David Mary (Collegeville: The Liturgical Press, 1962) pp. 1–27.

19. See *General Instruction, Rite of Christian Initiation of Adults,* no. 4. (Hereafter cited *RCIA.*)

20. See *General Instruction, Rite of Baptism for Children,* nos. 4, 9, 2. Even when a child is baptized who is in danger of death the new rite calls for a gathering of the Christian community: "parents, godparents, and if possible, some friends and neighbors of the family gather around the sick child." (no. 157)

21. The names of the rites indicate this shift: (I) Rite For Reconciliation of Individual Penitents; (II) Rite For Reconciliation of Several Penitents with Individual Confession and Absolution; (III) Rite For Reconciliation of Several Penitents with General Confession and Absolution.

22. *Rite of Penance,* no. 46, emphasis added. That this revised formula for absolution is not without flaws is described and addressed in David N. Power, "The Sacramentalization of Penance," *The Heythrop Journal* 18 (1977) 5–22, at 17–21. See, also by the same author, "Confession as Ongoing Conversion," *The Heythrop Journal* (1977) 180–190.

23. *General Instruction of the Roman Missal,* no. 45.

24. See "Sample Formulas for the General Intercessions," in *The Sacramentary* (New York: Catholic Book Publishing Co., 1974) pp. 992–1005.

25. On the place of intercessions within the eucharistic anaphora see Paul J. LeBlanc, "A Consideration of Intercessory Prayer Within the Eucharist," *The Dunwoodie Review* 8 (1968) 115–132, and Aidan Kavanagh, "Thoughts on the New Eucharistic Prayers," *Worship* 43 (January 1969) 6–7.

26. See, for example, Hans Küng, "Latin—The Church's Mother Tongue?" in *The Council in Action,* trans., Cecily Hastings (New York: Sheed and Ward, 1963) pp. 122–134.

27. See J. D. Crichton, *The Once and Future Liturgy* (Dublin: Veritas Publications, 1977) pp. 7–17.

28. In his standard work *A Short History of the Western Liturgy* (New York/London: Oxford University Press, 1979, second edition) Theodor Klauser characterizes the first two periods of the evolution of Western

liturgy as follows: "Creative Beginnings" (to 590) and "Franco-Germanic Leadership" (to 1073). By way of comparison to these more creative stages he characterizes the second millennium as follows: "Trend Toward Uniformity" (to 1545) and "Unification in Worship" (to the twentieth century). Certainly, the first millennium of the Church's life saw greater liturgical evolution and variety than that experienced in the second millennium.

29. It should be recalled, however, that Rome did see itself as responsible for reviewing liturgical texts and practices and for "correcting" texts where needed. That this is evidenced in our day is seen in the Apostolic Constitution of Paul VI promulgating the Roman Missal of 1970: "No one should think, however, that this revision of the Roman Missal has been suddenly accomplished. The progress of liturgical science in the last four centuries has certainly prepared the way. After the Council of Trent, the study 'of ancient manuscripts in the Vatican library and elsewhere,' as Saint Pius V indicated in the apostolic constitution *Quo Primum,* helped greatly in the correction of the Roman Missal." (*Sacramentary* p. 8.)

30. The question of cultural adaptation of the liturgy and liturgical indigenization is treated more fully below, Part Two, Chapter Seven, section on "Adaptation of Ritual."

31. See *Constitution on the Sacred Liturgy,* nos. 14, 19, 21, 37–40.

32. See, among others, William G. Storey, "The Liturgy of the Hours: Cathedral versus Monastery," in *Christians at Prayer,* pp. 61–82.

33. See, for example, *Ordo Romanus Primus,* an eighth-century document reflective of the liturgy of the papal court, conveniently translated and reprinted in R.C.D. Jasper and G. J. Cuming, eds., *Prayers of the Eucharist, Early and Reformed* (London: Collins, 1975) pp. 111–115. For the original see, M. Adrieu, *Les Ordines Romani du Haut Moyen Age,* Vol. II (Louvain, 1948) pp. 74–108.

34. *Music in Catholic Worship* (Washington: Bishops' Committee on the Liturgy, 1972) no. 17.

35. That the notion "family liturgy" is distinctly preferable to planning and celebrating liturgies for children only is derived from the ecclesial experience that there is always a certain diversity of ages, sexes, backgrounds, etc., present at liturgy. In addition the *Directory for Masses with Children* always refers to liturgies for children and adults, whether for "Masses with Adults in Which Children Also Participate" (Chapter Two) or for "Masses with Children in Which Only a Few Adults Participate" (Chapter Three).

36. *Music in Catholic Worship,* no. 18.

37. The question of how to plan liturgy for varied communities is addressed more fully below, Part Three, Chapter Ten, sections on "Liturgical Planning" and "Planning: Principles and Practice."

38. *Rite of Penance,* Form Two, no. 99.

39. "The parts [of the liturgy of the eucharist] preceding the liturgy of the word . . . have the character of beginning, introduction, and preparation. The purpose of these rites is to make the assembled people a unified community and to prepare them properly to listen to God's word and celebrate the eucharist" (*General Instruction of the Roman Missal,* no. 24).

Chapter Five
PROCLAMATION OF
THE WORD OF GOD

Closely allied with the primary element of liturgical prayer as a corporate work done in faith, is the revelation and proclamation of the word of God. When communities gather in the Judaeo-Christian tradition for moments of common prayer and worship they gather to hear the word of God once addressed to their ancestors and now addressed to them. They are nourished and formed by that word alone as the source of life. Liturgical prayer is the means for growing in the faith, the covenant relationship in faith concretely expressed through the liturgy. The revelation of the word of God is a privileged means through which contemporary communities grow in the image and likeness of the God they worship. Hence, the proclamation of the word became and remains a central feature of what was "done in faith" by the gathered community. While such an emphasis on the proclamation of the word at liturgy had not been the lived experience of Roman Catholics for centuries,[1] the restoration of the word to a position of prominence is one of the chief characteristics of the contemporary liturgical reform.[2] From the perspective of the liturgical tradition of the Roman Catholic Church, and in view of the aim of the Second Vatican Council in re-emphasizing the proclamation of the word, we may say that the sacred word of God holds a position of prominence and distinction when delineating the elements of liturgical prayer.

WORD OF GOD: ADDRESS AND RESPONSE

Contemporary Christians frequently tend to think of the word of God as the bound volume of the Scriptures, the seventy-two books that contain the foundational revelation of God to his covenanted people. We are so familiar with bound books, the printed word, published texts and phrases such as "the pen is mightier than the sword" that it is not surprising to find that we customarily regard the word as a collection of inspired texts and books. And certainly there is much to be said in favor of this interpretation and association, for, in fact, we are able to have ready access to the stories of God's dealing with his chosen people and the events of the history we call "salvation" through the books of the Bible easily available through the printed word. But it should be recalled that what we regard as books are collections of what were first compiled and edited in order to be proclaimed in the public liturgical assembly. The dynamic and living word of God, the Scriptures, found their dynamism and vitality in the event of proclamation, announcement and address to God's people. Throughout history Christian communities gathered (and continue to gather) to hear the word of the Lord in order that their identity as members of God's people might be renewed, revitalized and re-established. Christianity is an historical religion in that the foundation events of its origin— the paschal mystery of Jesus—happened in history and changed the face of history for those who believe. Communities of Christians themselves are remade and renewed again and again through liturgical prayer, particularly through the hearing and acceptance of the revealed word of God. The past deeds of salvation are "symbolically presented anew" in the sense that "whenever ... the Church, gathered by the Holy Spirit for liturgical celebration, announces and proclaims the word of God, it has the experience of being a new people in whom the covenant made in the past is fulfilled."[3] The identity of being the new people of God in Christ is confirmed and established each time the Christian community gathers for the liturgy. A fundamental means for this renewal and revival of being incorporated into God's saving love is the very announcement of the word.

Understanding God's word as texts alone can tend to distort this, for texts alone are oriented toward understanding and comprehension. The proclamation of the texts of the Scriptures, on the other hand, is for deepening faith and renewing life.

> Texts by themselves can be used as weapons of warfare. But when we view them . . . as the remains of a community . . . in response to God, we have shifted from the totalitarianism of "things" to the personalism of a living community whose core is a divine and living Person in dialogue with his people. We say living, and thereby mean to indicate a dynamic continuity of growth within the community as it responds to and is formed by the living God.[4]

The Hebrew Scriptures reflect this approach to the word of God, this dynamic, formative and challenging word of revelation. The authors assert that "not by bread alone does man live, but by every word that comes forth from the mouth of the Lord" (Dt 8:3),[5] and they challenge contemporary congregations: "Today, listen to the voice of the Lord" (Ps 95:7). In summarizing their relationship with God, the chosen of Israel would rely on confessions of faith such as that presented early in the Old Testament to accompany a thanksgiving festival for the harvest:[6]

> Then you shall declare before the LORD, your God, "My father was a wandering Aramean who went down to Egypt with a small household and lived there as an alien. But there he became a nation great, strong, and numerous. When the Egyptians maltreated and oppressed us, imposing hard labor upon us, we cried to the LORD, the God of our fathers, and he heard our cry and saw our affliction, our toil and our oppression. He brought us out of Egypt with his strong hand and outstretched arm, with terrifying power, with signs and wonders; and bringing us into this country, he gave us this land flowing with milk and honey. Therefore, I have now brought you the first fruits of the products of the soil which

you, O LORD, have given me." And having set them before
the LORD, your God, you shall bow down in his presence.
(Dt 26:5–10)

The creed of the people of Israel is contained here in summary
fashion. It is a creed based on what God did for them and
continues to do for those who gather to hear, proclaim, and
offer gifts in sacrifice to the Lord, the author of all these things.
The God believed in and trusted in the Scriptures is the God
who has acted favorably toward Israel and toward the "new
Israel," the Church. The intervention of God in sacred history
continues where and when contemporary communities gather
for liturgical prayer. Such "confessions of faith" summarize and
concretize the faith experience they presently share.

In addition the God of the covenant requires a ready response by those who enjoy a relationship in faith, for it is his
word and his commands which they are to obey.

If, then, you truly heed my commandments which I enjoin on
you today, loving and serving the LORD, your God with all
your heart and all your soul, I will give you the seasonal rain
to your land, the early rain and the late rain, that you may
have your grain, wine and oil to gather in. . . . But be careful
lest your heart be so lured away that you serve other gods and
worship them. (Dt 11:13–16)

This particular text is all the more significant since it forms part
of the daily synagogue service, and is the cherished confession
of faith, the *Shema*.[7] The relationship forged between God and
Israel is often poetically expressed in the prayerbook of Israel,
the Book of Psalms:

O give thanks to the Lord for he is good,
for his love endures forever.
Give thanks to the God of gods,
for his love endures forever.
Give thanks to the Lord of lords,
for his love endures forever.

It was he who made the great lights,
for his love endures forever. . . .
The first born of the Egyptians he smote,
for his love endures forever.
He brought Israel out from their midst,
for his love endures forever. . . .
He divided the Red Sea in two,
for his love endures forever. . . .
Through the desert his people he led,
for his love endures forever. . . .
He let Israel inherit their land,
for his love endures forever.
He gives food to all living things,
for his love endures forever.
To the God of heaven give thanks,
for his love endures forever.

                    (Ps 136:1–3, 7, 10, 11, 13, 16, 21, 25, 26)

The tradition of Judaism as an historical religion is clearly affirmed and reiterated when communities gathered for daily or weekly prayer, especially in the synagogue where texts were proclaimed and psalms prayed. The intervention of God on their behalf was experienced anew in these liturgical gatherings, through word and song; the offer of the relationship of the covenant was repeated and experienced anew in common prayer. The response of the assembly to the proclaimed text was in song, in prayer responses, and ultimately in action as they pledged themselves to obey continually the word of the Lord. The very identity of Israel as God's chosen people was ratified and reaffirmed when the community gathered to hear and to respond to the word of God. That the word of God was to be central in recalling and experiencing the relationship of faith between God and his people is evidenced even more clearly and fully in the Christian Church when we acclaim Christ himself as "the Word" incarnate, the image of the Father's glory.

The liturgy of Christmas provides ample evidence of how Christ as the word is the mediator of the new covenant relationship with God. The Gospel reading for the Mass during the Day on Christmas is the prologue from the Gospel of John:

> In the beginning was the Word;
> The Word was in God's presence,
> and the Word was God.
> He was present to God in the beginning.
> Through him all things came into being,
> and apart from him nothing came to be. (Jn 1:1–3)

> The Word became flesh
> and made his dwelling among us,
> and we saw his glory:
> the glory of an only Son coming from the Father,
> filled with enduring love. (Jn 1:14)

As a way of contrasting the old and new covenants, specifically the incompleteness of the former when compared to the fullness of revelation in Christ, the second reading for this same liturgy also speaks in terms of the incarnate word, the Son of God:

> In times past, God spoke in fragmentary and varied ways to our fathers through the prophets; in this, the final age, he has spoken to us through his Son, whom he has made heir of all things and through whom he created the universe. This Son is the reflection of the Father's glory, the exact representation of the Father's being, and he sustains all things by his powerful word. (Heb 1:1–3)

The texts from the Christmas liturgy reiterate the prominent place which the Word of God, Christ, has in the lives of Christians. Worshiping communities not only witness to the presence of the fullness of God's speaking in Christ, they share in that fullness through and in Christ:

> In the wonder of the incarnation
> your eternal Word has brought to the eyes of faith
> a new and radiant vision of your glory.

> Your eternal Word has taken upon himself our human weakness,
> giving our mortal nature immortal value.

So marvelous is this oneness between God and man
that in Christ man restores to man the gift of everlasting life.
(Prefaces, Christmas I and II)

The text of the eucharistic prayer used customarily on weekdays
refers to Christ when it states:

He is the Word through whom you made the universe,
the Savior you sent to redeem us.
By the power of the Holy Spirit
he took flesh and was born of the Virgin Mary.
(Eucharistic Prayer II)

A reference made to Christ in the preface that ends the Christmas season liturgically, the feast of the Baptism of the Lord,
gives an indication of the direct association of Christ as the
Word and hearing the voice of the Father:

You celebrated your new gift of baptism
by signs and wonders at the Jordan.
Your voice was heard from heaven
to awaken faith in the presence among us
of the Word made man.
(Preface, Baptism of the Lord)

These texts form part of the scriptural and liturgical foundation for understanding the voice of Christ as truly present and
active in the liturgy today. This is stated clearly in the Liturgy
Constitution of Vatican II as well as in documents of post-
conciliar liturgical renewal such as the Introduction to the Lectionary for Mass:

As a help toward celebrating the memorial of the Lord with
devotion, the faithful should be keenly aware of the one
presence of Christ in both the word of God—"it is he who
speaks when the holy Scriptures are read in the Church"—
and "especially under the eucharistic elements."[8]

With regard to the celebration of the Eucharist the parallel is
often drawn between the table of God's word and the table of

the sacrament: "The Church has honored the word of God and the eucharistic mystery with the same reverence, although not with the same worship, and has always and everywhere intended and endorsed such honor."[9]

The scriptural and liturgical evidence adduced here shows the important place given to the proclamation of the word of God in the liturgical gathering, especially since it is the *proclamation* of the sacred word that is revived and emphasized in our day. In Israel the proclamation of the word established the relationship of love between God and his chosen ones. It was through the "word of God breaking into their history that Israel became the people of God."[10] The same was true when the Christian community was formed by the announcement of the fulfillment of Israel's hopes and expectations in Jesus: "This is the time of fulfillment. The reign of God is at hand" (Mk 1:15). The required response to this announcement was "Reform your lives." Therefore, it is important to underscore the dynamic inherent in the liturgical assembly gathered in the name of the Lord: they come to hear and to respond to the word of the Lord addressed to them, in this time and place.

> The revealed and proclaimed word in the Bible is not primarily concerned with "things" but with people. It is more concerned with their will than their mind, with their moral response, than their information. . . . The word in the Bible demands submission and acceptance.[11]

> The virtue and force here attributed to the word of God is only intelligible if God himself is personally active when his word is heard. It implies not only the external act of proclamation of the word, but also the internal activity of the Holy Spirit disposing the hearer to accept the word presented . . . externally. Thus it becomes the medium of personal communion.[12]

The liturgical proclamation of the word involves the act of invitation by God and the response in faith of the assembled community. The texts of the Scriptures are for announcement and acceptance; the setting for this address and response is the event of liturgy.

LITURGICAL PROCLAMATION OF THE WORD

The structure and setting for the proclamation of the word of God in Christian liturgy derives from that established in Judaism. The synagogue service at the time of Jesus (in something of an idealized form)[13] contained Scripture readings, psalms, prayers, the decalogue and the recitation of the Shema. This liturgical structure influenced the earliest Christians as they continued to come together for this scripturally inspired prayer[14] and as they adapted it for the liturgy of the word when celebrating the Lord's Supper.[15] The proclamation of the Scriptures was accompanied by the response of the community in psalmody, intercessions, and in the sacrament celebrated. As is stated in the General Instruction on the Liturgy of the Hours:

> Following ancient tradition, sacred scripture is read publicly in the liturgy not only in the celebration of the Eucharist but also in the Divine Office. This liturgical reading of scripture is of greatest importance for all Christians.... In liturgical celebrations prayer always accompanies the reading of sacred scripture. In this way the reading may bear greater fruit, and conversely prayer, especially through the psalms, may be more fully developed by the reading and encourage more intense devotion. (no. 140)

Lectionary—Among the features which have marked the proclamation of the word in Roman Catholic practice is the use of the lectionary. Rather than rely on persons in the community to pick and choose passages at random, the lectionary is a way of establishing the texts to be proclaimed in the liturgical assembly. While pre-conciliar usage saw the same Scripture texts frequently repeated, the Liturgy Constitution of Vatican II called for "more reading from holy Scripture, and it is to be more varied and suitable" (no. 35) and "the treasures of the Bible are to be opened up more lavishly, so that richer fare may be provided for the faithful at the table of God's Word . . . (no. 51). It was determined that "a more representative portion of holy Scripture will be read to the people over a set cycle of years" (no. 51) through the re-establishment of a more complete lectionary system. The promulgation of the *Lectionary for Mass* in 1969 for the Roman Catholic Church and its subsequent adoption (in large measure) by many Protestant denominations[16] ushered in a new and revolutionary era in liturgical piety. The new lectionary for Mass stands beside the lectionary for Scripture readings in the liturgy of the hours (especially in the office of readings) and in the texts for the celebration of the various sacraments, as a major overturning and redirecting of liturgical prayer for Roman Catholics.

Two principles were used in the selection of the texts found in the new lectionary: "semi-continuous reading" and "harmony." Both of these principles derive from liturgical tradition where a biblical book was read in succession so that the whole of the Scripture was used at liturgy (semi-continuous readings) or when certain readings were carefully chosen to more adequately express the uniqueness of a feast or season (harmony). With regard to the principle of semi-continuous reading on Sundays at the Eucharist the lectionary introduction states: ". . . the Sundays of Ordinary Time do not have a distinctive character. Thus the texts of both the apostolic and gospel reading are arranged in an order of semi-continuous reading, whereas the Old Testament reading is harmonized with the gospel." (no. 67) "Harmony of another kind exists between texts of the readings for each Mass during Advent, Lent, and Easter, the seasons that have a distinctive importance." (no. 67)[17]

For Sundays, solemnities, and liturgical seasons (such as Lent and Easter), the readings assigned in the lectionary are to be used in the liturgy. On other days, particularly on days when the commemoration of a particular saint ("memorial") is optional, the readings for that weekday in the lectionary may be changed in favor of readings that reflect the saint commemorated. But preference and deference is generally given to the semicontinuous proclamation of a biblical book, thus respecting the principle of the lectionary itself, that the whole of God's word is to be proclaimed, prayed over and explored in the liturgy. One of the important advantages of the lectionary, therefore, is that it keeps the praying community honest in that it attempts to reflect the whole of Scripture: the uncomfortable words as well as words of comfort, texts that challenge as well as texts that console, lessons that provoke as well as lessons that reassure. *All* that has been written has been written for our instruction and our formation in the faith.

Feasts and Seasons—For an understanding of what is involved in a liturgical season or the theology underlying a particular liturgical feast, liturgists often have recourse to the Scripture texts proclaimed and the prayers of the day's Mass formula. In speaking of the place of the lectionary readings in the liturgy the new introduction to the Lectionary for Mass states:

> The many riches contained in the one word of God are admirably brought out in the different kinds of liturgical celebrations and liturgical assemblies. This takes place as the unfolding mystery of Christ is recalled during the course of the liturgical year, and as the Church's sacraments . . . are celebrated. . . . For then the liturgical celebration, based primarily on the word of God and sustained by it, becomes a new event and enriches the word itself with new meaning and power. (no. 3)

In addition, it is important to recall that the prayer texts from the sacramentary themselves have been inspired by the Scripture texts proclaimed. As is noted in the Liturgy Constitution of Vatican II:

> Sacred Scripture is of paramount importance in the celebration of the liturgy. For it is from Scripture that lessons are read and explained in the homily, and psalms are sung; the prayers, collects and liturgical songs are scriptural in their inspiration and it is from Scripture that actions and signs derive their meaning. (no. 24)

The examples cited in this chapter concerning the Scripture readings and the prefaces used for the feast of Christmas indicate the correlation noted by the Council. How we, the celebrating community at prayer, are joined to the mystery of the incarnation is specified in the sacramentary texts for the Mass of Christmas,[18] and in the solemn blessing for the Christmas season:

> When he came to us as man,
> the Son of God scattered the darkness of this world,
> and filled this holy night (day) with his glory.
> May the God of infinite goodness
> scatter the darkness of sin
> and brighten your hearts with holiness. ℟. Amen.

> God sent his angels to shepherds
> to herald the great joy of our Savior's birth.
> May he fill you with joy
> and make you heralds of his gospel. ℟. Amen.

> When the Word became man,
> earth was joined to heaven.
> May he give you his peace and good will,
> and fellowship with all the heavenly host. ℟. Amen.

There are clear references in this text to the Johannine Gospel of the Mass on Christmas day about "the Word," to the Isaiah reading that begins the liturgy of the word at midnight: "The people who walked in darkness have seen a great light . . ." (Is 9:1), as well as to the Gospel for the Mass at midnight: "The angel of the Lord appeared to them . . ." (Lk 2:9).

What the liturgical texts evidence especially on special feasts and seasons is a certain cohesion based on the Scripture readings. This need not (and should not) mean that every text, song, prayer, or comment should speak to the "theme" of a liturgy, for that would be to compress the varied images and messages of the Scriptures into one topic only. But it is to suggest that where a cohesion and subtle relationship among the scriptural and liturgical texts is evident, these may be chosen and emphasized in order to help orient worshiping communities to the mystery that is celebrated at the liturgy.

Preaching the Word—The restoration of the liturgy of the word to a position of great prominence in Roman Catholic liturgy has caused a consequent and no less important shift regarding the preaching of that word. It entails a movement in preaching from sermons to homilies. In conventional pre-Vatican II usage the giving of a "sermon" at the Eucharist often had little to do with the Scriptures just proclaimed.[19] The hoped-for return to biblically-based preaching and the homily form of preaching is nothing short of revolutionary. It is the purpose of the homily to comment on the Scriptures, to continue the announcement of the time-conditioned Scriptures to the conditions of a particular time and place (here and now) and to focus for contemporary congregations the message that is contained, revealed and proclaimed in the Scripture readings on a given occasion.

> . . . The liturgy's insights are more or less veiled; liturgical texts and forms tend to be immobilized. . . . What the homily does is extend the immemorial symbols to a particular time and place, a particular people. The old is expressed anew; it must be, to come alive, to keep alive, to make alive.[20]

The homily is different from a presentation, a lecture, or a class for theological instruction. Its purpose is to evoke, to deepen, to challenge, and to channel the faith of those assembled for liturgical prayer. Since the liturgy is the experience of salvation now, in the here and now, the homily is to help particularize this experience for those gathered together. The breaking of the eucharistic bread for this particular group of believers is preceded by a no less important breaking of the word of revelation, redemption and sanctification.

Pre-conciliar usage often underscored the "interruption" quality of the sermon with preachers making the sign of the cross before and after the preaching (now eliminated in the order of Mass), having left the main altar for the pulpit where the already recited Latin text was repeated in the vernacular, followed by announcements, then the sermon. The Liturgy Constitution puts it this way:

> By means of the homily the mysteries of the faith and the guiding principles of the Christian life are expounded from the sacred text during the course of the liturgical year. The homily, therefore, is to be highly esteemed as part of the liturgy itself. . . . (no. 52)

This same sentiment is reiterated for the liturgy of the hours and for sacramental celebrations, thus shifting the homily from an "interruption" at the liturgy to integration within the liturgy. The issue of biblical preaching in the homily form concerns the aptness, and the fittingness of the homily in that it reflects the genuine human concerns of the people assembled for liturgy, and what light the proclaimed Scripture texts may shed on those real needs. When and where this kind of integration between liturgical proclamation and human life is accomplished in the homily, one can say that the "immemorial symbols" of the liturgy are extended "to a particular time and place." The announcement quality of the liturgy of the word is carried on through the homily,[21] as well as in the effective proclamation of the Scriptures, the responsorial psalm, the alleluia, and the general intercessions. That the homily given at Sunday liturgy leads to the celebration of the Lord's Supper in the Eucharist and is set within a liturgical season (e.g., Advent, Christmas, Lent, Easter, and Ordinary Time) should somehow be reflected in what is preached, for it is "through the course of the liturgical year (that) the homily sets forth the mysteries of faith and the standards of the Christian life on the basis of the sacred text."[22] The alternate side of the fact that the Scriptures determine to some extent what is prayed in the texts of the liturgy is seen here where the homily itself is framed by and ought to reflect the liturgical season being experienced. In addition, the unity of the word and sacrament celebrated is signaled by the frequently repeated instruction that the homily is normally "given by the one presiding."[23] That the table of the word leads to the table of the Eucharist is to be underscored, ministerially. This involves a significant shift since conventional practice frequently emphasized guest preachers. The one presiding can more easily help in the transition between word and Eucharist by referring in the homily to the liturgy of the table to come.

Alongside the tried and true means preachers use to write and deliver homilies—biblical interpretation, reflection and prayer, understanding the liturgical context for the homily (season and sacrament or hour of prayer), and the needs of particular communities—there is another means available derived from the model of the reformed liturgy: liturgy planning. In determining how a particular liturgy should be shaped and celebrated in a given community, the planning group might well address the challenge of the word to be proclaimed and the needs, strengths, and assumptions of the people celebrating the liturgy.[24] While this is not to suggest that words are necessarily put in preachers' mouths, it is to suggest that careful and skillful homiletic preparation and delivery does depend in large measure on the integration achieved between sacred text and liturgical community. At times the preacher may well have to speak to needs other than those offered at the planning meeting for reasons of being faithful to the text or because of a real need that must be addressed by the community. One thinks of the issues of racial prejudice, human rights, social justice and nuclear armaments which continue to deserve emphasis in our day and the fact that there are times when such issues are not understood to be part of the implications which ought to result from Gospel living.[25] Liturgy planning should regularly include sharing prayer and thoughts about the word to be proclaimed as a primary emphasis. How the rest of the elements of the liturgy (song, gesture, intercessions, etc.) help complete this emphasis should derive from this as a focal point.

The challenge in implementing the reformed liturgy involves moving from preaching sermons to preaching homilies, and understanding their position as integral to the liturgical celebration, not an interruption during it.

The Word at Liturgy—The variety and distinction in liturgical roles is clearly envisioned and emphasized in the reformed liturgical rites. "Liturgical tradition assigns responsibility for the biblical readings in the celebration of Mass and other sacraments and at the Hours to ministers: to readers and the deacon."[26] The role of the deacon during the liturgy of the word is to proclaim the Gospel, sometimes to preach, and to propose the intentions of the general intercessions. The reader exercises his or her function in the liturgy "and should exercise this even though ministers of a higher rank may be present."[27] The introduction to the lectionary emphasizes the role of reader, addresses his preparation for this ministry, and offers the pastoral judgment that "whenever there is more than one reading before the gospel it is better to assign the readings to different readers" (no. 52). It is assumed that readers take part in planning the liturgy (no. 51).

In terms of the space designated for worship, the lectionary introduction speaks of designing a lectern that is "rather large" (no. 34), and that should be in a "place in the church that is somewhat elevated, fixed, and of a suitable design and mobility." "It should reflect the dignity of God's word and be a clear reminder to the people that in the Mass the table of God's word and of Christ's body is placed before them" (no. 32). The intention of these instructions is to point out the renewed emphasis which the liturgy of the word deserves in every act of Christian worship. Readings are always to be done from a fitting lectern, and only the proclamation of the word should be done from here. By its nature the lectern is reserved for "the readings, the responsorial psalm, and the Easter proclamation (*Exsultet*). The lectern may rightly be used for the homily and general intercessions. . . . It is better for the commentator, cantor, or director of singing, for example, not to use the lectern."[28]

The reverence given to the scrolls in Israelite worship by having lamps burning near them, encasing them with elaborate covers, and carrying them in dignified procession during the liturgy has traditionally been adopted in the Christian use of the word in liturgy. Such traditional emphasis is reiterated in recent documents on liturgical implementation. It is envisioned that two books be used for proclamation in the liturgical assembly, one a book of the Gospels, the other the lectionary containing the other readings. Since the proclamation of the Gospel always stands as the high point of the liturgy of the word during the eucharistic liturgy, "the Book of the Gospels was always designed with the utmost care and was more ornate and shown greater respect than any of the other books of readings."[29] It may be carried in procession by the deacon and it receives marks of respect in the celebration of the liturgy such as kissing and incensation. When it is carried in procession it is placed on the main altar and left there until the procession with it to the lectern. To show the parallel between word and Eucharist, the present missal notes that the Gospel book may be left on the altar before the liturgy begins if it is not carried in procession, and during the Gospel acclamation be carried to the lectern. In comparison with the many lectionaries available for use in the liturgy, there are relatively few Gospel books available. Using one lectionary for the other readings and another for the Gospel is a way of differentiating between these two books. For the Gospel book to receive greater attention and emphasis, it might be helpful to cover it with a cloth cover that matches or contrasts with the church decor or vestments used for the liturgy. Changing these covers for the various seasons would be a way of enhancing the Gospel proclamation and of offering communities a non-verbal way of focusing attention on a worthy book for proclamation.

A final comment about our experiencing the word at liturgy concerns silence. The reformed liturgy presents us with a rich fare to assimilate in the liturgy of the word—most often three readings interspersed with sung psalm and Gospel acclamation. But what is also envisioned is short periods for silence, for meditative prayer and reflection. In fact, the introduction to the lectionary envisions periods of silence after each of the readings and after the homily (no. 28). Silence coupled with purposeful singing of the psalm and acclamation helps set a balance between hearing the proclaimed word and assimilating it. The intention in the revision and reintroduction of the liturgy of the word is for it to be an experience of hearing, singing and silent reflection. In addition to times for silence, "the liturgy of the word must be celebrated in a way that fosters meditation; clearly, any sort of haste that hinders reflectiveness must be avoided."[30]

In order for the word to be heard and assimilated by the kind of reflection envisioned, ushers would do well to refrain from seating people during the proclamation of the texts and perform this service during the psalm or Gospel acclamation. Other liturgical ministers help focus attention on the proclamation of the Scriptures when, during the liturgy itself, they all give their full attention to the word as it is being proclaimed. Unnecessary movement or reading along in missals or pamphlets while the reader is proclaiming the word sets up a division between what is taking place liturgically and what is taking place among those gathered, whether ministers or assembly. "Faith, then, comes through hearing, and what is heard is the word of Christ" (Rom 10:17). Part of the dynamic involved in assimilating what is heard at liturgy is prayer and quiet reflection. The liturgy itself should provide time and an atmosphere within which this can occur.

SACRAMENTS—VISIBLE WORDS

In addition to emphasizing the proclamation of the word as the direct address and present announcement of the good news of salvation, another scriptural notion about the importance of the word that is being revived and understood anew in our day concerns its power and effect. Far from being "merely" a word or the news about salvation, the biblical understanding of the word is that this very announcement accomplishes what it is intended to accomplish—through it believers *experience* salvation. There is a direct relationship between announcement and accomplishment of salvation in and among communities which gather for the liturgy. Specifically, this concerns the relationship between the proclamation of the word and the celebration of sacraments.

In the first account of creation in the Book of Genesis God is pictured as the one who brings creation out of what was formless, order out of what was chaos. In the process the author specifically notes that all this was accomplished because of what God "said." "Then God said 'Let there be light,' and there was light" (Gen 1:3) is a paradigm for the way the days of creation are structured in Genesis 1:1–2:2. In anthropomorphic language this first creation account relates that the author of all things made and sustains all life because of what was said and declared "in the beginning." The Hebrew Scriptures are filled with references to the power of God's word, as the psalmist sings: "By his words the heavens were made, by the breath of his mouth all the stars" (Ps 33:6). "He spoke; and it came to be. He commanded; it sprang into being" (Ps 33:9). The vehicle for the act of creation and the sustaining of the people of Israel as chosen was by means of the word, the announcement, the call of the Lord.

It is this Old Testament background which is reflected in the New Testament accounts of Jesus where evangelists use similar idioms to express the power and creative force of the word of Jesus, that it too accomplished what it intended to do. It is not coincidental that the account of creation in Genesis containing the words: "In the beginning God said" (Gen 1:1, 3), is repeated in the introduction to the Gospel of John referring to Christ: "In the beginning was the Word" (Jn 1:1). The creative, power-filled word of God in creating the sun, the moon, the stars, and our first parents is now personified and incarnate in Jesus, the word of the Father. As the word, the unique expression of the fullness of revelation, Jesus continues the work of salvation in history through his words and deeds. It is these very words, just like those of the Father, which accomplish what they intend; it is by his words that Jesus performs the work of salvation. The life of Jesus is marked by powerful preaching and teaching, as well as by inspiring healings and miracles. And all of these have their origin and source in the announced, spoken, and proclaimed word.

In the Gospel of Mark, for example, it is Jesus' proclamation that cures the leper—"He stretched out his hand and touched him and said to him, 'I will; be clean' " (Mk 1:41)—and it is the same kind of announcement that not only cures the paralytic of physical infirmity, it also reveals Jesus' power to forgive sins: "When Jesus saw their faith, he said to the paralytic, 'My son, your sins are forgiven'" (Mk 2:5). In fact, the evangelists want to emphasize this point so strongly that they offer the example of the centurion's faith in the word of Jesus as model of faith confession for succeeding generations: "Lord, I am not worthy to have you come under my roof; but only say the word, and my servant will be healed" (Mt 8:8). The placing of a modified form of this text in the eucharistic liturgy before the reception of the Eucharist, and in pericope form (Mt 8:5–11) on Monday of the First Week of Advent, points directly to the important place accorded to the word of the Lord in the liturgical practice of the Church. The word of the Lord is powerful in that it not only announces and states, it accomplishes and does what it intends. In Jesus, words and deeds are complementary.

All of this has reference to the experience of the Church in continuing the mission and work of Jesus in liturgy and sacraments. Augustine, among others, points to the fact that sacraments are visible words, visible and real demonstrations of the dynamism and effect which the word of the Lord has. "The Word comes to the element; and so there is a sacrament, that is, a sort of visible word."[31] While the Roman Catholic Church and the Reformation churches have been divided over the relative importance of the word (emphasized in the Protestant tradition) or of sacrament (the Roman Catholic tradition) in liturgy and in the lived spirituality of the churches, a prior experience in the life of the Christian Church (and in fact a more substantial tradition in the history of the Christian Church) views these as complementary rather than separate, parts of one sacramental event rather than as separate and distinct liturgies. While the renewed emphasis on the word in Roman Catholic liturgical and sacramental life is of rather recent vintage, the roots of this unity are strong and deep. However, up until the recently revised sacramental rituals were implemented, it was common to celebrate Christian marriage with an exchange of consent and rings preceded by an "instruction,"[32] to celebrate infant baptism with the briefest reference to proclaiming the word,[33] to "receive" the sacrament of penance with no reference to the Scriptures,[34] and to celebrate the sacrament of the anointing of the sick with no proclamation of the word.[35] The restoration of lectionaries for the sacraments is among the most traditional yet revolutionary reforms achieved in recent years in Roman Catholic liturgy.[36]

In the documents of reform the priority of reuniting the proclamation of the word with the accomplishment of the sacraments is clearly stated: "That the intimate connection between word and rites may be apparent in the liturgy . . ." (Liturgy Constitution, no. 35) there is to be more reading from the word at the liturgy. "In the Christian community itself . . . the preaching of the Word is needed for the very administration of the sacraments. For these are sacraments of faith; faith is born of the Word and nourished by it."[37] With regard to the unity of word and Eucharist the Lectionary introduction states: "The Church is nourished spiritually at the table of God's word and at the table of the eucharist: from the one it grows in wisdom and from the other in holiness" (no. 10).

Theologically what emerges in the revival of the proclamation of the Word as that which grounds the sacramental event is an emphasis on sacraments as true "visible words," as manifestations of the powerful force of the word of the Lord. To suggest that the sacraments are preceded by a liturgy of the word (and that the preacher breaks the word as well as the bread of Eucharist) is somewhat tentative when compared with the more forceful (and more Augustinian approach) which states that in fact the word of the Lord is proclaimed, active, and made real in the liturgical assembly when it gathers for sacraments which are themselves so founded on the word that they are called "visible words."

Karl Rahner puts it this way: "We can arrive at a concept of the sacraments in which the sacrament is understood as one quite specific word-event within the theology of the word."[38]

I believe that it is a conviction common to all Christians, and in the last analysis transcending the differences between the confessions, that the word pronounced in the Church in the name and at the behest of God and Christ has in principle an exhibitive character, that it effects what it signifies. . . .[39]

In the restored sacramental practice of the Church this intrinsic relationship between the word and sacrament is brought out in the way sacraments are celebrated. For example, the Rite of Christian Initiation for Adults is predicated on communal celebrations of the word with preachers directed to focus the attention of the gathered community on the relationship between the Scripture readings and the initiation which the catechumens presently await, prepare for, and ultimately experience after the liturgy of the word at the Easter Vigil.[40] Infant baptism is celebrated in a ceremony involving emphasis on both word and sacrament:

> After the reading, the celebrant gives a short homily, explaining to those present the significance of what has been read. His purpose will be to lead them to a deeper understanding of the mystery of baptism and to encourage the parents and godparents to a ready acceptance of the responsibilities which arise from the sacrament.[41]

While every sacramental ritual that has been revised since Vatican II contains a lectionary with Scripture texts chosen to reflect the announcement of salvation through the word and the sacrament celebrated, the restoration of a liturgy of the word in the liturgy of penance and in the rite of the worship of the Eucharist outside of Mass is particularly instructive. Even here, in what had become among the most private and individual experiences of sacrament, the Church emphasizes the *liturgy* of penance (in two of the three sacramental forms) with a liturgy of the word. Even in the form of penance for the individual confession of sins, a form of word service is provided as a means of expressing the presence of Christ the shepherd who reconciles all to himself through word and sacrament.[42] With regard to exposition of the Holy Eucharist the instruction states that "shorter expositions of the eucharist are to be arranged in such a way that the blessing with the eucharist is preceded by a suitable period for readings of the word of God, songs, prayers, and sufficient time for silent prayer" (no. 89).

The biblical evidence of God speaking and acting in the Old

Testament and of Jesus accomplishing his mission in words and deeds is thus continued in the sacramental experience of the Church where sacraments are properly understood as visible words, as the means whereby contemporary Christians share in the proclamation of the good news of salvation, the Gospel of Jesus Christ.

CONTEMPLATING THE WORD

In order for the proclamation of the word to accomplish its purpose of deepening the faith experience of the assembled community, the lectionary introduction continually refers to effective proclamation, to listening to the texts proclaimed and to silent prayer. Dispositions of heart are stirred when reverence for and care in the proclamation of the Scriptures is coupled with silence at its hearing for contemplation and prayer. The experience of the liturgy itself should establish a setting in which the word is proclaimed and truly heard, not merely listened to, or noted.

In addition, those charged with liturgical proclamation (and by extension we can say those who hear the word proclaimed) are to receive proper preparation including biblical and liturgical formation, not only in technique but in the theology of what is taking place at liturgy.

> The purpose of their biblical formation is to give readers the ability to understand the readings in context and to perceive by the light of faith the central point of the revealed message. The liturgical formation ought to equip the readers to have some grasp of the meaning and structure of the liturgy of the word and of the significance of its connection with the liturgy of the eucharist.[43]

That the experience of liturgical prayer can help form and direct personal prayer is one of the aims of the restoration of the liturgy in the Church, and it is often cited as one of the ways in which the liturgy exercises a formative influence on the spirituality of those who participate in common prayer.[44]

> The more we read the word of God the more we can ponder the meaning of our own existence and of our relationship with God against the background of God's dealings with humankind in the world that God created, sustains, and redeems in Christ.[45]

When we search and probe the Scriptures as they are set out for us in the liturgy we come to know the God of invitation and covenant relationship, of reconciling love and forgiveness, the God of challenge and moral commands, and the God whose enduring power and love is mediated once-for-all ages through a Son whom we acclaim as Lord. Searching and probing the Scriptures brings us to the very roots of our faith, and religious practice, as based on the word of the Lord which endures forever.

In this experience, both in personal reflection on the word and in its liturgical proclamation, we come to know something of the struggle and pain that must be a part of the life of the Christian on this earth. And yet through this same means we come to know the peace and lasting joy that comes to us through knowing God's word and will, which alone gives life. In the words of Gregory the Great:

> The place of battle is the heart of the one who hears the word of God. It is called a place of battle because there the word which is received makes war on well-worn ways of life. The heavenly things it hears begin to have their attraction, but longstanding habit arises and suggests that the message should be despised. The struggle, then, gets worse because what the teacher commands, the evil spirits cry down by dissuasion. Like warriors they rise up against God's holy ones, destroying in conflict whatever the teacher has been saying. What does it mean, then, to come to the place of battle if not by the approach of acute discernment, to come to the very depths of the heart of the listener, where the enemies may most quickly be found and most ruthlessly cut to pieces? For those who do not know how to wage an internal conflict can never come to the true battlefields.[46]

The rule of life in this passing world is the revealed word of God. Pondering it and keeping it leads to life eternal with God. In the meantime, living the word gives us in the here and now a share in the joy that will be complete in the kingdom forever. As we pray in the liturgy:

> May almighty God keep you from all harm
> and bless you with every good gift. ℟. Amen.
>
> May he set his Word in your heart
> and fill you with lasting joy. ℟. Amen.
>
> May you walk in his ways,
> always knowing what is right and good,
> until you enter your heavenly inheritance. ℟. Amen.

The assembly of believers who gather for Christian worship gather together to experience again and again their gifted, covenant relationship with God. This is primarily accomplished through the proclamation and contemplation of the word of the Lord as embodied in the canon of the Scriptures. These inspired books are intended for proclamation, hearing and acceptance by those who share common worship. The address from God to his people is continued and concretized in the experience of liturgical prayer. It is through the liturgy that Christian communities have their identity confirmed yet challenged, renewed yet stimulated toward growth—all accomplished when the word of the Lord is seen to be central and essential for the faith already shared to grow and develop. Whether in the liturgy of the hours or in the celebration of the sacraments, emphasis is always placed on the revealed word in Christ who himself is the word, the source of all life and holiness. And yet it is in personal contemplation of the word as well as in the liturgical announcement of that same word that we grow into the fullness of the mystery which is Christ. It is his voice that is heard and his way that is accepted when Christians assemble to pray. An essential foundation of liturgical prayer is, therefore, the revelation and proclamation of the word of God.

NOTES

1. While the liturgy was never removed from the celebration of the Eucharist, for example, and the singing of the Scripture texts did mark solemn high Mass celebrated in Latin in conventional pre-conciliar practice, the issue here concerns the re-emphasis placed on the proclamation of the word in post-conciliar liturgical practice.

2. *Constitution on the Sacred Liturgy*, no. 24.

3. *Lectionary for Mass, Introduction* in Liturgy Documentary Series 1 (Washington: USCC, 1982) no. 7, p. 15.

4. Aidan Kavanagh, "The Tradition of Judaeo-Christian Worship: Our Debt to Each Other," in Philip Scharper, ed., *Torah and Gospel.* Jewish and Christian Theology in Dialogue (New York: Sheed and Ward, 1966) p. 49.

5. It is significant that this Old Testament text is used by the evangelists when recounting the temptation of Jesus (see Mt 4:4 and Lk 4:4). That this text is of central importance on the day when this Gospel is proclaimed on the First Sunday of Lent is evident in the fact that it is chosen as the verse for the Gospel acclamation in all three cycles of the lectionary for this day.

6. On the central significance of this text see Gerhard von Rad, *Old Testament Theology*, Vol. One, trans. D.M.G. Stalker (New York: Harper and Row, 1962) pp. 120–121.

7. See C. W. Dugmore, *The Influence of the Synagogue upon the Divine Office* (London: Oxford University Press, 1944) and as reprinted (London: The Faith Press, 1964) pp. 18–20. It is fitting that the *Shema* begins with the words "*Hear,* O Israel."

8. See *Lectionary for Mass, Introduction,* no. 46, p. 24, quoting the *Constitution on the Sacred Liturgy,* no. 7.

9. *Ibid.,* no. 10, p. 16.

10. Aloysius Church, *The Theology of the Word of God* (Notre Dame: Fides, 1970) p. 20.

11. *Ibid.,* p. 15.

12. *Ibid.,* pp. 17–18.

13. The elements included: (Lessons), Psalms (145–150), Shema, Decalogue, *Teffilah* or *Amidah.*

14. See, for example, Acts 3:1, 10:9 and 16:25. See also *General Instruction, Liturgy of the Hours*, no. 1.

15. See, for example, the witness of Justin cited in Part Two, Chapter Four, section on "God's Presence to a Redeemed Community."

16. James F. White, "Preface," *A Lectionary* (Princeton: Consultation on Church Union, 1974) p. 1. It should be pointed out, however, that the Roman lectionary at present is not without flaw; indeed it has received the scrutiny of Scripture scholars who have found it wanting in places. Among the more significant commentaries see Gerard S. Sloyan, "The Lectionary as a Context for Interpretation," *Interpretation* 31 (April 1977) 131-138. See also William Skudlarek, *The Word in Worship*. Preaching in a Liturgical Context (Nashville: Abingdon, 1981) pp. 3-39.

17. For a more complete description see, *Lectionary for Mass, Introduction*, nos. 66-77.

18. See Part One, Chapter Three, section on "Incarnational Spirituality."

19. See Paul E. Dinter, "Preaching and the Inquiring of God," *Worship* 52 (May 1978) 223-236.

20. Walter J. Burghardt, *Tell the Next Generation*. Homilies and Near Homilies (New York/Ramsey: Paulist Press, 1980) p. 11, quoting Yves Congar.

21. See *Fulfilled in Your Hearing*, The Homily in the Sunday Assembly (Washington: USCC, 1982) from the Bishops' Committee on Priestly Life and Ministry.

22. *Lectionary for Mass, Introduction*, no. 24, p. 19.

23. *Ibid.*, p. 24. See, also, *General Instruction of the Roman Missal*, no. 42.

24. See, for example, the suggestions on planning in *Music in Catholic Worship*, nos. 10-14, and in *Fulfilled in Your Hearing*, pp. 36-38.

25. See Walter J. Burghardt, "Preaching the Just Word," in Mark Searle, ed., *Liturgy and Social Justice* (Collegeville: The Liturgical Press, 1980) pp. 36-52.

26. *Lectionary for Mass, Introduction*, no. 49, p. 25.

27. *Ibid.*, no. 51, p. 25; on the role of the reader, see *General Instruction of the Roman Missal*, no. 66 and the motu proprio of Pope Paul VI, *Ministeria quaedam*.

28. *Lectionary for Mass, Introduction*, no. 33, p. 21; see also *Environment and Art in Catholic Worship*, nos. 74-75.

29. *Lectionary for Mass, Introduction*, no. 36, p. 21.

30. *Lectionary for Mass, Introduction*, no. 28, p. 20.

31. Text as found in Robert W. Jenson, *Visible Words* (Philadelphia: Fortress Press, 1978) p. 3. The author also cites the text of John Gerhard: "By 'the word' is to be understood: first a mandate ... by which an element ... is separated from ordinary use and destined for sacramental use; and second a promise, and indeed the gospel itself as it is to be applied and sealed by the sacrament."

32. Rite for Celebrating Marriage, "Exhortation Before Marriage," *The Roman Ritual* (Milwaukee: Bruce, 1964) p. 269. The rubrics state: "If there is no homily the priest may read the following exhortation, a custom of very long standing in the U.S."

33. *The Roman Ritual*, pp. 51–52, cites the use of Psalms 99 and 22 as "hymns." There is no other reference to Scripture.

34. *The Roman Ritual*, pp. 190–191.

35. *The Roman Ritual*, pp. 208–215.

36. The common bond established through the word and especially as presently proclaimed in the sacramental event is the basis for Karl Rahner's approach to ecumenical dialogue and interchange in "What Is a Sacrament?" in *Theological Investigations* Vol. XIV (New York: Seabury, 1976), trans. David Bourke, pp. 135–148.

37. *Decree on the Ministry and Life of Priests*, no. 4.

38. Karl Rahner, "What Is a Sacrament?" p. 138.

39. *Ibid.*, p. 139.

40. See *RCIA*, nos. 19, 52, 106, 161, 168, 175.

41. See *Rite of Baptism for Children*, nos. 17, 45, as well as 44.

42. *Rite of Penance*, no. 17: "The the priest, or the penitent himself, may read a text of holy Scripture, or this may be done as part of the preparation for the sacrament. Through the word of God the Christian receives light to recognize his sins and is called to conversion and to confidence in God's mercy." See also no. 24 regarding the nature of the homily to be given at communal celebrations of the sacrament.

43. *Lectionary for Mass, Introduction*, no. 55, p. 26.

44. See Part One, Chapter One, section on "Formative Nature of Liturgical Prayer," and *Constitution on the Sacred Liturgy*, nos. 13 and 17.

45. Alan Bouley, "Scripture, Personal Prayer, and Liturgy," in *Scripture and the Assembly*, Liturgy Vol. 2 (Summer 1982) p. 64.

46. Quoted in Aelred Squire, *Summer in the Seed* (New York/Ramsey: Paulist Press, 1979) pp. 55–56.

Chapter Six
PARTICIPATION IN MEMORY AND HOPE

There is a saying among the rabbis: "To remember is to give life; to forget is to let die." This can be applied to the Christian liturgy in the sense that it is the communal act of commemorating and remembering what is the source of all life for the believer: the mystery of Jesus dead and risen. The experience of liturgy is our collective act of memorial through which we experience the saving deeds of the dying and rising of Jesus, the paschal mystery. In liturgical shorthand we would say that the liturgy is our participation in Jesus' dying and rising; the means to achieve this identification with Christ is communal remembering.

The notion of "participation" is frequently used to describe our active involvement in the act of worship: in word, song, gesture and silence. And this is a correct (though somewhat limited) usage of the term. However, a more traditional understanding of "participation" that can help us understand what occurs at liturgy is that it is through these sacred rites, symbols and celebrations that we experience the very life of Christ, we participate and share (take part in and become part of) his paschal, saving mystery. Our insertion into this central "mystery of faith" is what liturgy is all about. What is effected and accomplished is our being drawn into the very act of Jesus' dying and rising, into this timeless event which we can and do experience in the present time through the liturgy.

This fundamental notion of *remembering* in community prayer offers and ensures for us a share in the mystery of Christ, in his death and resurrection. "Lord, by your cross and resurrec-

tion you have set us free. You are the Savior of the world." This
central notion of remembering is the underpinning and foundation of what liturgy is all about. Hence, remembering, memorial
and commemoration comprise an essential element of liturgical
prayer. A liturgy (as opposed to other forms of prayer) essentially is an act of remembering what God has done and does in and
through Christ; the act of liturgy insures our participation in the
life of God through Christ. In asserting the priority of liturgical
prayer over other kinds of prayer the Church underscores that it
is through the liturgy fundamentally that we experience the
mystery of Christ's paschal victory.

LITURGICAL MEMORIAL

It is axiomatic to assert that the more we understand and appreciate the theology and spirituality of Judaism as experienced at
the liturgy, the more we will be able to appreciate the generative
source of what has evolved into the forms of liturgical prayer in
the Christian Church.[1] There is, however, no aspect of Christian
liturgical prayer that yields such a rich understanding and appreciation than that which is understood by the notion of communal remembering at the liturgy, or what is more accurately
described as liturgical "memorial." Specifically, the rediscovery
of the understanding of time that is operative in Jewish liturgy
and the meaning of how this is unfolded and experienced in the
actions that comprise Jewish liturgy offer significant insight
when we try to appreciate what is involved in Christian liturgy.

The basis of Jewish piety is remembrance. While the covenant between God and this chosen people was forged and sealed
once in history for "ancestors" or "forefathers," the covenant
relationship was continually experienced and forged anew for
succeeding generations who would gather for the communal
actions of Jewish liturgy. The relationship between God and
Israel was renewed at the liturgy. Through the liturgy God was
remembered by his people and God *remembered* these as his own.
God's remembering has an effect: it gives life. "Whoever Yahweh does not remember has no existence."[2]

The communal gathering of the people of Israel to hear the

revealed word of God and to experience his remembrance of them formed a significant part of Jewish liturgical prayer. Similarly, this action of gathering for the hearing of God's word and for rites of remembrance is what Christian liturgy is all about. For both forms of liturgy the end result is the same: renewal of the covenant forged by God for his chosen people. When God "remembers" or "is mindful," worshiping communities experience a share (participate) in his very life. When God "forgets" or turns from his people they are cut off from this source of peace, love and forgiveness. They die. "To remember is to give life. To forget is to let die."

Examples of the kind of action involved in the Jewish notions of "remembering" and "memorial" are found throughout the Scriptures. At morning prayer each day the Christian community prays in the words from the song of Zachary: "He promised to show mercy to our fathers/and to remember his holy covenant" (Lk 1:72). Similarly, at evening prayer in the song of Mary we pray: "He has come to the help of his servant Israel/for he has remembered his promise of mercy, the promise he made to our fathers,/to Abraham and his children forever" (Lk 1:54–55). These New Testament canticles, which form an important and very traditional part of the morning and evening prayer of the Church's liturgy, are best understood when seen against the background of the Old Testament notion of remembering the covenant (Gen 9:15; Ex 2:24; 6:5; Lev 26:52).

The psalms take up this same idea and give it depth and rich expression: "He gives food to those who fear him,/keeps his covenant ever in mind" (Ps 111:5, used at Sunday Evening Prayer, Week III). "The Lord has made known his salvation;/he has shown his justice to the nations./ He has remembered his truth and love/for the house of Israel" (Ps 98:5, used at Wednesday Evening Prayer, Week III). In a more revealing personal prayer the psalmist pleads: "Remembering your mercy, Lord,/and the love you have shown from of old./ Do not remember the sins of my youth./ In your love remember me" (Ps 25:6–7, used at Thursday Daytime Prayer Week I).

What is involved in liturgical memorial, therefore, is a communal remembering: of what God did and does for his people in offering and sustaining them in the covenant relationship. "Remembering" is not just a category involving thought or individual recollection of past events. "Remembering" at the liturgy is an action which the gathered community does (as opposed to "thinks about") in order to receive life from God; it involves an action which God performs for his people in the here and now. Liturgical remembering is through the doing. In the words of Robert Taft:

> A religion is different from a personal philosophy of life in that it is a *shared* perspective, a common outlook on reality. As such it depends on *history*, on the group's collective remembrance of things past, of events that have been transformed in the collective memory of the community into key symbolic episodes determinative of the community's being and self-understanding.[3]

To get to the heart of what Taft is saying about the past and about time requires taking a look at our common assumptions about time and using the Jewish understanding of liturgical time to illuminate what is at stake here. The basis of what is done in the present liturgy is based on what God has done in the past ("salvation history") and on what God will complete and fulfill at the end of time (to bring time to an end). Once again, what stands in the center is our present experience of the liturgy, the experience of prayer which, through remembering, bridges what for us are usually separable and separated periods: past, present, future. At liturgy these are merged and experienced together. At liturgy we "recall the past," we "shape the present" and "summon the future."[4]

Recalling the Past. The events which formed the people of Israel into the chosen of God, and those which formed the new people of God into the Christian community are the foundational events of a history we call "salvation." Hence, the term "salvation history" is used to describe the interventions of God who called and calls a people to himself. Yet, there is another, richer sense in which these events of salvation history can be understood, for they are not only events that are relegated to the past. These saving events are of a nature and kind that they have enduring value and implications. They are, in one sense, historically verifiable and yet they are also experienced again and again at the common prayer of the community—the liturgy. In this sense, the present liturgical prayer of the Church is a time when the past deeds of salvation are experienced anew, not in the sense that they are redone, repeated or remade, but in the sense that by their very nature these deeds of God have enduring power and lasting effects for communities removed in time and place from the time when they first occurred. Later generations in the history of Israel experienced (and still experience) the acts of redemption (Exodus, Red Sea) although they were not present when these deeds were first accomplished for Israel. The place of experiencing them was and is the liturgy. In the liturgy "there was an immediate encounter, and actual participation in the great acts of redemption. The Old Testament maintained the dynamic, continuing character of past events without sacrificing their historical character."[5]

What occurs in Jewish liturgy is an action performed by the community, at God's gracious invitation, to recall and remember the foundational events of redemption and to experience those same events in such a way that they would become a part of and truly "participate in" that same redemption in the present. What is involved is not a repetition, a re-enactment, or a redoing of any of the saving events. Rather, what occurs is a direct contact with them through liturgical memorial. The community remembers what God did and through the very act of remembering receives salvation from the God remembered. This God who saves is acclaimed as "greater than all gods." The Mishnah states that when celebrating the Passover, each generation of the people of Israel should consider as though they themselves "had personally gone forth from Egypt,"[6] in the sense that the same redemption, the very same deliverance is offered in every time and place where believers gather for worship. The past is not repeated; rather the past events are contemporized, made actual and real, through liturgy. In order to avoid the sometimes overused (and also polemical) term "re-

enactment" of the past, another way of describing the full impact of the past on the present through liturgy is to say that in
this memorial the foundation events of redemption are actualized and made available to the community. "Actualization is the
process by which a past event is contemporized for a generation
removed in time and space from the original event."[7] For the
people of the old covenant at worship:

> the act of remembrance is not a simple inner reflection . . .
> [it] involves an action, an encounter with historical events.
> Each successive generation in Israel witnessed to a reality
> which it encountered when remembering the tradition. The
> biblical events have the dynamic character of refusing to be
> relegated to the past.[8]

Hence, we can say that just as Jewish piety was based on a
very dynamic understanding of the action of God in history and
in the present, so Christian liturgical memorial is characterized
by this same understanding. In Christian worship we do not
repeat the life-giving death of Jesus at Calvary, nor do we repeat
the original event of his rising from the dead to the fullness of
life with the Father at Easter. Rather, through the liturgy we
share in what was accomplished for our salvation, we are remade
and made new through the paschal mystery of Christ. Because
God has redeemed us in Christ we gather in community to
remember and to experience this life again and again.

> So Christian worship is not how we seek to contact God; it is
> a celebration of how God has touched us, has united us to
> himself and is ever present to us and dwelling in us. It is
> ritual perfected by divine realism; ritual in which the symbolic
> action is not a memorial of the past, but a participation in the
> eternally present salvific Pasch of Christ.[9]

Christian liturgy is, therefore, our participation in the accomplished death and resurrection of Christ. This center of salvation was accomplished once for all and it is actualized for us at
the liturgy. Through liturgical prayer all that has been accomplished in salvation history can sanctify us and bring us closer to

the Father. The means to accomplish this is the liturgy at which we "remember" and receive the very "life" of God. "To remember is to give life."

That the paschal mystery is an accomplished deed of God for our salvation and the pattern according to which we are conformed for the present sanctification is stated clearly in the liturgy. The historical and temporal distance between Christ's dying and rising and our experience of this one mystery is transcended and eliminated when Christians gather for liturgy. As we pray in the Sunday preface: "By suffering on the cross he freed us from unending death, and by rising from the dead he gave us eternal life" (Sunday Preface II). And as we proclaim at the memorial acclamation: "Dying you destroyed our death, rising you restored our life." It is at moments of common liturgical prayer that the past events of redemption are experienced anew in the present by means of liturgical remembering. It is through the liturgy that we participate in the paschal mystery and so are transformed and made holy.

Summoning the Future. But this "recalling the past" in present rituals of worship is only half of what is really involved in liturgical memorial. The other part involves the present rites of liturgy (as based on the past) acting to "summon the future," the complete accomplishment of our redemption in Christ. We participate now in liturgy not only to *remember* the past, which itself is significantly more important and substantial than engaging in "nostalgia." We celebrate the liturgy to pray for the "coming of the kingdom" when we shall all be united with God forever, in the heavenly liturgy.[10] Our present participation in all that redemption is and signifies will be consummated in the future. It is that longed-for elusive future that we summon at the liturgy.

> "To commemorate is not to stand afar off from what happened in the past; on the contrary, it is to eliminate the distance between present and past." To commemorate is to give the past a new existence; it is to think that each of us is contemporaneous with historical events whose consequences we still endure or whose effects we still prolong in time. At

the same time the Jewish liturgy is oriented toward a future. The Passover meal is not an imaginary commemoration of the Exodus from Egypt; at the Passover meal, a place is set for the prophet Elias, showing hope and expectation of fulfillment.[11]

Central to this understanding is the notion that through liturgical memorial we break the boundaries of historical time to experience what is timeless and eternal—life with God. What was accomplished in Christ for the Christian is renewed and offered again and again at the liturgy so that believers can share and truly participate more fully in the very life of God through Christ.

> By his birth we are reborn.
> In his suffering we are freed from sin.
> By his rising from the dead we rise to everlasting life.
> In his return to you in glory
> we enter into your heavenly kingdom.
> (Preface, Sundays in Ordinary Time IV)

> In you we live and move and have our being.
> Each day you show us a Father's love;
> your Holy Spirit, dwelling within us,
> gives us on earth the hope of unending joy.
> (Preface, Sundays in Ordinary Time VI)

In Jewish and Christian worship as based on God's intervention in human history, the past is never over and done with; past deeds of redemption perdure and are experienced in the liturgy. Similarly, viewed from the perspective of what happens at liturgy we say that the future glory for which we long[12] is already experienced in the liturgy to a limited degree (as compared to the second coming itself). The "future" for which we long is not, in fact, a "time and place" category so much as it is our looking forward to the fullness of what we experience only partially in the liturgy—the whole mystery of Christ. We look not for a calculable time and place for Christ to "come again" so much as we long for the fullness of what was accomplished by his paschal mystery.

At liturgy, the past recalled is the once-for-all event of redemption won in the paschal sacrifice of Jesus. The future summoned is the *parousia,* the final coming of Christ at the end of time. The Christian Church stands "between the times" of what has been accomplished in Christ and what will be completed at his return. Hence, liturgical memorial is the means we now have of actualizing the past and summoning the future. While we can say that all has been accomplished in Christ's dying and rising, the very repetition and continual celebration of the liturgy reminds us that the completion and fulfillment of what was begun in Christ has not yet come to pass. In Christ it is accomplished but for us we still "wait in joyful hope for the coming of our savior Jesus Christ" to take us all to the kingdom of heaven.

> In all true Christian worship the basic emphasis must always be on this eschatological element; on salvation history, yes, but as one indivisible, eternally present reality which is the Kingdom of God realized in its fullness in the Passover of Christ.[13]

What is pointed out here is a helpful insight into the fundamentally eschatological basis of Christian liturgy. It is also a helpful corrective to the tendency of Western Christians to emphasize the juncture of past and present in the liturgy and ignore the completion of all liturgy in the coming of the kingdom, which kingdom is paradoxically experienced in liturgy but not in its fullness.

Examples of this eschatological emphasis in the liturgy are many. At the Communion rite of the liturgy of the Eucharist the priest holds the broken breads to be distributed and states: "This is the Lamb of God who takes away the sins of the world. Happy are those who are called to his supper."[14] The first part of the text refers to the sacrificial Lamb of God (Jn 1:29) in whose sacrifice we share at the Eucharist. In addition, the invitation to Communion contains another, more eschatological reference. The translation "Happy are those ... called to his supper" is in some ways unfortunate because it can seem to refer only to the present celebration of the Eucharist. In reality it refers to the table-fellowship in the kingdom, at the wedding feast of the Lamb. The text itself is inspired by Revelation 19:9: "Happy are they who have been invited to the wedding feast of the Lamb." What should be recalled in the light of this text is the dual reference to the redemption won for us by the sacrificial death and resurrection which we share at Eucharist, and the completion of our participation in this mystery at the eternal banquet in the kingdom.

The prefaces for the dedication of a church also express this same twofold notion:

> We thank you now for this house of prayer
> in which you bless your family
> as we come to you on pilgrimage.
> Here you reveal your presence
> by sacramental signs,
> and make us one with you
> through the unseen bond of grace.
> Here you build your temple of living stones,
> and bring the Church to its full stature
> as the body of Christ throughout the world,
> to reach its perfection at last
> in the heavenly city of Jerusalem,
> which is the vision of your peace.
>
> (Dedication of a Church I)

> Your house of prayer
> is also the promise of the Church in heaven.
> Here your love is always at work,
> preparing the Church on earth
> for its heavenly glory
> as the sinless bride of Christ,
> the joyful mother of a great company of saints.
>
> (Dedication of a Church II)

It is not only sacramental liturgy which unfolds this eschatological dimension, it is also seen and understood when we hear and proclaim the word of God in liturgical assemblies:

The word of God proclaimed in the celebration of his mysteries does not address present conditions alone but looks back
to past events and forward to what is yet to come. Thus God's
word shows us what we should hope for with such a longing
that in this changing world our hearts will be set on the place
of true joy.[15]

Specifically, with regard to the liturgy of the hours we can assert
that

it is incorrect, then, to view the Office as primarily "historical" rather than "eschatological." Theologically the coming
of Christ is one indivisible event, though it can intersect with
human history at different points in time. The *eschaton,* the
final fulfillment of history, has already occurred in Christ.
The time of the kingdom, the beginning of the final days, is
already begun.[16]

What the liturgy offers is a memorial of all that has been
accomplished in Christ and all that is to be completed in the
kingdom forever. Liturgical time can be understood as a succession of moments in our present historical time which allows us
to participate in the whole Christ, the Jesus whose dying and
rising is the center of our piety and whose second coming will
complete the inauguration of his kingdom, which itself was
begun through the paschal mystery. To "participate" in liturgy
means that we share in the very life of God, we take part in this
life and are transformed by it. What occurs in liturgy is our
participation in Jesus' paschal mystery and the means to achieve
this profound identification is communal remembering. Memorial, remembering is what the Christian liturgy is all about.

PARTICIPATION THROUGH LITURGY

While the intrinsic connection between Christ's paschal mystery
and the community's participation in this mystery has been
argued with reference to liturgical texts and the theology of
what occurs at worship, it must also be admitted that such a
close harmony and identification between Christ and the com-

munity in the act of worship has not always been so clear. In fact, it was the progressive separation between the doing of liturgy on the one hand, and the community's involvement in popular devotions on the other, that caused a great gulf between "liturgy" and "spirituality" over the centuries.[17] While the action of liturgy itself has always been regarded in the tradition of the Church as the privileged time of the Christian community's prayer, sometimes the union between the paschal mystery of Christ and the community's participation in this mystery was not so evident in experience or in commenting on what liturgy was all about. Two particularly striking examples of these other approaches may be termed "historicization" and "dramatization" as opposed to "commemoration" or "liturgical memorial." What remains constant through the Church's tradition is the important place which the liturgy plays in the piety of the people; but the issue here concerns to what extent historicization and dramatization understood the liturgy to be the setting (only) for uniting oneself with the mysteries of Christ and to what extent memorial in its fullest sense was appreciated as the action for the whole Church joining contemporary communities with the redemptive acts of Christ.

"Historicization" may be understood to be that approach to celebrating the memorial of the paschal mystery which gives undue emphasis to the historical details (names, dates, and places) of how and where these events originally occurred. Such an overemphasis can set up a dichotomy between the worshiping community's present life and the historical past of the time and place of Jesus' life, death and resurrection. This tendency sees a highly objective emphasis at work where Christ's passion, death and resurrection (although the latter is sometimes less emphasized) are made separate facts of history to recall individually so that each is commemorated in isolation from the others. What this approach does is to set up a clear separation between what is really one mystery—the obedient life, sacrificial death and resurrection of Christ. Once these essentially interrelated events become separated out, then there is a tendency to objectify each to the extent that "passion piety," for example, can reign as isolated from the rest of the whole paschal mystery. The liturgy seeks to underscore the fundamental unity of this mystery by stating: "Christ has died. Christ is risen. Christ will come again"; "Lord, by your cross and resurrection you have set us free. You are the savior of the world." What makes liturgical commemoration so important is that in the liturgy a different notion of time is operative wherein the whole of Christ's paschal mystery is celebrated and experienced anew as one mystery. Historicization can so break up this unity that individual parts become objects to be pondered and recalled but without the essential unity and identification established by liturgical commemoration.[18]

"Dramatization" is another approach to what is celebrated liturgically, but unlike the historicization emphasis, this seeks to imitate the events that comprise Christ's dying and rising so that the liturgy is seen to be a tableau that unfolds the events of the passion, for example, and neglects the essential quality of liturgy—that the liturgy does not repeat or redo any of these events; rather it commemorates all of them in the language of memorial. A misconstrued notion of dramatization of the liturgy occurs when commentators like Amalarius of Metz (ninth century) seek to "explain" the gestures of the liturgy in such a way that each gesture serves as a "reminder" (as opposed to memorial) of a part of the "drama" that led to the crucifixion of Christ and his burial in the tomb. The liturgy now becomes the setting for individual recollections of the suffering and death of Jesus as opposed to the means through which contemporary congregations can commemorate and experience the self-same redemption that was accomplished and is continually made available through the liturgy. Once again, the balance of the factors of suffering, dying, rising, and exaltation to the right hand of the Father is lost in favor of imitating the historical events through which the paschal mystery was accomplished. Once a form of piety "imitates" the events of the passion, or a school of interpretation emphasizes only the deeds of Christ as accomplished historically, then it is a short leap to understand the liturgy as merely the redoing of the paschal mystery without reference to the community's incorporation into this mystery. Historicization and dramatization misconstrue the essential unity between

Christ and community, and the notion of memorial on which the liturgy is based. Memorial as a means of *participation* in Christ's mystery is lost in favor of a notion of liturgy where individuals recall the events of Christ's dying and rising and witness them performed in the sanctuary (dramatization or historicization) or use them as matter for individual meditation. They are objectified in the sense that they are watched and thought about during the liturgy as opposed to being experienced and participated in through the memorial of liturgy.

The point of liturgical commemoration is to establish the participation of the community in Christ's paschal mystery, not by repeating any of those events or by imitating them in drama. With this in mind it is helpful to review the texts of the "memorial" prayer that is proclaimed at the Eucharist (the *anamnesis*) to see how the liturgy itself unites the events of the paschal mystery and joins contemporary communities with these deeds of redemption.[19]

In memory of his death and resurrection,
we offer you, Father, this life-giving bread,
this saving cup.
We thank you for counting us worthy
to stand in your presence and serve you.
May all of us who share in the body and blood of Christ
be brought together in unity by the Holy Spirit.
(Eucharistic Prayer II)

Father, calling to mind the death your Son endured for our
salvation,
his glorious resurrection and ascension into heaven,
and ready to greet him when he comes again,
we offer you in thanksgiving this holy and living sacrifice.
(Eucharistic Prayer III)

Father, we now celebrate this memorial of our redemption.
We recall Christ's death, his descent among the dead,
his resurrection, and his ascension to your right hand;
and, looking forward to his coming in glory,
we offer you his body and blood,

the acceptable sacrifice
which brings salvation to the whole world.
(Eucharistic Prayer IV)

We do this in memory of Jesus Christ,
our Passover and our lasting peace.
We celebrate his death and resurrection
and look for the coming of that day
when he will return to give us the fullness of joy.
Therefore we offer you, God ever faithful and true,
the sacrifice which restores man to your friendship.
(Eucharistic Prayer for Masses of Reconciliation I)

Lord our God,
your Son has entrusted to us
this pledge of his love.
We celebrate the memory of his death and resurrection
and bring you the gift you have given us,
the sacrifice of reconciliation.
Therefore, we ask you, Father,
to accept us, together with your Son.
(Eucharistic Prayer for Masses of Reconciliation II)[20]

The memorial prayers of the eucharistic liturgy are derived from the prayers of liturgical commemoration of the Jewish liturgy. They express succinctly what liturgical commemoration is all about—the essential union between Christ's dying and rising and the community which commemorates, and thus shares in, that same mystery of faith. These prayers demonstrate that the key to understanding the memorial of Christ as experienced in the liturgy is that, through the liturgy, congregations removed in time and place from the events of redemption are themselves true participants and sharers in those saving deeds. In fact, to have been an eye-witness at Christ's death on the cross would have been to see an historical event, one part of the paschal mystery; to celebrate the liturgy is to share in the fullness of Christ's dying, rising and intercession at the Father's right hand in glory. Participation in Christ's mystery at the liturgy is a full and real experience of redemption; in fact it expresses a unity and fullness that was not present at the events of the Last Supper or the crucifixion. The liturgy, as a ritual, does not historicize or dramatize the paschal mystery at all. What the ritual of the liturgy does is to commemorate historical events in such a way that these verifiable happenings are combined and transformed—they are no longer "merely historical." In and through the liturgy they are transformed in the light of the resurrection and exaltation in such a way that those who share in them now participate in the whole of the paschal mystery. Through the ritual of liturgy these deeds of redemption are shared intensely by the celebrating community who, through this sharing, are transformed and made new by, in and through them. In addition, liturgical commemoration looks toward the future realization of all that is expressed and intended by this memorial, for it orients believers to the final revelation and accomplishment in the kingdom of all Christ came to do. The Eucharist, for example, is the place of communal remembering, which gathering and ritual gives life to all who recall, call to mind, and remember. The liturgy is our participation now in the whole of the paschal mystery of Christ who has died, is risen and who will come again.

The prefaces for the dead express this participation in Christ when they state:

> He chose to die
> that he might free all men from dying.
> He gave his life
> that we might live to you alone forever.
>
> (Christian Death II)

> By your power you bring us to birth.
> By your providence you rule our lives.
> By your command you free us at last from sin
> as we return to the dust from which we came.
> Through the saving death of your Son
> we rise at your word to the glory of the resurrection.
>
> (Christian Death IV)

Also in the funeral liturgy the participation of the community in the saving life, death and resurrection of Christ is affirmed and acclaimed:

> By your coming as man
> > Lord, save your people.
> By your birth
> > Lord, save your people.
> By your baptism and fasting
> > Lord, save your people.
> By your sufferings and cross
> > Lord, save your people.
> By your death and burial
> > Lord, save your people.
> By your rising to new life
> > Lord, save your people.
> By your return in glory to the Father
> > Lord, save your people.
> By your gift of the Holy Spirit
> > Lord, save your people.
> By your coming again in glory
> > Lord, save your people.

(Final Commendation)

What is to be underscored when understanding and appreciating what occurs at the liturgy is the delicate balance established in the liturgy among all the events that comprise the paschal mystery (obedient life, free acceptance of death, rising to glory, exaltation to the right hand of the Father)[21] and the union that occurs in the liturgy between Christ's dying and rising and the community's real and enduring participation in this mystery through liturgy. Eucharist, for example, is not a word service followed by the distribution of Communion; rather, it is a liturgy of word and a liturgy of celebrating and sharing in the very action and mystery of Christ in the eucharistic prayer which leads to sharing in the eucharistic bread and wine.[22] The Eucharist is incorrectly understood and appreciated when it seems to be the passive listening to the word and receiving Communion. Rather, what occurs in liturgy is the actualization of the paschal mystery (especially in the act of praying the eucharistic prayer) for the *participation* of the community gathered together.

The experience of liturgical prayer is thus the privileged time to experience the whole of the mystery of Christ. By "recalling the past" and "summoning the future" at common prayer Christians "shape the present" in the sense that life is viewed from the perspective of Christ, and the memorial of Christ at the liturgy gives us a real share in the reality of God in Christ through the power of the Holy Spirit.

TO "BLESS" GOD

It was argued above that the eucharistic prayer (among other texts) is a most important prayer in the liturgy because it is through this prayer that worshiping communities experience the memorial of Christ's saving mysteries. In order to understand the full force of this prayer (and others like it) it is important once again to retrace the pattern of Jewish liturgical prayer on which it is based. This will provide a basis for interpreting the significance of the prayers which Christians use at central points of the liturgy.

Essentially this form of prayer is a declaration of dependence on God, the God who intervened in history and who continues his gracious intervention for the present Church. It is a prayer of praise, thanks, and blessing by means of which praying communities acknowledge their dependence on God and glorify God for the enduring power of the deeds of salvation realized and experienced again and again through the liturgy. The prayer is called the prayer of "blessing" because it is derived from the Jewish *berakah* prayer, a word whose meaning includes blessing, thanksgiving, acknowledgement, praise, glory, and honor. As we say at the beginning of the eucharistic prayer: "Let us give thanks to the Lord our God. It is right to give him thanks and praise." "Father, all-powerful and ever-living God, we do well always and everywhere to give you thanks (and glory)."

> Praising the mighty deeds of God wrought for his people throughout salvation history, the *berakah* gathered all these

together in a context of blessing and offered . . . thanksgiving to the source of all things. . . .This prayer is intimately personal: it reposes upon the community's faith knowledge of, and its faith-commitment to the divine goodness constantly being manifested. . . .[23]

The Old Testament provides many examples of this kind of piety and prayer which recall and remember God's intervention in history. At liturgy this same God is asked to intervene again to sustain those whom he has called to be his own. What occurs in these prayers is a declaration of praise and thanks and a description of the motive why the blessing is offered. In the Book of Exodus God is "blessed" and acknowledged because he led his people through the Red Sea. The song of Miriam puts it this way:

I will sing to the Lord, for he is gloriously triumphant;
horse and chariot he has cast into the sea.
My strength and my courage is the Lord,
and he has been my savior.
He is my God, I praise him;
the God of my father, I extol him.

Who is like to you among the gods, O Lord?
Who is like to you, magnificent in holiness?
O terrible in renown, worker of wonders,
when you stretched out your hand, the earth swallowed them!
In your mercy you led the people you redeemed;
in your strength you guided them to your holy dwelling.

The Lord shall reign forever and ever.

(Exodus 15 used at Saturday Morning Prayer I)

The psalms continue this same kind of approach to praising and thanking God for leading Israel to freedom and for sustaining them in life and peace:

Praise the name of the Lord,
praise him, servants of the Lord,

who stand in the house of the Lord
in the courts of the house of our God.
Praise the Lord for the Lord is good.
Sing a psalm to his name for he is loving.
For the Lord has chosen Jacob for himself
and Israel for his own possession.

The first-born of the Egyptians he smote,
of man and beast alike.
Signs and wonders he worked
in the midst of your land, O Egypt,
against Pharaoh and all his servants.

He let Israel inherit their land;
on his people their land he bestowed.

Sons of Israel, bless the Lord!
Sons of Aaron, bless the Lord!
Sons of Levi, bless the Lord!
You who fear him, bless the Lord!

(Ps. 135, used at Friday Evening Prayer III)

The sense of these prayers involves "remembrance" of the God who is active in history, the God who delivers his people and the same God who continues to act on behalf of his people. The praying of psalms and canticles invited communities to remember this intervention of God and to offer petitions and prayers in faith and trust because this same God continued to save and sustain them in the present. The language used includes praise, thanks, and acknowledgement. The understanding on which it is based is dependence on the God who accomplished deeds of salvation for his people.

This form of prayer (and piety) becomes more stylized and developed in succeeding generations in Judaism. What eventually develops is the liturgical form of blessing prayer (*berakah*) which takes as a model and outline much of what is contained in the psalms and canticles of the Old Testament. This form of prayer begins with declarations of praise, thanks and glory, and continues with a statement of where and how God saved his chosen people. This recounting of what God has done (the statement of the *mirabilia Dei*) reminded and assured communities gathered for prayer that the same God who saved their ancestors would continue to save and redeem them. The very same relationship that formed Israel into God's chosen people would continue to form them into new communities that inherit God's favor and mercy. Hence, it is on the basis of this declaration of God's actions in history that contemporary communities would offer prayer of petition for what they needed to continue in the covenant relationship of life and peace with God. The final part of the prayer is a doxology that ends the prayer as it began: praising and thanking God for his mercy and love.

The skeleton of this form of prayer may thus be constructed (albeit somewhat artificially) in the following outline: praise, thanks, blessing, recounting of God's acts in history, petition, doxology. What must be borne in mind, however, is that this prayer is not just a succession of words or of statements offered to God. Rather, it is the setting and framework within which the memorial of God's graciousness is "recalled" and "remembered"—therefore truly *experienced anew.* The memorial of what salvation is all about is experienced again and again when liturgy is celebrated and God's graciousness is remembered. The liturgical form for this is the blessing form of prayer. Liturgical memorial is an event, an experience now of God's divine action; the setting for this liturgical event is the prayer of blessing.

Examples of this kind of blessing prayer abound in the experience of Christian liturgy.[24] The background for these prayers from the Old Testament should be kept in mind, along with an appreciation of what is inherent in the accounts of the Last Supper. The authors recount that Jesus "blessed" the bread, "had given thanks" and declared "Do this in remembrance of me." Over the cup "when he had given thanks" he said "Do this, as often as you drink it, in remembrance of me."[25] The key words used over and over in Jewish liturgical prayer are seen here: bless, thanks, remember. The institution accounts of the Lord's Supper were themselves stylized early on in the Christian era with the eucharistic prayer taking on something

akin to the outline noted above for Jewish piety: praise and
thanks, recounting of salvation history, memorial of the Lord
Jesus and the supper, petition and doxology.[26]

Some phrases from the fourth eucharistic prayer can help
underscore the importance of this form of prayer for Christian
liturgy and for an understanding of the context within which the
memorial of Christ's dying and rising is set:

> Father in heaven,
> it is right that we should give you thanks and glory. . . .
> Source of life and goodness, you have created all things,
> to fill your creatures with every blessing. . . .
> Again and again you offered a covenant. . . .
> Father, you so loved the world
> that in the fullness of time you sent your only Son to be
>   our Savior. . . .
> In fulfillment of your will
> he gave himself up to death;
> but by rising from the dead,
> he destroyed death and restored life. . . .
> Father, may this Holy Spirit sanctify these offerings.
> Let them become the body and blood of Jesus Christ our Lord
> as we celebrate the great mystery
> which he left us as an everlasting covenant.
> While they were at supper,
> he took bread, said the blessing, broke the bread,
> and gave it to his disciples, saying:
> Take this, all of you, and eat it:
> this is my body which will be given up for you.
> In the same way, he took the cup, filled with wine.
> He gave you thanks, and giving the cup to his disciples, said:
> Take this, all of you, and drink from it:
> this is the cup of my blood,
> the blood of the new and everlasting covenant.
> It will be shed for you and for all
> so that sins may be forgiven.
> Do this in memory of me. . . .
>
> Father, we now celebrate this memorial of our redemption.
> We recall Christ's death, his descent among the dead,
> his resurrection, and his ascension to your right hand;

and, looking forward to his coming in glory,
we offer you his body and blood,
the acceptable sacrifice
which brings salvation to the whole world.
Lord, look upon this sacrifice which you have given to your
    Church;
and by your Holy Spirit, gather all who share this bread and
    wine
into the one body of Christ, a living sacrifice of praise.
Lord, remember those for whom we offer this sacrifice,
especially N. our Pope,
N. our bishop, and bishops and clergy everywhere.
Remember those who take part in this offering. . . .
Remember those who have died in the peace of Christ. . . .
Father, in your mercy grant also to us . . .
to enter into our heavenly inheritance. . . .
Then, in your kingdom, freed from the corruption of sin and
    death,
we shall sing your glory with every creature through Christ our
    Lord,
through whom you give us everything that is good.
Through him,
with him,
in him,
in the unity of the Holy Spirit,
all glory and honor is yours,
almighty Father,
for ever and ever.
Amen.

This eucharistic prayer (whose outline is basically followed
in all the eucharistic prayers we now use except for the Roman
canon) is an important example of the elements inherited from
Jewish piety and how the Christian Church developed the genius
and genus of this prayer for its own use.[27] What is involved here
is not merely a succession of statements that lead to consecration and Communion. Rather, what is evident here is a carefully
worded prayer whose inherent structure develops themes which
are central in Judaeo-Christian piety: that the God who acted in
history acts now on behalf of his people. It is within this impor-

tant prayer of blessing that the memorial of the whole paschal mystery is revealed and shared in by the community.

With regard to the eucharistic piety of Christians, the restoration of the whole eucharistic prayer to a position of great prominence in the liturgy, to the extent that it is called "the center of the entire celebration,"[28] helps situate the words of institution (consecration) in its traditional setting and context— a prayer of blessing. What is thus actualized in the liturgy of Eucharist is the entire paschal mystery of Christ. Through this kind of blessing prayer they have the structure for recalling the past, sharing the present and summoning the future. The eucharistic prayer as a unified prayer of thanks, praise and blessing is far more than an appendix to the words of institution alone.[29] One of the most significant factors of contemporary eucharistic practice among the Christian churches has been the revival of interest in and emphasis on the eucharistic prayer as a prayer of central importance in the liturgy.[30] Contemporary eucharistic piety, as illuminated and shaped by eucharistic practice using these prayers, cannot but help in shaping other liturgical and personal prayer as well.

Another significant example of how important the texts of liturgical prayers are for a full appreciation of the sacrament celebrated is found in the prayer used to bless the baptismal water in the rites of initiation. The joining together of baptismal references from the Old and New Testaments in this prayer attests to the importance of understanding the gesture of blessing water within the context of the full prayer:

> Father,
> you give us grace through sacramental signs,
> which tell us of the wonders of your unseen power.
> In baptism we use your gift of water,
> which you have made a rich symbol of the grace
> you give us in this sacrament.
>
> At the very dawn of creation
> your Spirit breathed on the waters,
> making them the wellspring of all holiness.

The waters of the great flood
you made a sign of the waters of baptism
that make an end of sin
and a new beginning of goodness.

Through the waters of the Red Sea
you led Israel out of slavery,
to be an image of God's holy people,
set free from sin by baptism.

In the waters of the Jordan
your Son was baptized by John
and anointed with the Spirit.

Your Son willed that water and blood should flow from his side
as he hung upon the cross.
After his resurrection he told his disciples:
"Go out and teach all nations,
baptizing them in the name of the Father, and of the Son, and of
    the Holy Spirit."

Father,
look now with love upon your Church,
and unseal for it the fountain of baptism.

By the power of the Spirit
give to the water of this font
the grace of your Son.

You created man in your own likeness:
cleanse him from sin in a new birth to innocence
by water and the Spirit.

We ask you, Father, with your Son
to send the Holy Spirit upon the water of this font.
May all who are buried with Christ in the death of baptism
rise also with him to newness of life.
We ask this through Christ our Lord.
Amen.[31]

What emerges from this review of the blessing form of prayer is the understanding of how important the whole prayer is in delineating the theological and spiritual meaning of what occurs in liturgy. To isolate the last part of the prayer for blessing water cuts it off from its appropriate context, the recounting of the intervention of God throughout history for his people. Just as isolating the words of institution can put undue emphasis on these words apart from recounting all that is realized in the actualization of the memorial of Christ, so too stressing the blessed water apart from the prayer that is used to bless it cuts it off from the rich associations between initiation and salvation history. Salvation is expressed and experienced in initiation for the first time, as based on the history of God's intervention in human history. Once again, it is the setting of the blessing prayer which gives us the fullest context for the experience of memorial. The blessing prayer is a prayer of remembrance.

CENTRALITY OF MEMORIAL

> This is the core of biblical [and liturgical] prayer: remembrance, praise and thanksgiving—which can then flow into petitions for the continuance of this saving care in our time of need. Remembrance, *anamnesis,* is also at the heart of all ritual celebration, for celebrations are celebrations of something: through symbol and gesture and text we render present—proclaim—once again the reality we feast.[32]

What Christians "feast" is Christ; the center of our feasting is his paschal mystery. To celebrate his memory, to commemorate his victory over sin and death, is what the liturgy is and does. Hence, over all other forms of prayer, it is the liturgy alone which is regarded as *the* prayer of the Church. It is at the liturgy that the gathered community realizes its identity as a people redeemed by the death and resurrection of Christ. The actualization of this sacred mystery is what makes Christian liturgy so unique. "All that the Son of God did and taught for the reconciliation of the world we not only know through the narration of past events; we also experience the effects of it in virtue of these present deeds [the liturgy and sacraments]."[33]

Especially in light of the structure and theology of the blessing form of prayer, however, it is important to underscore the pattern which liturgical prayer establishes for personal prayer as well. The balance struck in the blessing prayer between praise and petition and the importance of recounting God's graciousness throughout history is particularly illustrative. What the ritual of the Church helps to underscore is an equilibrium whereby petition is set in the context of praise and thanksgiving. To overemphasize petition and present needs (as is sometimes the case in novena-like prayers and some intercessory prayers) is challenged by the fact that liturgical prayer strikes an important balance here. In addition, the recounting of the foundation events of salvation history in the liturgy helps to shape our attitude in terms of asking our Father for all that we need. The confident trust which is expressed liturgically by this narration should also mark the disposition of believers when involved in personal prayer as well. The God worshiped and adored by Christians is the God who became incarnate in his Son and who is present to his Church in the liturgy. This is the same God who continually offers us a relationship of reconciliation and hope. The very narration of the events of salvation history in the blessing prayers can offer hope and encouragement for those struggling with belief in God. The election of the people of God was (and is) never based on perfect response and total conformity to his will. In fact, it is God's intervention precisely when his chosen people went (and go) astray that offers hope to us whose faithful response is often less than faith-filled and total. In the context of remembering God's faithfulness and love and sharing new life because of this remembrance, it is illustrative and encouraging to learn that the God we worship understands our weakness and forgives us our sins.

The pattern of the blessing prayer and the notion of memorial also guides our personal prayer in that it helps us realize that the fullness of all life and peace lies beyond this mortal life. It exists in the fullness of life with God in the kingdom forever. This eschatological emphasis, an essential aspect of memorial, helps underscore that all prayer, all liturgy, all Christian life is oriented to final union with God. In the meantime liturgical and personal prayer are indispensable means to achieve in the here and now a share in what will one day be completed—union with God.

The rabbis' quote "To remember is to give life; to forget is to let die" is indeed central to understanding Jewish and Christian liturgical prayer. It is in the liturgy that contemporary congregations share in the actualization of all that is meant by redemption in Christ. In these privileged moments of common prayer we ponder the word of revelation and celebrate the presence of that same salvation in symbol, gesture and prayers of blessing. This is accomplished in all liturgy and in the sacraments, but it is accomplished in a particular and unique way in the Eucharist with the notion of "memorial" so apparent and operative. It is at moments of common liturgical prayer that we in the present recall and experience all that happened in the past of salvation history and long for the fullness of what is already experienced in the liturgy, the coming of the kingdom of God. At the liturgy we stand "between the times" of the past and the future. It is the liturgy alone which enables us to experience a share in the fullness of life with God "as we wait in joyful hope for the coming of our Savior." The liturgy contains an important and sustaining balance between past and future. The matrix of this is the present liturgy.

> As long as we are going through the desert of this world, as long as we are walking by faith and not by sight, we need these goods desperately [the liturgy]. We are fed in our minds by reading and hearing the word of God, we are fed in our mouths by eating the bread of eternal life from the table of the Lord, and drinking the chalice of salvation. But when we come to the land of the living, to the blessed Sion, where the God of gods is seen face to face, we shall not need the word of doctrine, nor shall we eat the bread of angels under the appearances of bread and wine, but in its own proper substance.[34]

Until that time, however, the act of remembering and the doing of memorial are essential—these are the foundation upon which the liturgy is based. It is through these that we experience the reality of God. "To remember is to give life; to forget is to let die."

NOTES

1. See, among others, Louis Bouyer, "Jewish-Christian Liturgies," in Lancelot Sheppard, ed., *True Worship* (Baltimore: Helicon Press, 1963) pp. 29–44, and Aidan Kavanagh, "The Tradition of Judaeo-Christian Worship: Our Debt to Each Other," pp. 47–59.

2. Brevard S. Childs, *Memory and Tradition in Israel* (London: SCM Press, 1962) p. 33.

3. Robert Taft, " 'Thanksgiving for the Light': Toward a Theology of Vespers," *Diakonia* 13 (1978) 27–28.

4. See the outline of the interesting work of liturgy by Marianne H. Micks, *The Future Present. The Phenomenon of Christian Worship* (New York: Seabury, 1970). The two main sections of the work are "Summoning the Future" and "Shaping the Present."

5. Brevard Childs, *Memory and Tradition,* p. 84.

6. Quoted in Aidan Kavanagh, "The Tradition" p. 52.

7. Brevard Childs, *Memory and Tradition,* p. 85: "Later Israel, removed in time and space from the original event, yet still in time and space, found in her traditions a means of transforming her history into redemptive history."

8. *Ibid.,* p. 88.

9. Robert Taft, "Thanksgiving for the Light," 29.

10. The term "heavenly liturgy" is meant to indicate the coming of the fullness of the kingdom where we shall be drawn into the fullness of the mystery of Christ's intercession at the right hand of the Father. Sometimes this term is an adaptation of the parallels made in the Letter to the Hebrews between the rituals of the old covenant and the new covenant established through the one high priest, Jesus.

11. Adrien Nocent, *The Liturgical Year,* Vol. One, trans. Matthew O'Connell (Collegeville: The Liturgical Press, 1977) p. 15.

12. See Part One, Chapter Two, section on "Until the Kingdom Comes."

13. Robert Taft, "Thanksgiving for the Light," 43.

14. The Latin original in the Roman Missal is: "Beati qui ad cenam Agni vocati sunt."

15. *Lectionary for Mass, Introduction*, no. 7, p. 15.

16. Robert Taft, "Thanksgiving for the Light," 43.

17. See Gabriel Braso. *Liturgy and Spirituality*, pp. 3–55 and Louis Bouyer, *Liturgical Piety*, pp. 1–9.

18. Liturgists often refer to the events that occurred over a number of days in fourth century Jerusalem causing the expansion of the earlier commemoration of the Easter mysteries of two or three days only, as an "historicization" of the primitive observance of Easter. The suggestions made in this chapter about historicization are not intended to imply that the expansion of the Easter celebrations in this period is a harmful or unfortunate development. For more about the primitive unity of the Easter liturgy and the intended unity as seen in the present liturgy of Holy Week and Easter, see Part Two, Chapter Eight, section on "The Paschal Celebrations."

19. The text of the memorial prayer in the Roman Canon is not included here because the import which should have been given to this text had frequently been ignored in liturgical text and piety because of the exaggerated emphasis in this prayer on the idea of offering and the acceptance of the gifts. "The disordered insistence upon the idea of the offering of the *oblata* obscures the idea that what we offer above all in the Mass is Christ our Lord himself, and ourselves with him. We lose sight of the fact that the real and primary offering of the Mass takes place after the institution with the *Unde et memores*" (from Cipriano Vagaggini, *The Canon of the Mass and Liturgical Reform*, p. 97).

20. This is not to suggest that these memorial prayers are without defect. With regard to the memorial prayer in the fourth eucharistic prayer specifically see Aidan Kavanagh, "Thoughts on the New Eucharistic Prayers," *Worship* 43 (January 1969) 2–12, at p. 8 where he states that the offering section of the fourth eucharistic prayer is an "offering of the Blessed Sacrament rather than that of the Church."

21. This notion has been very helpful in advancing the progress of ecumenical conversations on liturgy and on the theology of the Eucharist, especially regarding the sacrifice of Christ. See, for example, "The Eucharist: A Lutheran-Roman Catholic Statement," no. I, 1, in *Lutherans and Catholics in Dialogue: The Eucharist as Sacrifice* (Washington: USCC, 1967) pp. 187–188.

22. This important distinction between "Communion services" and the "Eucharist" is part of the issue raised when laypeople lead

Sunday worship services. See Joseph A. Komonchak, " 'Non-ordained' and 'Ordained' Ministers in the Local Church," in Concilium 133, *Right of the Community to a Priest* (New York: Seabury, 1980) 44–50. He states: "Whatever may happen at their Sunday services without priests—and it would be incorrect to say that they have no religious and ecclesial significance—they are not the Eucharist. The assembly may pray and sing together; they may hear the Word of God proclaimed and preached; they may offer prayers of thanksgiving and petition; they may share communion; but they do not celebrate the Eucharistic *actio* and the Church-constitutive *memoria Christi* is not reactualized for their appropriation" (p. 46).

23. A. Kavanagh, "The Tradition," p. 50.

24. For an introduction to the relationship between the Jewish forms of blessing prayer and the Christian adaptations and extensions of this practice see, for example, Louis Bouyer, *Eucharist.* Theology and Spirituality of the Eucharistic Prayer, trans. Charles U. Quinn (Notre Dame: University of Notre Dame Press, 1961); Aidan Kavanagh, "Thoughts on the Roman Anaphora," *Worship* 39 (November 1965) 515–529, *Worship* 40 (January 1966) 2–16; Thomas Talley, "From *Berakah* to *Eucharistia:* A Reopening Question," *Worship* 50 (March 1976) 115–137.

25. See, among others, the texts as presented and commented upon by L. Deiss, *Springtime of the Liturgy,* pp. 24–26.

26. The outline of the new eucharistic prayers as stated in the General Instruction of the Roman Missal is as follows: Thanksgiving, Acclamation, Epiclesis, Narrative of the Institution, Anamnesis, Offering Intercessions, Final Doxology (no. 55).

27. On the question of the development of this prayer through its formative period to a stabilization see Alan Bouley, *From Freedom to Formula.* The Evolution of the Eucharistic Prayer from Oral Improvisation to Written Texts (Washington: Catholic University of America Press, 1981).

28. *General Instruction of the Roman Missal* no. 54 states: "The eucharistic prayer, a prayer of thanksgiving and sanctification, is the center of the entire celebration."

29. That the words of institution dominated in the piety of the Roman Catholic and Reformed Churches is clear. A review of the texts of the Eucharist as revised by Luther himself attests to how Christians fundamentally misunderstood the importance of this prayer in this period. See R.C.D. Jasper and G. J. Cuming, *Prayers of the Eucharist: Early and Reformed,* pp. 122–128.

30. It is precisely because of Luther's opposition to and editing of the eucharistic prayer that the inclusion of anaphora prayers in some of the contemporary Lutheran liturgies is especially significant: see, for example, *Lutheran Book of Worship* (Minneapolis: Augsburg, 1978) 68–71.

31. *RCIA* no. 215 and *Rite of Baptism for Children,* no. 91. Other options for the blessing of water are found in nos. 223–224; these are especially instructive because they contain the important words "praise" and "blessed be God."

32. R. Taft, "Thanksgiving for the Light," 42.

33. Adrien Nocent, *The Liturgical Year,* Vol. One, p. 18. Nocent here relies on the important insight of Leo the Great about the *sacramentum redemptionis.*

34. From Rupert of Deutz, as quoted in A. Squire, *Asking the Fathers,* p. 122.

Chapter Seven
A PATTERNED EXPERIENCE
OF PRAYER

By its very nature, Christian liturgy shares in what characterizes all religious rituals—it is a repetitive, structured, familiar and common action of a community of people gathered to experience the very presence of God within that ritual. The frame and structure of ritual itself is not co-terminous with the experience of God, nor is the correct performance of the ritual all that is necessary for effective liturgical celebration;[1] but it is nonetheless true that the notion of liturgy as a patterned (ritual) experience of prayer is an important element in Christian liturgical prayer. It is undoubtedly true that in our day "ritual" is often associated with that which is stuffy, boring, and endlessly the same. While such terminology may well represent popular interpretations of ritual and underscore the negative connotations which rituals can and do have, it is also true that the Christian liturgy especially need not have such negative associations. This is to suggest that liturgy as ritual need not mean that liturgy is necessarily ritualistic or that it is a cult of forms alone that necessarily puts an end to spontaneity and freshness in liturgical celebration. Ritual as a pattern of prayer helps preserve liturgy from becoming a kind of prayer that changes with the whims and prejudices of those who celebrate it. The ritual structures inherent in liturgy help preserve the tradition of what the whole Church believes and celebrates at any particular celebration. The ritual celebrated is the Church's, not that of any individual community exclusively, and it is precisely this conserving role which liturgy plays in Church life. Through the liturgy the very identity and life of the communion of the Christian Church is disclosed, made real and celebrated. Hence, the ritual structure that operates in liturgy makes a positive contribution to Church life—through liturgy the Church acknowledges its "roots" and it reaches beyond the "now" of this present celebration to God who is timeless and to the truths which God reveals which are eternal.

By calling this element of liturgical prayer "a patterned experience" two things are meant. First, it suggests that Christian liturgical prayer is a ritual in this positive sense, some aspects of which are discussed here. Second, it is to suggest that at the same time we are affirming the ritual nature of liturgy we are not necessarily saying that the ritual experienced is exactly the same for all who gather for worship. Hence, attention will be given to understanding what structures of ritual are operative in all liturgy, whether one is engaged in a daily round of liturgical prayer (hours and Eucharist, as in a monastic community) or whether one is involved in an experience of liturgy once weekly (the Sunday Eucharist), or whether one finds oneself involved in variations within either example (a person who is faithful to weekly Eucharist and daily personal prayer). The importance of ritual in the liturgy will be the same for each person, but the type and frequency of celebration will not necessarily be the same. Yet, whenever Christians "gather together to ask the Lord's blessing" in the common prayer called liturgy, by that very fact they engage in an act that by its very nature is ritual.

PARTICIPATION THROUGH RITUAL

When commenting on the "structured" (ritual) character of the liturgy of the hours, Nathan Mitchell makes some important observations which can be applied to all liturgy.

> No one would deny that informal, spontaneous, and unstruc-
> tured prayer has vital importance in Christian life. The free-
> dom fostered by the meditation revolution and charismatic
> prayer groups is a genuine value. But the utter absence of all
> structure in prayer leads to experiences that are seedy, chaot-
> ic, and, ultimately, unparticipable. Like other forms of wor-
> ship the Liturgy of the Hours is a multi-leveled act of

communication. Its levels include the *verbal* (short readings, psalms, songs, etc.), the *nonverbal* (gesture, movement, silence), the *overt* (varieties of external expression) and the *covert* (internal moods and dispositions), the *interpersonal* and the *transcendent*. Any liturgical celebration activates messages on all these levels. Such celebrations are *structured* in order to insure optimum conditions for both communication and participation. Structure lets all messages on all levels get through with a minimum of distortion.[2]

This important statement helps to underscore the positive contribution which the liturgy, precisely as ritual, makes to the ongoing development of forms of prayer in the contemporary Church. Liturgy is a complex unity of a variety of means of communication; it is the ritual of liturgy which keeps these in balance and shapes them into a coherent whole. The experience of liturgy is based on maintaining the delicate balance inherent in this variety and complexity. What reminds us of this complexity and what informs our participation in these aspects of communal activity is ritual. The ritual inherent in liturgy provides the frame and structure within which prayer takes place. The intent of its repetition and familiarity is to enhance and invite participation. In the words of Margaret Mead:

> To speak of ritual is to speak of patterns of human behavior
> . . . behavior that is repetitious and different from the ordinary. We do not normally talk about the things that people do every day, although they are both patterned and habitual, as is ritual. Ritual has an extra degree of intensity. A fair amount of bodily behavior is normally included in a ritual action, although this does not necessarily mean active behavior.
>
> . . . ritual is concerned with relationships, either between a single individual and the supernatural, or among a group of individuals who share things together. There is something about the sharing and the expectation that makes it ritual.[3]

Following along with Mitchell's reflection on the liturgy of the hours it is important to be aware of the many kinds and levels of communication involved in the celebration of the hours. (This is especially important when applied to the hours because they themselves are often experienced as "wordy" and as "heavy" when compared with the more obvious use of symbol and gesture in sacramental activity.) Like all liturgy, the hours contain the gathering of the community for the proclamation and hearing of the word, for participation in liturgy through gesture (standing, sitting, bowing, making the sign of the cross), the use of elements (lights, candles, incense, especially at evening prayer), singing (hymn, psalms, canticles) and the experience of variety in liturgical roles in the liturgy (assembly, leader, reader, cantor). While it is true that when compared with sacramental worship the liturgy of the hours is more word-oriented, it is not necessarily the case that this word predominance means passivity or boredom for those worshiping. It is the contribution of the ritual of the hours that makes it a participatory and evocative liturgy. Where "boredom" and "passivity" are often associated with the worst aspects of ritual as popularly understood, it is something of a paradox that it is precisely through ritual that liturgy need not be boring or a passive experience.

It is particularly instructive to understand that in establishing the rites and ceremonies that came to comprise the liturgy, Christians adopted and adapted pre-existing rituals (including myths and symbols) by means of which they handed on, conveyed, and celebrated the Christian faith. The process involved here is often called "valorization" whereby Christian rites are a reinterpretation and adaptation of what were in origin (largely) Jewish ceremonies which themselves were reinterpretations and adaptations of pre-existing Canaanite rituals.[4] "They were infused with new meanings that completely transformed their inner nature, but they have the rites and symbols of natural religion and the specific reinterpretation of those rites by Judaism as their necessary foundation."[5] In addition to this background for the early experience of ritual in Christianity is the part played by transposing Christian liturgy to Rome and to other areas of Europe, as well as the impact which Eastern practices had on Western liturgy.[6] Christian liturgical ritual evolved and developed as the religion established itself in new and varying cultures. It is important to recall the valorization process in order to underscore both continuity and variety in Christian liturgy.

The continuity established in the formative years (after the resurrection into the Constantinian era) consisted in a number of things among which are: the establishment of the canon of Scripture for liturgical proclamation, the taking over of the liturgy of word and meal from Judaism, and the use of the calendar which respected the seasons of nature as background for the central celebrations of the Christian faith, the resurrection at Easter and the incarnation at Christmas. This continuity is seen to our own day. To appreciate ritual as a conserving element of liturgy is to respect the symbols, myths, rites and ceremonies which comprise Christian worship. On the other hand, an historical review of the evolution of forms of Christian worship also points to the fact that the ritual in Christian liturgy does not mean identical ceremonies always and everywhere. The variety between the liturgy at Rome and the liturgy in Gaul, for example, points to a unity in the liturgy with variety in expression and ceremony. In this sense a more accurate understanding of the Christian liturgy with its evolving forms of prayer is underscored in a description of ritual that sees it as "a recognizable and repeatable form of activity within which innovation is possible, and which is transformed only rarely at a peak of creativity."[7]

What is important to assert at this point is the tradition of ritual in Christian liturgy where the central myths and symbols of Christianity are experienced again and again at common prayer. This same heritage is shared everywhere the Christian liturgy is celebrated. But Christian liturgy (for most of its life) was not inflexible and so fixed that variety was not possible. What is necessary, therefore, is to underscore the ritual aspect of Christian liturgy in terms of the forms of prayer and the tradition preserved within them, and at the same time the flexibility involved within this ritual structure.

Christian liturgy is meant to invite and lead to communal participation in the mystery of Christ. It is meant to be a familiar and participable means whereby the tradition of the good news is preserved, transmitted and celebrated. As St. Paul writes in one of the most ancient texts of the New Testament: "I handed on to you first of all what I myself received, that Christ died for our sins in accordance with the Scriptures; that he was buried and, in accordance with the Scriptures, rose on the third day" (1 Cor 15:3–4). It is this "handing-on" which liturgy is all about. Ritual is meant to serve and preserve this "traditional" process.

An appreciation of ritual as it operates in Christian liturgy requires that we have a respect for the inherent logic of a liturgical celebration. This is to suggest that appropriate liturgical activity involves celebrating the rites of the Church in such a way that the ritual opens up the way for communities of faith to experience the Gospel proclaimed in word and action in and through the liturgy. The structure of the Eucharist is to be respected: the liturgy of the word leads to presenting gifts, their transformation during the eucharistic prayer, and sharing in the body and blood of Christ in Communion. This ordering should be respected precisely because this familiar pattern and structure enables those present to take part "knowingly, actively, and fruitfully."[8] This form of participation in the ritual is meant to establish the deeper meaning of liturgical participation[9] whereby contemporary communities are made sharers in the very life and mystery of God in and through Christ.

In addition to the liturgy of the Eucharist, all sacramental celebrations have their own inherent logic whereby the newly-emphasized liturgy of the word leads to the liturgy of the particular sacrament celebrated. For example, in the structure of the ritual of penance it would be important to underscore and respect the kinds of prayer and all the elements involved in communal rites of reconciliation which follow the liturgy of the word. These include (after the homily) a general confession of sins (the "I confess" prayer said by all, a litany form of prayer with deacon and community involved, the Lord's prayer and a concluding prayer), individual confession and absolution (or general absolution), a proclamation of praise for God's mercy (for example, the canticle of Mary or Psalm 135), the concluding prayer of thanksgiving, final blessing and dismissal. The inherent structure of penance calls for much more than a word service and confessions; it calls for a ritual of word and rite in which various liturgical roles are respected, a variety of prayers is offered to choose from, and a number of possible gestures to accompany the rite are possible (kneeling for the litany, standing for the song of thanksgiving, sign of peace to conclude). It is the ritual structure of the liturgy that invites familiarity with the particular sacrament celebrated and yet offers variety within that celebration.

Our participation in the mystery of Christ is assured in the liturgy, especially when the ritual patterns of this form of common prayer are observed. The liturgy is not meant to be ritual for its own sake, for the ritual is meant to offer and assure worshipers a repeated share in the mystery of Christ, the center of all liturgical ritual. Nor is the liturgy meant to be "made up" or created each time it is celebrated, for such a tradition-less and "unstructured" ritual (if one can exist!) invites curiosity and chaos, not involvement, familiarity and prayerful participation. It is this prayerful participation, in and through ritual to the person and paschal mystery of Christ, that the liturgy is meant to foster and achieve.

RHYTHM OF LITURGICAL RITUAL

Closely allied with the notion of ritual containing a framework and structure within which the liturgy takes place is the notion that the Church's experience of ritual prayer itself establishes a pattern for the times and occasions when liturgical rituals should take place. As was noted above, the exact determination of when liturgy should be celebrated and by whom is not an easy question to answer; in fact the issue as it is raised here is not meant to impose such a structure. However, the issue does involve reviewing the Church's tradition and practice of experiencing ritual in varying communities. In this way we can discover what are possible rhythms and patterns for contemporary Christians to experience liturgical prayer (with no specification as to which is better). For example, a monastic pattern of ritual prayer is obviously fuller with more frequent meetings than the pattern which is possible for persons not living in monastic community. There are points which intersect for both, but the rhythm and concrete expression will be different for each. Just as there is no one form of community for all Christians[10] so there is no set formula for the rhythm of liturgical prayer for all communities.

Clearly, from the earliest tradition of Christianity it is the weekend which receives greatest attention liturgically. The Sunday Eucharist was clearly the primary feast day.[11] This was the day which differentiated Christians from Jews who would gather on the sabbath. "On the day called after the sun,"[12] says Justin, the Christian community gathers for the hearing of the word, prayer, and the sharing of the bread and cup. The day was chosen to recall the first day of creation, the day of the Lord's rising from the dead, and the looked-for "eighth day" of fulfillment and completion of all that was begun in Christ. The Fathers of the Church are fond of calling Sunday the "day of light," the "day of resurrection," the "day of Spirit" and the "eighth day."[13] As we pray in the hymn:

On this day, the first of days,
God the Father's name we praise;
Who creation's Lord and Spring,
Did the world from darkness bring.

On this day, th'eternal Son
Over death His triumph won;
On this day the Spirit came
With His gifts of living flame.

Word made flesh, all hail to Thee!
Thou from sin hast set us free;
And with Thee we die and rise
Unto God in sacrifice.

Holy Spirit, You impart
Gifts of love to every heart;
Give us light and Grace, we pray,
Fill our hearts this holy day.

God, the blessed Three in One,
May Thy holy will be done;
In thy word our souls are free,
And we rest this day with thee.[14]

That this day has central priority in the calendar of all Christians is seen by the fact that from earliest times (fourth century) it was preceded by a vigil service commemorating the resurrection of Christ from the dead.[15] This service consisted in three psalms (the three days Christ was in the tomb), an incensation (the spices of the women), the reading of the resurrection account from the Gospels (the angel announcing that the Lord had risen), and a procession.[16] Clearly, the weekend has long been established as the pivotal point for Christian worship for all the baptized. Unlike Judaism, which celebrated the sabbath (begun on Friday night), the Christian Church celebrates Sunday with its traditional vigil the evening before, or, more commonly now, evening Masses on Saturday for Sunday.

> For Christian worshipers, then, Sunday remains radically different from the Sabbath. Whereas a contemporary Jewish scholar summarizes the meaning of the Sabbath ... in the magnificent and appealing phrase "an exodus from tension", a Christian writer speaks instead of "the weekly disturbance occasioned by Sunday." The day is seen as essentially a repeated entry into tension —an eschatological tension between the already and the not-yet. It is a day on which Christians rejoice and give thanks for the resurrection of Jesus Christ, for God's new creation, but also a day on which they acknowledge the urgency and responsibility which the End imposes.[17]

The tradition of Christianity asserts that this day, above all, is the day for Eucharist—for sharing in the revealed word of God and for the sharing of the Lord's Supper. In recent years the separation between Catholics and non-Catholic Christians was so severe that the former held to Sunday Mass, often with little regard for the preaching of the word, and the latter held to

Sunday worship (word service and preaching) often separated from the eucharistic meal. The divergence in practice here signified different emphases as a result of the Reformation; but at least in the mainline Christian churches these assemblies were on the day of the Lord, Sunday.

What is established as the fundamental basis for the rhythm of liturgical celebration, therefore, is that Sunday worship is for all the baptized. That the Eucharist was and is the means of renewing identification with and participation in the paschal mystery begun in baptism is clear from the revised use of the rite of blessing and sprinkling with holy water on Sunday as a way to begin the Eucharist (the former *Asperges Me*). Sunday worship is the primary day of feasting for all Christians.

Another liturgical pattern of prayer that relates to establishing a rhythm of Christian prayer is the liturgy of the hours, especially morning and evening prayer. The practice of temple worship in the morning and evening, and synagogue worship on a similar rhythm in Judaism, influenced the practice of earliest (and subsequent) Christianity.[18] In the restoration of the liturgy of the hours in recent years these two hours once again receive greater emphasis than the others (the "minor hours" of terce, sext, none and compline from the monastic usage). Traditionally the hours of prayer in both urban and cenobite monasticism[19] as well as the daily prayer in parish churches[20] emphasized morning prayer to consecrate and dedicate the day to the Lord, and evening prayer to give thanks for the day and to beg forgiveness for any misdeeds done.

In the present reform of the hours, the clear intention is to give priority to these hours of prayer, whether prayed in religious or monastic community, or in other pastoral settings.[21] This non-eucharistic form of daily prayer, interestingly enough, found its way into common practice for all peoples, even those who did not pray the hours in common (as did monks and religious). For example, Martin Luther spoke of the importance of beginning and ending the day with the sign of the cross, and recent conventional Roman Catholic piety stressed morning and evening prayers (or at least beginning the day with the "morning offering"). Whether the custom of daily hours of prayer can be restored in parochial settings is still an issue for pastoral ministers to face; but what should not be lost sight of is the possibility that the traditional rhythm of morning and evening prayer be imitated as occasions for daily prayer in common or in private.[22] What the tradition of the Church and the documents of the present reform of the hours suggest is the important place to be occupied by prayer morning and evening (in addition to Eucharist on Sunday).

While it is clear that the full expression of the monastic hours of prayer is unrealistic and unrealizable for most Christians, the rhythm established by the ritual of non-eucharistic prayer is worth pondering. This daily, regular, structured form of prayer is held as an ideal and as an important form of prayer for all Christians. What this suggests from the perspective of what can be gleaned from the ritual of liturgical prayer is that one element of liturgical prayer which should influence our spirituality is precisely this regular, patterned, structured daily prayer. Daily prayer and reflection on the word helps avoid what can be a temptation that is all too real in the modern Church— spiritual "binges." Shoring up one's "spiritual life" with periodic days and weekends of prayer without attention to daily application to prayer makes little sense (for many spiritual, physical and psychological reasons) and it has no justification in the liturgical tradition of the Church. For some, one of the many pastoral adaptations of the liturgy of the hours[23] will be useful for personal prayer. For others, daily reading and reflection (e.g., the daily readings from the Eucharist when not attending) could be a very appropriate way to learn from and imitate what is inherent in the liturgical ritual of the Church.

> The prayerful reading of scripture need not consume hours each day, and for most of us that is impossible anyway. But a regular, relatively brief period of time set aside each day for *lectio* is more fruitful in the long run than going on spontaneous binges of bible reading or waiting for the intermittent urgings of the Spirit. The regular self-discipline of *lectio* helps us sort out priorities in our lives and makes us more aware of our strengths and weaknesses as we struggle to be faithful;

but also—and this is more important—it gives God freedom
to speak to us because it makes us free to listen.[24]

In some ways this last statement takes us back to a point
made earlier and gives it a new dimension. It is not so much that
liturgical ritual is followed with exactitude and precision by all;
it is that fidelity to the regular and repeated aspect of ritual
allows us to experience God's presence and to focus how our
lives are lived through incorporation and participation in God
through Christ, in the holiness of the Holy Spirit. Being attentive to the ritual pattern of daily prayer allows God to act within
and among us as his people.

Naturally, where and when Christians are able to gather
together for daily prayer, so much the better (whether in homes,
churches, schools, etc.). But the lack of a church community
should not be cause to ignore the important role played by the
rhythm of daily engagement in liturgical prayer, or in prayer as
derived from the liturgy (such as the daily meditative reading of
the Bible). Christian liturgical tradition offers us the challenge
that weekly sharing in Eucharist and some form of daily prayer
mark the lives of Christians. It is this tradition which is revived
in the reformed liturgy in both the Roman Catholic and other
Christian Churches.[25] The rhythm that was established from the
earliest days of Christianity has been revived and given due
emphasis in the documents of the contemporary liturgical reform. The usual ritual rhythm of Christian prayer involves Sunday (Eucharist) and daily (non-Eucharist prayer).

CREATIVITY AND OPTION

There can be no doubt that today there is a strong tendency
to seek the freshness of new expressions, of spontaneity and a
sense of close community when Christians worship together.
And there is also an urgent search for the strong bases on
which a life of faith, love and service can grow. This tension
between the spontaneous and the deeply-rooted, the new and
the ancient, is a healthy one so long as one is not sacrificed in
favor of the other. Liturgical prayer ideally comprises both

the spontaneous and the traditional, the free-flowing and the structured.[26]

This section from an adaptation of the Taizé Office describes well the post-Vatican II challenge that faces worshiping congregations: how to achieve the delicate balance between what is established as a needed part of the ritual of the Church and what can be varied and adapted so that the liturgical ritual is not always and everywhere the same. This is no small task for Roman Catholics becuase pre-conciliar ritual was determined and fixed,[27] as compared with the model of liturgical reform ushered in by the recently revised rites of the Church. Before Vatican II there was little in the way of creativity and variety within the ritual except what was already determined by handbooks of ceremonies, the rubrics, and in sacristy manuals. Finding the right text for the right sacrament or prayer for a blessing insured that the liturgy of the Church would be accomplished; it was all set down in text and direction. Where variety did exist—for example, solemn, high, and low Mass—the only option was for the *type* of Mass chosen (one of these); there was no variety within the type selected.

The era of liturgical adaptation and flexibility ushered in by the Council is nothing short of revolutionary as compared with post-Tridentine usage. The Liturgy Constitution of Vatican II states:

> Even in the liturgy, the Church has no wish to impose a rigid uniformity in matters which do not involve the faith or the good of the whole community. Rather, she respects and fosters the spiritual adornments and gifts of the various races and peoples. Anything in their way of life that is not indissolubly bound up with superstition and error she studies with sympathy and, if possible, preserves intact. Sometimes in fact she admits such things into the liturgy itself, as long as they harmonize with its true and authentic spirit. (no. 37)

> Provided that the substantial unity of the Roman rite is maintained, the revision of liturgical books should allow for legitimate variations and adaptations to different groups, regions,

and peoples, especially in mission lands. Where opportune, the same rule applies to the structuring of rites and the devising of rubrics. (no. 38)

What is operative in the model of liturgical reform established by the Council is an approach which respects the traditional ritual structure of liturgy and which removes anything that detracts from clarity in ritual expression or which causes unnecessary repetition and confusion.[28] In addition, the post-conciliar reform offers great latitude within the rites for flexibility and option. Hence, there is a wealth of text and option provided in each recently revised liturgical ritual in order that the particular worshiping community may derive maximum benefit from the experience of worship. As Pope Paul VI stated in the *Apostolic Constitution on the Missal:*

> Even though, in virtue of the decree of the Second Vatican Council, we have accepted into the new Roman Missal lawful variations and adaptations, our own expectation in no way differs from that of our predecessor. It is that the faithful will receive the new Missal as a help toward witnessing and strengthening their unity with one another; that through the new Missal one and the same prayer in a great diversity of languages will ascend, more fragrant than any incense, to our heavenly Father, through our High Priest, Jesus Christ, in the Holy Spirit.

Choosing prayers and options that best suit the needs, preparation and disposition of particular communities[29] is a task most often assigned to the planning committee. The responsibility of such groups is to provide a liturgy in which the ritual structure of the rite is respected, but which also allows for creativity and variety based on the needs of the individual liturgical community.

Part of the challenge involved here is to see that what a particular group feels it wants and should have is evaluated and some determination is made as to whether "wants" should be the only determinative of what should occur liturgically. True creativity involves an understanding of what fidelity to the word of God means so that the Scriptures challenge communities to new growth as well as comfort them in their lives of faith. (Communities may "want" to hear about forgiveness and the mission of the Lord to the lost, but at the same time they may often also "need" to hear about their leading lives in conformity with the challenge and self-sacrifice required by the Gospel.)

In addition true creativity means respecting an individual element within the liturgy as it has evolved over the centuries and as it is intended to be used in the present rite. Respect for the ritual derived from liturgical study can help communities grow in understanding how present rituals come from the tradition of the Church and as such deserve appreciation and understanding. By combining a knowledge of the liturgy with the flexibility inherent in the present liturgical reforms, planning groups can serve best as they seek to provide variety and flexibility within the ritual itself. In this way the "prayer of the Church" is understood not as the same ritual everywhere, but the same pattern of prayer adapted to the needs of varying worshiping communities. Two examples which can illustrate what is at stake in trying to achieve the delicate balance between ritual and creativity concern the general intercessions at Eucharist and the hours of morning and evening prayer.

The restoration of the general intercessions to a position of some prominence to complete the liturgy of the word has been one of the accomplishments of the post-Vatican II reform.[30] A review of the structure of this prayer as it has been experienced in the tradition of the Church and as it is presently reinstated can help direct planners in exercising creativity and option. With regard to the nature of the prayer it should be recalled that the "general intercessions are a sign of communion of this particular assembly with other assemblies and with the universal Church."[31] Hence, local needs ought to be set within the context of prayer for the needs of the universal Church. This is particularly important to remember when designing intercessions for celebrations of individual sacraments (such as marriage, initiation) which can tend to be preoccupied with the needs of the individuals celebrating the sacrament. The general intercessions are primarily universal in scope. With regard to the style of prayer it should be noted that these are prayers of petition, not thanksgiving, hence to offer gratitude at this point in the liturgy is to misconstrue the nature of this prayer. These prayers, like all prayers, should retain the rhythm and idiom of prayers; they are not teaching devices. They should not be didactic, but should reflect biblical imagery of the readings, the sacrament celebrated, or the season during which the liturgy takes place.[32] With regard to the structure of the prayers the tradition of the Church is reflected in the contemporary usage which is structured:

Introduction—by the presider; it is an invitation to the community to be attentive and confident in prayer; it is not a prayer to God. It is a variation on the simple "let us pray".

Intentions—by the deacon or other minister (reader). These are intentions stated, again not prayers to God. There is no fixed structure for the petitions, but a simple statement: "for the needs of the Church throughout the world, especially . . . we pray to the Lord" might be a helpful way to structure them.

Response—by community. This can vary but the response should match the intention offered.

Silence—this should be part of the prayer even when members of the assembly can voice their own intentions. All too often the ritual of liturgy is associated with doing and saying; silence is part of the liturgy as well.

Concluding Prayer—by the presider. This is a prayer to God that sums up and completes the intercessions; generally speaking nothing new by way of intention or need is added here.

With this structure in mind (and with the sample intercessions contained in the appendix to the sacramentary for Mass and in the sacramental rituals) planning committees and celebrating communities are free to adapt and construct intercessions which reflect present needs. Creativity within the structure of ritual aids in the participation of the entire community in liturgical prayer.

On a much larger scale, the example of the structure of the morning and evening prayer from the liturgy of the hours can help offer suggestions for structuring the daily prayer of a variety of Christian communities, even when they cannot gather in churches to pray daily. In planning these celebrations or in structuring daily prayer it is important to bear in mind that we are dealing with a pattern of prayer which can be adapted for use in many and varied circumstances. The hours may be used in parish settings and religious communities in a rather full form. They can be trimmed and adapted for use in school settings or for family prayer. It should be remembered that these are forms of liturgical prayer; hence a balance of speaking as well as silence, and a variety of gestures (stand, sit, kneel, etc.) might well be employed to express bodily involvement in worship.

The great latitude possible in the liturgy of the hours as restored by the Council invites creativity and option in order that these hours of prayer not be relegated to religious communities or clerical obligation only. In the accompanying diagram the structure of the hour is underlined, with an indication of the liturgical role involved and options which can help individual communities pray morning and evening.[33]

Once again the issue here is to illustrate the fact that the post-Vatican II reform of the liturgy involves creativity and option within the framework of the structure provided by the revised rituals of the Church.

ADAPTATION OF RITUAL

In addition to the flexibility and option which is built into the model of liturgical reform begun by the Second Vatican Council the Constitution on the Sacred Liturgy of Vatican II gives encouragement to another stage in liturgical reform. This involves the question of cultural adaptation or indigenization of the liturgy. By "indigenous" is meant what originates or occurs naturally in a place; it reflects what is "native"—"not exotic" but

MORNING/EVENING PRAYER

Element	Role	Nature and Option
Invitatory (AM)	Leader	May be "Lord, open my lips.—And my mouth will proclaim your praise." OR "God, come to my assistance. — Lord, make haste to help me." May be accompanied by: Psalm 95, the Invitatory Psalm (sung?).
Invitation to Prayer (PM)	Leader	"God, come to my assistance. — Lord, make haste to help me."
Morning/Evening Hymn	Cantor	May be selected from any hymnal or from those provided in the liturgy of the hours. These should express the hour of the day (primarily) or they may express the feast celebrated (if the feast is particularly notable).
Psalmody	Cantor/Reader	At morning prayer there is a morning psalm, an Old Testament canticle and a praise psalm. The antiphon at the beginning may be repeated at the end. Psalm prayers (often found in the texts of the hours) are optional. Psalms may be sung (or said) antiphonally, responsorially or straight through by an individual.

At evening prayer there are two psalms and a New Testament canticle of Christ. When there is a special solemnity or feast and the psalms of Sunday are prescribed, these need not always be those of week one in the psalter. |
| Reading | Reader | Those provided are short, random selections, followed by a responsory. These may be expanded to longer selections, or |

they may be changed. The principles of continuity and harmony in the lectionary should be remembered here so that "favorite passages" do not supersede the reading of the whole Scripture. The responsory may be omitted altogether, or changed to reflect the adjusted reading.

Canticle	Reader/Cantor	The canticle of Zechariah (AM) and of Mary (PM) are invariable parts of the hours. Standing for them and beginning them with the sign of the cross are traditional ways of emphasizing the "new" covenant as opposed to the psalms of the "old" covenant.
Invocations/Intercessions	Leader and Reader	Invocations at morning prayer are to dedicate the events of the day to God; they are to consecrate the day and its work. At evening prayer the intercessions parallel those of the liturgy of the Eucharist.
Lord's Prayer	Leader	The restoration of the Lord's prayer to the morning and evening hours represents the restoration of a traditional element of the hours.
Collect	Leader	May be of the day, of the hour. The prayers of the day may be changed in favor of one from among the thirty-four prayers provided as options.
Blessing and Dismissal	Leader	May be the blessings that end the hours or these may be replaced by one of the Solemn Blessings from the sacramentary for Mass (especially appropriate on solemnities and during special seasons) or it may be replaced by one of the prayers over the people from the sacramentary.

"innate" and "inherent." Hence, the process of indigenization involves adapting the liturgy to meet the needs of varying cultures whose customs and usages may well be at variance with the cultural usages and assumptions on which the liturgy is based.

In addressing this more radical phase of cultural adaptation[34] the Council fathers state:

> Within the limits set by the typical editions of the liturgical books, it shall be for competent territorial ecclesiastical authority . . . to specify adaptations, especially in the case of the administration of the sacraments, the sacramentals, processions, liturgical language, sacred music, and the arts, but according to the fundamental norms laid down in this Constitution. (no. 39)

> In some places and circumstances, however, an even more radical adaptation of the liturgy is needed and entails greater difficulties.

> Therefore:
> (1) The competent territorial ecclesiastical authority . . . must, in this matter, carefully and prudently consider which elements might appropriately be admitted into divine worship. Adaptations which are judged to be useful or necessary should then be submitted to the Apostolic See, by whose consent they may be introduced.
> (2) To insure that adaptations are made with all necessary circumspection, the Apostolic See will grant power to this same territorial ecclesiastical authority to permit and to direct, as the case requires, the necessary preliminary experiments over a determined period of time. . . . (no. 40)[35]

With these statements the Council fathers called for a phase of liturgical adaptation and reform quite unlike that undertaken at Trent. This renewed approach sets the question of adaptation alongside the sense of unity experienced by the use of the Roman rite throughout the world. Liturgical indigenization is not an opportunity for gimmicks or facile judgments about changing rubrical details or creating liturgies at whim. At stake here are the very roots of ritual within a culture and the expression of the one Roman liturgy in a number of varied cultures throughout the world.[36] The question of the inter-relationship between the two (liturgy and culture) is a complex issue, and yet when faced carefully and thoroughly it can lead to much rich insight about the possibility of varying liturgical structures because of the very variety among cultures.[37]

Historically what occurred in the evolution of liturgy was a certain indigenization process whereby the Greco-Roman world indigenized the Jerusalem liturgy by adopting popular customs into the liturgical structure it received. These accommodations were influenced, in turn, by the variety experienced in the liturgies of the rest of Europe. What resulted, therefore, was a "Roman rite" which was thoroughly influenced by Jerusalem origins, Roman customs and European practices. Liturgical historians raise the question of how genuinely "Roman" was the pre-conciliar Roman rite because of such a variety and complexus of influences. Yet, the "Roman rite" came to dominate after Trent with the publication of the Roman Breviary (1568) and the Roman Missal (1570).[38] What the Vatican Council did was to restore the principle of cultural adaptation in liturgy to a place of prominence once again. As can be seen in the Rite of Christian Initiation of Adults and the Rite of Baptism for Children there is clear provision made for "Adaptations by Episcopal Conferences Which Use the Roman Ritual" (RICA no. 64; RB nos. 23–26) and "Adaptations by the Minister" (RCIA no. 67; RB nos. 27–31).

Pastorally, what is at stake is the issue of how the liturgy of the Church can more adequately nourish the lives of faith and growth in faith of the community at common prayer. The questions raised by "popular religion" and religious "folk customs" are to be taken seriously in the sense that these practices have often been the means of sustaining people's religious lives, as opposed to (or at least alongside of) the liturgy of the whole Church.[39] From the perspective of the Filipino experience Anscar Chupungco states:

> . . . while the Greco-Roman world indigenized the Jerusalem
> liturgy by adopting popular customs into the sacramental
> structure itself, Filipinos did not bother to incorporate their
> native traditions into the official worship of the Church. Thus
> a clear line was drawn between the folk "liturgies" and the
> official liturgy which was celebrated with extreme fidelity to
> the Roman rite. Filipinos went to church for Mass and sacra-
> ments, but their interest as a community was focused on their
> folk "liturgies." With these they felt at home. And these they
> cherished and faithfully preserved through the centuries.[40]

Chupungco argues that cultural adaptation of the liturgy is
not an option, it is a theological and liturgical imperative. He
also speaks about the homage of the variety of cultures in which
the liturgy is presently celebrated which cultural variety can be
more effectively integrated into the forms of the liturgy. And
finally he argues that true liturgical adaptation requires fidelity
to the spirit of the liturgy. By emphasizing the latter as an
essential part of the indigenization process we are reminded of
what ritual does by way of preserving the tradition of a religious
group. Christian liturgy ought to retain features that have been
emphasized more fully as a result of the recent reforms which
are based on the liturgical tradition of the whole Church. Adaptations should respect the nature of liturgy which is a celebration of the paschal mystery of Christ, a sharing in the word of
God, enacted because of the presence and action of the Spirit,
which involves the active participation of the community, made
possible especially because there is a simplicity in the rite in
which a variety of roles is operative.[41] Proper catechesis should
accompany the liturgical reforms as we have them so that they
can be understood and implemented fully; similarly, proper
catechesis should also accompany any change in the ritual because of the process of indigenization.

For Americans some steps have been taken in the direction
of at least some cultural adaptation of the liturgy. The many
American editions of the reformed liturgy of the hours attest to
local initiative in the introduction of this post-conciliar revision.
The use of a wide variety of music in these printed editions, for

example, gives evidence of the adaptation of the Roman original for Americans. The introduction to the sacramentary for Mass gives an "Appendix to the General Instruction for the Dioceses of the United States of America" containing most of the adjustments made in implementing the revised Missal in America.[42] There is some debate about the saints whose feasts are presently commemorated in America and the number of days of obligation in the calendar. These are matters for national adaptation.[43] Many liturgists today call for a thorough study of the possibilities of liturgical adaptation in the United States; to be sure such a task involves respect for liturgical tradition and variety to suit local needs.[44]

But what needs to be recalled throughout is the fact that liturgy, as a ritual, involves much more than changing ceremonies which affect externals only. As rituals, as public actions, the liturgy affects people on many levels, not the least of which is self-identity. To have changed the rituals from the Tridentine Missal to the present reforms is to have changed a set of assumptions about the self-identity of the Christian communities that gather for worship:[45] from "I" believe to "we" believe; from watching to participating; from receiving to celebrating. In some ways it is better to suggest that ritual adaptation evolves rather than is pre-determined and easily accomplished. By its nature as ritual, good liturgy preserves the identity of the celebrating community. Through the liturgy communities share in the paschal mystery of Christ and in the values of his kingdom. Changing ceremonies too quickly or facilely can cause disruption and pastoral harm. But moving toward a new phase of reintegrating liturgy and culture is important (and part of the Vatican II agenda) precisely because all too often the official liturgy of the Church spoke a language and idiom that was foreign and not indigenous.

To speak of ritual as an element of liturgical prayer is to affirm the place which ritual plays in the identity of the Christian Church and in the on-going identification of those who gather for liturgical prayer.

One of the features of good ritual and good church life is a kind of stability that allows people to feel quite comfortable, knowing what to expect when they turn to rites or to other church services. At the same time, we must adapt church life, as has always been true in the history of the church, to changing cultures, situations, and events. The life of the church must relate to the experience of the people. Again both values warrant consideration in pastoral practice. Some balance must be struck between the two and adaptations must be seen as consistent with what is foundational for the church. Stability without adaptation is traditionalism. Adaptation without continuity appears as sheer novelty and leads to disorientation.[46]

In Christian liturgy two extremes ought to be avoided: the idolatry of rubrics and usage that is tradition-less. Good ritual insures a frame and structure for liturgical prayer and offers variety within it so that it does not become boring or ritualistic. The structure of ritual invites participation because of its familiarity; the variety achieved within it invites interest. Ideally, Christian liturgy does both.

NOTES

1. See *Constitution on the Sacred Liturgy,* no. 11.

2. N. Mitchell, "Useless Prayer," p. 22.

3. Margaret Mead, "Ritual and Social Crisis," in James Shaughnessy, ed., *The Roots of Ritual* (Grand Rapids: Wm. Eedrmans, 1973) pp. 87–89.

4. Lionel L. Mitchell, *The Meaning of Ritual* (New York/Ramsey: Paulist Press, 1977) pp. 23–62.

5. *Ibid.,* p. 26.

6. See, among others, Anscar J. Chupungco, *Cultural Adaptation of the Liturgy,* "A History of Liturgical Adaptation," pp. 3–41.

7. Patrick J. Quinn, "Ritual and the Definition of Space," in *The Roots of Ritual,* p. 103. See discussion below on "Creativity and Option," Part Three, Chapter Ten," section on "Liturgical Planning."

8. See above, note 1, and *Constitution on the Sacred Liturgy,* no. 14: "In the restoration and promotion of the sacred liturgy, this full and active participation by all the people is the aim to be considered before all else; for it is the primary and indispensable source from which the faithful are to derive the true Christian spirit."

9. See Part Two, Chapter Six, section on "Participation Through the Liturgy."

10. See Part Two, Chapter Four, section on "Variety and Community."

11. In the *General Norms for the Liturgical Year and the Calendar* it states: "The Church celebrates the paschal mystery of the first day of the week, known as the Lord's Day or Sunday. This follows a tradition handed down from the Apostles, which took its origin from the day of Christ's resurrection. Thus Sunday should be considered the original feast day." (no. 4) In some popular treatments of the liturgy, Sunday has been referred to as "little Easter" because of the centrality of the paschal mystery celebrated on this day. However, it would be more accurate and precise to call Easter the "great Sunday."

12. From Justin's *First Apology* cited above, Part Two, Chapter Four, section on "God's Presence to a Redeemed Community."

13. See, for example, H. Boone Porter, *The Day of Light.* The Biblical and Liturgical Meaning of Sunday (Greenwich: Seabury, 1960).

14. Text from *Worship II* (Chicago: G.I.A. Publications, 1975) no. 219.

15. This option has been restored in the recent revision of the hours; see *The Liturgy of the Hours,* Four Volumes (New York: Catholic Book Publishing Co., 1975), Appendix I: Canticles and Gospel Readings for Vigils.

16. See Juan Mateos, "The Origins of the Divine Office," *Worship* 41 (October 1967) 483, and William Storey, "The Liturgy of the Hours: Cathedral versus Monastery," in *Christians at Prayer,* p. 70.

17. Marianne Micks, *The Future Present,* p. 40.

18. *Ibid.,* p. 64.

19. See, "The Liturgical Code in the Rule of Benedict," *The Rule of St. Benedict,* ed. Timothy Fry *et al.* (Collegeville: The Liturgical Press, 1981) pp. 379–414.

20. See William Storey, "Parish Worship: The Liturgy of the Hours," *Worship* 49 (January 1975) 2–12.

21. *General Instruction, Liturgy of the Hours,* nos. 6, 20–32.

22. In reviewing the evolution of the liturgy of the hours Juan

Mateos uses the phrase "Christian Prayers of Private Devotion" to describe the Christian adaptation of the Jewish hours of prayer (see J. Mateos, "The Origin of the Divine Office").

23. For example, William Storey, *Bless the Lord,* A Prayerbook for Advent, Christmas, Lent and Eastertide (Notre Dame: Ave Maria Press, 1974); *Praise Him,* A Prayerbook for Today's Christian (Notre Dame: Ave Maria Press, 1974); see also *Praise God in Song,* Ecumenical Daily Prayer (Chicago: G.I.A. Publications, 1979).

24. Alan Bouley, "Scripture, Personal Prayer, and Liturgy," in *Scripture and the Assembly,* p. 64.

25. See, for example, *Lutheran Book of Worship,* pp. 131–160 for the order of Morning Prayer, Evening Prayer, and Prayer at the Close of the Day.

26. *Praise in All Our Days,* Common Prayer at Taizé (London: The Faith Press, 1975) p. 7.

27. The words "pre-determined" and "fixed" should not be misunderstood, since there was evolution (albeit limited) and liturgical changes from Trent to the present. However, generally speaking, once changes were made they were fixed.

28. *Constitution on the Sacred Liturgy,* no. 34: "The rites should be distinguished by a noble simplicity; they should be clear, and unencumbered by useless repetitions; they should be within the people's powers of comprehension, and normally not require much explanation."

29. *General Instruction of the Roman Missal* no. 313; see also *Music In Catholic Worship* nos. 10–14.

30. *General Intercessions* (a booklet prepared by) Bishops' Committee on the Liturgy (Washington: USCC, 1979), p. 1.

31. *Ibid.,* p. 5.

32. *Ibid.,* p. 7.

33. As sources for the adaptation see *General Instruction, Liturgy of the Hours,* nos. 34, 41, 46, 49, 51, 112, 169, 188, for example.

34. A. Chupungco (*Cultural Adaptation,* pp. 51–57) calls this the "second degree of adaptation."

35. See, *ibid.,* Chapter Two: "The Magna Carta of Liturgical Adaptation," pp. 42–57.

36. See above for a review of the importance of rites and liturgical families in the non-Roman Western rite, Part Two, Chapter Four, subsection on "Roman and Local Liturgy," under section on "Variety and Community."

37. See, among others, David N. Power, "Cult to Culture: The

Liturgical Foundation of Theology," *Worship* 54 (November 1980) 482–495.

38. The Missal published in 1570 was not essentially different from that published in 1474; however, the fact that it was to be used by all communities (save for those with a ritual of their own existing for at least two hundred years) was what made it a book of lasting significance.

39. This very significant field of research is being taken very seriously by liturgists. See, for example, David Power and Hermann Schmidt, eds., *Liturgy and Cultural Religious Traditions,* Concilium 102 (New York: Seabury, 1977).

40. Anscar J. Chupungco, *Towards a Filipino Liturgy* (Manila: Benedictine Abbey, 1976) pp. 2–3.

41. See, for example, an English translation of the Filipino Mass, in *Towards a Filipino Liturgy,* pp. 119–139.

42. *Sacramentary,* pp. 49–52.

43. See John A. Guerrieri, "Holy Days in America," *Worship* 54 (September 1980) 417–446.

44. See John Gallen, "American Liturgy: A Theological Locua," *Theological Studies* 35 (June 1974) 302–311; Charles Gusmer, "A Bill of Rites: Liturgical Adaptation in America," *Worship* 51 (July 1977) 283–289; Louis Weil, "Liturgy in a Disintegrating World," *Worship* 54 (July 1980) 291–302.

45. See the fine essay of Matthias Neuman, "Self-Identity, Symbol, and Imagination: Some Implications of Their Interactions for Christian Sacramental Theology," *Symbolisme et Théologie,* Sacramentum 2 (Rome: Editrice Anselmiana, 1974) *Studia Anselmiana 64,* pp. 91–123.

46. Philip J. Murnion, "Dilemmas in Ministry," *Clergy Report* 4 (December 1974).

Chapter Eight
LITURGICAL TIME:
FEASTS AND SEASONS

The Christian Church sees itself as the people redeemed in time but who look forward to the end of time; as a people situated between the first coming and the second coming of Christ; between his incarnation in human form and his return as the Lord the God of power and might; between his resurrection (and ascension) and his coming again in glory. We are a people who celebrate the memorial of redemption by participating in Christ's death and resurrection as we await his coming again in glory. When we celebrate the feasts and seasons of the liturgical year we "recall the past," "summon the future"[1] and experience in the present all that is implied in the paschal mystery of Christ.

The purpose of our feasting in the seasons of the Church calendar is to enter into the sacrifice of Christ who intercedes for us at the Father's right hand. We do not redo Christ's paschal mystery; rather, through the liturgy, we continually share in his paschal triumph and joy.

> For the Fathers of the church the liturgical year is not an edifying commemoration of the past, but a making real in the present for the sake of the future . . . [it] is not a simple recall of the past but a remembering that enables us to share in the mysteries of Christ.[2]

Since we are a people "between the times" the liturgical commemoration and celebration of word and sacrament is a privileged time for us to experience the very life of God in Christ. When we "gather together to ask the Lord's blessing"

we "proclaim the death of the Lord until he comes in glory."
Hence, the experience of the liturgy in time (our present) is the
occasion when we experience all that was promised in Christ
and look forward to all that will be fulfilled when the kingdom
comes. In the meantime at liturgy we share deeply and as fully as
we can in the life of God. The liturgical year is the setting of our
participation in and appropriation of the mystery of Christ.
What is commemorated and celebrated at every act of liturgy
(the paschal mystery) is explicitated and commemorated over
the feasts and seasons that comprise what we call "the liturgical
year." What is at stake is our participation in Christ,[3] the framework for this to occur is the pattern of ritual we call Christian
liturgy,[4] and the setting is offered in the feasts and seasons that
together comprise the liturgical year.[5]

LITURGICAL TIME

From the perspective of an appreciation of the spirituality
involved in Christian liturgy it is important to recall that in the
valorization process Judaism adopted many of the customs
which were operative in Canaanite rituals of common prayer.
One aspect of this heritage (and as exemplified in many other
"primitive religions") is the notion of time and its relation to
liturgical rites. Such primitive religions based their spirituality
and experience of common prayer on the repetition of myths
and rituals in order to recreate time and space. The "new year"
was a time when new beginnings would occur; the past ("old
year") was wiped away. The ingathering of the crops was often
the occasion for this festival and such festivity often lasted for
days (for example, the number twelve for the "days of Christmas" as derived from *Saturnalia*). By these annual new year
celebrations the community was given hope; they shared a new
perspective on life, for in a sense life was beginning all over
again for them each year. Something of this same sense of new
opportunities and new possibilities is involved in our "new
year's resolutions" and the custom in some European countries
of throwing things out on New Year's Day. The "old" is cast out
so the new can begin. Especially if the previous year was bad

(bad luck) the new year is greeted more enthusiastically because of the possibilities offered for renewal and literal re-creation.

The notion of time that is operative here is cyclic in that the annual repetition of the myth (of creation) and the ritual that accompanied this retelling of the foundational events was the means whereby present communities were renewed and saved. The myths were passed from one generation to another and the ritual offering involved symbols of what was most real to that society. Examples of these symbolic offerings include the first fruits of creation or a prized lamb from the flock. The myth and ritual combined in liturgy to give hope, promise and new beginnings.[6]

> The myths which presented the contents of pagan festivals did not refer to events within history but were rather situated at the time of the beginnings of all things, *en arche.* The cosmogonic ritual, as analysed by phenomenologists of religion, seeks to escape the mounting influence of the past— what Mircea Eliade calls the "terror of history"—by the ritual expulsion of malign influences (sin, disease, etc.) and the regeneration of time through the repetition of the cosmogony. The regular return of such festivals marks a "death" and "rebirth" of time itself, and thus points to such a cyclical view of time as was characteristic of Greek thought and which Eliade has described as "a refusal of history".[7]

For biblical religion, however, there would be a new understanding of time and of the place of human beings in history. This involves the shift from cyclical time to linear time, and such a shift included a change of understanding of what happens at liturgy. The contribution of Judaism to this pre-existing round of rituals was to take essentially agrarian and nomadic cyclical festivals and to make them over into the means whereby Judaism commemorated and experienced anew the redemptive events of history. Where time has previously been wiped out, now time was taken seriously in the Jewish perspective. The events of God's intervening in time (the exodus) made all the difference in their understanding of themselves and of history. Time was now viewed both cyclically and linearly.[8] Annual renewal festi-

vals would continue in Judaism but they were made to celebrate
not an annual end of time and a new beginning from nothing,
but the event of the exodus. This was an historically verifiable
and annually commemorated event that made Israel a people.
This was the moment of their "creation," for an irrevocable
bond had thus been forged between God and his covenanted
people. Identity for Israel was renewed at such rituals because
they shared a common salvation event, an event that was first
accomplished by God on their behalf. These celebrations, like
those in Canaan before them, were annual events. Thus cyclic
time was sustained within a view of history that was linear. What
was commemorated now was the once-for-all salvation event of
redemption through the Red Sea and the promise of a land in
which to dwell as God's chosen. The event of being made a
people once for all by the event of the Passover was celebrated
annually; hence the intersection of linear and cyclic time.

The new beginnings promised by the primitives' celebrations were no longer possible for Judaism. Theirs was one new
beginning; it was that one event that was commemorated and
actualized in the liturgy of Judaism (daily, weekly, annually). It is
from this pattern that Christianity inherited its daily, weekly and
yearly commemorations of the memorial of Christ.[9]

> Thus for the first time, the prophets placed a value on his-
> tory, succeeded in transcending the traditional vision of the
> cycle (the concept that ensures all things will be repeated
> forever), and discovered one-way time. . . . For the first time,
> we find affirmed, and increasingly accepted, the idea that
> historical events have a value in themselves, insofar as they
> are determined by the will of God. This God of the Jewish
> people is no longer an Oriental divinity, creator of archetypal
> gestures, but a personality who ceaselessly intervenes in his-
> tory, who reveals his will through events. . . . It may . . . be
> said with truth that the Hebrews were the first to discover the
> meaning of history as the epiphany of God, and this concep-
> tion . . . was taken up and amplified in Christianity.[10]

All of this is taken a step further in the fact that Judaism was
also a religion of eschatology as well as of current events and

past history. Judaism looked to the exodus as its origin. It also looked to the time when, as God promised, a Savior would come and bring its exalted status to fulfillment. Judaism's linear notion of time looked to the future as well as to the past. What this does is make Jewish liturgy a juncture in the linear time (recalling the past and summoning the future) and cyclical time (repeated, regular observances on a cycle).

Christian worship adopts this same juncture of linear and cyclical time in its liturgy, except for the difference that what was longed for in Judaism has been accomplished in the coming of Christ. This event in history has changed the way Christians view the counting of history itself, for now all things are "in the year of our Lord." The center of history is this coming of Christ and the redemption he accomplished once-for-all. Christian liturgy is celebrated in the present by means of which the fullness of life in Christ is repeatedly shared and commemorated. But like the liturgy of Judaism, Christian ritual looks beyond itself, even as privileged occasions of sanctification, to the completion of all liturgy, beyond linear time in the kingdom of God forever.

Hence, it can be asserted that one of the bases on which Christian liturgy is grounded is this fusion of cyclical and linear time. While the circle is conventionally used to illustrate the annual round of feasts and liturgical seasons in Christianity, this can also be less than totally helpful because it leaves out the notion of linear history (from Christ's birth to his second coming). Therefore, one way of illustrating the annual celebration of the liturgical year is a spiral with both circle and line in evidence. The spiral continues to expand as long as time and history "in the year of our Lord" continue. But each year is also respected as a unit within the line by a circle suggesting annual commemoration.

Besides the close association of cyclical and linear time in liturgy is an understanding of time that associates "sacred" and "profane" time.[11]

> Ordinarily our experience of time is rather continuous. Sometimes we are busy and the time passes quickly; sometimes we are bored and it seems to drag. But it is always the

same time, it is always passing, and one moment seems just like the next. But on certain occasions our consciousness of time is altered and we enter a special time, a sacred moment. . . . But when the moment arrives, time feels different. . . . In sacramental experiences the time that is experienced is similarly sacred.[12]

For the Christian Church the essential aspect of religious time is that of an occasion for gathering together to celebrate its identity as a people who share in the paschal mystery of Christ. This takes place in a number of ways and on many different occasions. The setting forth of these ways and occasions is what is meant by the "sacramental life" of the Church and "the liturgical year." What is important to remember is that "sacred time" is not an escape from "profane time" so much as it is an experience of communal prayer in time (the present) which discloses the ultimate meaning of life in Christ. Liturgical celebrations are not occasions to flee from the world and from historical time; they are important moments in historical time to disclose what is meant by salvation in Christ. This is what is meant by "liturgical time."

ONE MYSTERY OF CHRIST

In the words of Marianne Micks:

At least since the fourth century, the Church Year has invited [believers] to think about the past and about the future. And at least since the fourth century some Christians have dissolved the tension by choosing what might well be called a tourist's view of time, while others have elected to affirm it through their understanding of mystery in holidays.[13]

What is involved here is the perennial problem of how to view the Church year. As was noted above concerning our participation in the commemoration of Christ at liturgy,[14] the most important focus for liturgical commemoration is to view it as a means of participating in the very action of Christ actualized in and through the liturgy. When this central focus is lost, for example under the pressure of "historicization" and "dramatization," the significance of memorial in its wholeness as a concept that is at the basis of Christian liturgy is lost. When the process of historicizing and dramatizing takes over within liturgical celebration there is a misunderstanding of the delicate balance of factors which are at the heart of commemoration.

Something similar happens in trying to understand and appreciate the liturgical year when we opt for the "tourist's view of time," that is, a chronological approach to feasts. According to this view the Church year offers us glimpses into the life of Christ in such a way that this series repeats itself annually like a continuous slide show. "The approach is chronological in the sense that the events of the Church year happen as if 'by the clock'."[15] In this approach the Church year can appear to be separate from the present needs and concerns of the community that is (paradoxically) celebrating them! The Church year would seem to move along with the flow of chronological time, day by day, month by month.

> When the church year is approached chronologically, the tendency is to perceive it as a liturgical device, extraneous and optional to present human existence. We remain outside as onlookers. When we approach the Church year chronologically, we dissociate the years of our lives from the year of the Church, as if we were standing on solid "rock" observing the liturgical seasons flow by.[16]

Just as our "participation" in the paschal mystery is what memorial is all about, so too our participation in the paschal mystery of Christ is what the liturgical year is all about. The flaw in the chronological approach to the Church year is that we interpret the mystery of Christ as separate and distinct events. In fact, the mystery of Christ is unique and indivisible, and it is through our present experience of this mystery that we are redeemed and sanctified. What makes a round of feasts and seasons in the liturgy one year different from another year's observance is that we ourselves are different and changing, and it is always the "who we are" that God calls into his life in the liturgy. The heart and center of the liturgical year is the making present among us of the saving act of Christ. Christ's presence is not a "past" or "future" presence. It is an eternal now, an enduring presence for us. By no means is the liturgy a biography of Jesus, a dramatization of his death (and resurrection), or a chronology of the events of his earthly life. It is always the continual commemoration of the one sacrifice of Christ which we enter ever more fully at common worship.

One way of understanding this is to use an "eschatological approach" to the calendar. This approach

> recognizes the vicissitudes and emptiness of chronological time. It also recognizes that we and the whole creation will "pass away" (Lk 21:33a). Therefore, the eschatological approach seeks to hear the "last word" (eschatology), the word which will not pass away (Lk 21:33b). We seek the "last word" of Christian eschatology which will transform both the "meantime" and the "end time" of our lives. In our use, eschatological time refers to any chronological time which is transformed by being perceived and lived in the light of God's "last word".[17]

This is to suggest that during the liturgy we are not viewing a series of scenes from the life of Christ, nor are we merely recounting Christ's birth, life or death. What occurs in the liturgy is the actualization of the mystery of Christ and our being made sharers in this mystery.

> Liturgical catechesis must always be based on the actualization of the mystery being commemorated and celebrated. It must insist incessantly on the fact that to celebrate a mystery is not to celebrate a past but rather a "today" for tomorrow.

> Each celebration is, in effect, the celebration of Jesus Christ in his present activity for the salvation of the world and of humankind. This fundamental aspect provides catechesis with its specific character: it is not confined to simple instruction; it affords access to the reality of salvation.[18]

Hence, whatever the feast celebrated during the course of the liturgical year, it is always the paschal mystery of Christ that is the center. By way of example the illustrations below will serve to show how both the "paschal celebrations" and the "incarnation celebrations" are essentially commemorations of the paschal mystery of Christ.

In addressing the question of how to appreciate what is involved in celebration during the year, Pope Paul VI stated:

> The purpose of the restoration of the liturgical year and the revision of its norms is to allow the faithful, through their faith, hope, and love, to share more deeply in "the whole mystery of Christ as it unfolds throught the year".[19]

He suggests that the liturgical year exerts a "special sacramental power and influence which strengthens Christian life." As the Liturgy Constitution of Vatican II states:

> Within the cycle of a year, moreover, [the church] unfolds the whole mystery of Christ, but not only from His incarnation and birth until His ascension, but also as reflected in the day of Pentecost, and the expectation of a blessed, hoped-for return of the Lord. Recalling thus the mysteries of redemption [in the liturgy] the church opens to the faithful the riches of her Lord's powers and merits, so that these are in some way present at all times, and the faithful are enabled to lay hold of them and become filled with saving grace. (no. 102)

In the revision of the liturgical year the paschal mystery is given special emphasis as that which is central in all Christian celebration. An understanding and exploration of the central seasons of the Church year (to follow below) help orient our prayer toward what is truly celebrated in gesture, word and symbol in the liturgy. Such an appreciation also helps us celebrate these seasons fully, as experiences of Christ in which we share. The Church year is not meant to be a spiritual straitjacket confining prayer and devotion. Rather it is a helpful structure whose prayers, rites and texts help us appropriate the mystery of Christ. Just as the daily and weekly common prayer of the

Church was noted above as the central means through which Christians participate in the dying and rising of Christ, so too (and in some ways more explicitly) through the liturgical year communities of Christians celebrate and share the memory of Christ. What is offered in liturgy is the active presence of Christ for us; what is required of us is our coming to the liturgy with faith and openness so that the very ordinariness of our lives can be transformed by Christ. Liturgical prayer does not mean in any way that we separate our needs, concerns and our very selves from what is happening in the liturgy. Rather all that we are and all our needs are presented to the Lord so that the liturgy might transform us again and again into the image and likeness of God. What is celebrated is the one mystery of Christ over the course of the year through feasts and seasons. But what is at the center of liturgical commemoration through the year is our being made one with God through Christ and Christ as mediator making us one with God. The concretization of this takes place in the unfolding of the liturgical year.

THE PASCHAL CELEBRATIONS

The Easter Triduum[20]—The *General Norms* for the Liturgical Year and the Calendar state:

> Christ redeemed us all and gave perfect glory to God principally through his paschal mystery: dying he destroyed our death and rising he restored our life. Therefore the Easter triduum of the passion and resurrection of Christ is the culmination of the entire liturgical year. Thus the solemnity of Easter has the same kind of preeminence in the liturgical year that Sunday has in the week.

> The Easter triduum begins with the evening Mass of the Lord's Supper, reaches its high point in the Easter Vigil, and closes with evening prayer on Easter Sunday. (nos. 18–19)

In light of the distinctions made above regarding the notion of historicization and dramatization of what ought to be seen as essentially commemoration in liturgy, and the notion of how an

eschatological understanding of the liturgical year is preferable
to one that is chronological (or biographical), it is interesting to
note how often our associations with the "three days" of the
celebration of Easter liturgy do, in fact, reflect an historical and
chronological approach to "Holy Week." One evidence of the
lack of appreciating the three days as our progressive assimila-
tion into the dying and rising of Jesus is that popular devotions
often overshadowed the liturgy in emphasis. As far back as 1955
in the document revising the rites of Holy Week Pope Pius XII
had this to say about the priority which should be given to the
liturgy over other devotions:

> The liturgical rites of Holy Week not only have a special
> dignity, but have also a special sacramental power and effica-
> cy in nourishing the Christian life, and cannot be adequately
> replaced by those pious exercises of devotion usually called
> extraliturgical, which take place during the sacred triduum in
> the hours after noon [e.g., Good Friday between noon and
> three o'clock].[21]

The Holy Father clearly enunciated a principle that is very
traditional and one which can be used to illuminate our understanding of the liturgy of Easter and Christmas, that the rites
themselves have a "special sacramental power and efficacy," and
hence they are to be preferred to other devotions.

In addition, another way of understanding the liturgy of
these days is to discover what the liturgy itself—texts, prayers,
symbols and actions—reveals about the mystery celebrated.
What the liturgy of these days reveals is the *unity* of the paschal
mystery of Christ commemorated during the triduum from Holy
Thursday evening to Easter with its preceding Vigil. This is in
opposition to some conventional understandings that place each
day of these three in isolation as though the suffering and death
of Christ could be understood apart from the resurrection. If we
look at the liturgy without pre-conceived ideas or other devotions in mind, it reveals that on each day of the triduum there is
explicit reference to the whole of the paschal mystery. What
occurs on an individual day is a liturgy which commemorates the
whole of this mystery while at the same time emphasizing one

aspect of the events which together comprise this mystery of faith. For example, on Good Friday it is clear that emphasis is placed on Jesus' death on the cross. And yet this commemoration includes reflection on his free acceptance of death, for on this day the passion account of John is read (18:1—19:42) in which there is no reference to any agony in the garden; the redemptive death was "freely accepted." According to John the crucifixion is the event where the fullness of Christ's *glory* is revealed (not just humiliation and suffering), which glory was seen at the incarnation (Jn 1:14: "And we saw his glory" from the Mass of Christmas Day) and manifest at the wedding feast at Cana (Jn 2:12): "Thus did he reveal his glory, and his disciples believed in him"). In addition, the prayers of Good Friday speak both about the dying of Christ and the whole of the mystery commemorated over the three days:

> Lord,
> by shedding his blood for us,
> your Son, Jesus Christ,
> established the paschal mystery.
> In your goodness, make us holy
> and watch over us always.
>
> (Opening Prayer)

> Lord,
> send down your abundant blessing
> upon your people who have devoutly recalled the death of your
>   Son
> in the sure hope of the resurrection.
> Grant them pardon; bring them comfort.
> May their faith grow stronger
> and their eternal salvation be assured.
>
> (Prayer Over the People)

> Almighty and eternal God,
> you have restored us to life
> by the triumphant death and resurrection of Christ.
> Continue this healing work within us.
> May we who participate in this mystery
> never cease to serve you.
>
> (Prayer After Receiving Communion)

This last text is especially illustrative of the unity of the death and resurrection. In addition this prayer notes the understanding of the dying of Jesus as triumphant, a notion fully in accord with that of the evangelist John. It also stresses our present "participation" in the mysteries commemorated. That our present celebration of Good Friday recalls the past and looks to future glory is noted in the prayer over the people which speaks about the assurance of eternal salvation, celebrated and signified in the present in the liturgy. There is no "tourist's view of time" operative here; it is a notion of liturgical time that is traditional in the best sense of being commemorative and eschatological.

That this traditional and very rich understanding of liturgy is operative throughout the whole of the "three days" is especially clear in the high point of the triduum, the Easter Vigil. This liturgy is the culmination of the preparation period of Lent and it is extended beyond Easter Day for the rest of the Easter season. The Vigil is the juncture of the "forty days" of Lenten preparation and the "fifty days" of Easter as a season. What we bring to the Vigil is our personal and communal dying in Lent and our collective rejoicing in hope throughout Easter. That this night is a celebration of new life is clear just from its celebration in springtime, with the context provided by the spring equinox and full moon. These cosmic elements project and support the paschal themes of creation, rebirth, light and the presence of salvation. "While the mystery of human salvation is brought about by the death and resurrection of Christ and shared by the Church through the paschal sacraments, it is ushered in by the season which alone eloquently portrays it."[22] With this as a physical setting it is most significant, therefore, that the Vigil takes place at night, that it necessarily includes a service of light shattering natural darkness, and that it involves a liturgy of baptism through which new members of the community of Christ share in the new life of Christ (at the very time when nature is coming to birth, to rebirth, to new life). These most significant symbolic actions help articulate what the Christian celebration is all about.[23]

The idea of spring as a renewal of creation is underscored in the first reading for this liturgy, the creation account from the Book of Genesis (1:1–2:2). In many ways the proclamation of this text harkens back to the time when spring festivals in primitive societies were concerned with the renewal of life at this time of year, which was effected by the annual repetition of this kind of cosmogenic myth. The notion of birth and rebirth in faith is underscored in the reading from Exodus (14:15—15:1) about how the Israelites were saved as they made their way through the Red Sea. In the words of the responsorial psalm: "I will sing to the Lord, for he is gloriously tiumphant; horse and chariot he has cast into the sea."[24] Clearly notions of creation, re-creation (cycles of nature) and identity as part of God's people (Jewish celebration of the Passover) frame what Christians celebrate this night, and why this time was chosen for Christian celebration:

> This is the passover of the Lord:
> if we honor the memory of his death and resurrection
> by hearing his word and celebrating his mysteries,
> then we may be confident
> that we shall share his victory over death
> and live with him forever in God.
>
> (Introduction to Easter Vigil)

The Vigil liturgy begins with the service of light: blessing the new fire, lighting the paschal candle, carrying the candle in procession, and the singing of the Easter Proclamation (*Exsultet*). This rich symbol of light in darkness is applied to the celebrating community who are made sharers in the light of Christ through the liturgy:

> Father,
> we share in the light of your glory
> through your Son, the light of the world.
> Make this new fire holy, and inflame us with new hope.
> Purify our minds by this Easter celebration
> and bring us one day to the feast of eternal light.
>
> (Blessing of Fire)

Clearly, the intention of the liturgy with all members of the assembly carrying and holding lighted candles and hearing this prayer is for the community to share deeply in the events commemorated this night until the fullness of divine life is made real and shared in the kingdom.

The classic text of the Easter Proclamation recounts the events of salvation history which lead to our annual celebration of Easter, and, in the action of recounting, these events are made real once again in the liturgy. The Jewish background for the Easter feast is abundantly clear: "This is our passover feast, when Christ, the true Lamb, is slain, whose blood consecrates the homes of all believers." The original "passing over" is recalled and transcended here, both in the waters of the Red Sea and in the sprinkling of blood on the doorposts of believers. On this night Christian liturgy celebrates the passover of Christ by the water of baptism and the body and blood of Christ at the Eucharist—the paschal sacraments.

> Father,
> even today we see the wonders
> of the miracles you worked long ago.
> You once saved a single nation from slavery,
> and now you offer that salvation to all
>   through baptism.
>
> Lord God,
> in the new covenant
> you shed light on the miracles you worked in
>   ancient times:
> the Red Sea is a symbol of our baptism,
> and the nation you freed from slavery
> is a sign of your Christian people.
>   (Prayers following the reading of Ex 14)

That the proclamation of the word is an essential and most significant aspect of this liturgy is clear from the introduction which is provided in the sacramentary:

Let us now listen attentively to the word of God,
recalling how he saved his people throughout history
and, in the fullness of time,
sent his own Son to be our Redeemer.
Through this Easter celebration,
may God bring to perfection
the saving work he has begun in us.

What particularizes and specifies the Vigil liturgy this night from all others is that after the liturgy of the word there is the initiation of new members, especially adults, into the communion of the Church and the solemn renewal of baptismal promises from the faithful. The rite of initiation is followed according to which there is the significant moment of blessing the water of the font,[25] the renunciation of sin, the profession of faith, water baptism, and the celebration of confirmation. For those renewing baptismal promises the liturgy states:

Dear friends,
through the paschal mystery
we have been buried with Christ in baptism,
so that we may rise with him to a new life.
Now that we have completed our Lenten observance,
let us renew the promises we made in baptism. . . .

The final part of the Easter Vigil liturgy is the liturgy of Eucharist. This is the culminating action of the Church gathered in prayer this vigil night. The Eucharist takes on particular meaning and enjoys special emphasis this night because from Thursday night on the Church does not celebrate Eucharist (it distributes Communion on Friday from hosts remaining after the liturgy of the Lord's Supper on Holy Thursday). This first Eucharist of Easter is fittingly the first sharing in Communion by the newly-initiated. The passover connotations are not lost at this point, for the use of unleavened bread and wine and the sharing in a sacrificed lamb are the foundation on which this celebration is based. That Christ is acclaimed "Lamb of God" and that the bread is broken and wine is poured out are central

actions of the Eucharist. On this night, however, they take on
special significance, for the Church shares in this sacrament on
the very night which celebrates new life in Christ:

> We praise you with greater joy than ever
> on this Easter night,
> when Christ became our paschal sacrifice.
> He is the true Lamb who took away the
>   sins of the world.
> By dying he destroyed our death;
> by rising he restored our life.

(Preface, Easter I)

The Solemn Blessing for Easter succinctly states what has been
accomplished in the celebration of the three days and it also
looks beyond them to the kingdom of heaven:

> You have mourned for Christ's sufferings;
> now you celebrate the joy of his resurrection.
> May you come with joy to the feast which
>   lasts for ever.

Lent—With regard to the season of Lent, the *General Norms* for
the Liturgical Year and the Calendar state:

> Lent is a preparation for the celebration of Easter. For the
> Lenten liturgy disposes both catechumens and the faithful to
> celebrate the paschal mystery: catechumens through the sev-
> eral stages of Christian initiation; the faithful, through re-
> minders of their own baptism and through penitential
> practices.
>
> Lent runs from Ash Wednesday until the Mass of the Lord's
> Supper exclusive. (nos. 27–28)

While the season of the "forty days" has been conventionally
understood as a season for penance and preparation for Easter,
the reformed liturgy gives this preparation a sharper focus and a
more careful delineation. Lent is a communal season during

which communities of the faithful welcome new members into their number at the Sunday liturgies of Lent (the Rite of Christian Initiation of Adults)[26] and it is a time for communal reflection on those things which need to be purged in preparation for reconciliation and the renewal of the promises of baptism during the Easter Vigil. The prayers used during the liturgy of Ash Wednesday are to be understood in this light:

> Lord,
> bless the sinner who asks for your forgiveness
> and bless all those who receive these ashes.
> May they keep this Lenten season
> in preparation for the joy of Easter.
>
> (Blessing of Ashes)

> Lord,
> bless these ashes
> by which we show that we are dust.
> Pardon our sins
> and keep us faithful to the discipline of Lent,
> for you do not want sinners to die
> but to live with the risen Christ.
>
> (Alternate Prayer, Blessing of Ashes)

What is particularly significant about these prayers is that both of them look beyond the important symbol of ashes to their underlying meaning and use in liturgy, for the prayer and reflection of those who are blessed by them. The fact that this liturgy and the Lenten season is to lead us "to live with the risen Christ" is significant; but in addition there is the obscure but real reference to sharing life with God in the kingdom of heaven implicit in the text "in preparation for the joy of Easter." The original (and ancient) form of this prayer speaks clearly of the fact that all Lent and all liturgy is to lead beyond ceremonies (even Easter celebrations) to the kingdom. As we often pray in a classic hymn for this season:

> And through these days of penitence,
> And through thy Passiontide,

Yea, evermore, in life and death,
Jesus! with us abide.

Abide with us, that so, this life
Of suff'ring over past,
An Easter of unending joy
We may attain at last![27]

Lent is thus best understood as a season which leads to the paschal celebration of "the death and resurrection of Christ our Savior" (prayer after Communion) and yet which also looks to the fullness of resurrected life in the kingdom forever.

The Sundays of Lent are structured so that on the First Sunday we proclaim the Gospel of the temptation of Jesus, and thus we are faced with reflecting on those things which prevent us from living totally with God. We hear about Christ being tempted by Satan and thus are led to reflect on what are the allurements, the distractions, the temptations in our own lives. As we hear in the preface for this Sunday

His fast of forty days
makes this a holy season of self-denial.
By rejecting the devil's temptations
he has taught us
to rid ourselves of the hidden corruption of evil,
and so to share his paschal meal in purity of heart,
until we come to its fulfillment
in the promised land of heaven.

On the Second Sunday of Lent we reflect on the event of the transfiguration of Christ. Just as there can be no liturgy without clear emphasis on the resurrection of Christ, so there can be no Lenten liturgy without the hope, promise and glory which is ours in Christ, revealed to the disciples on the mountain of the transfiguration. In the preface for this Sunday we pray:

On your holy mountain he revealed himself in glory
in the presence of his disciples.

He had already prepared them for his approaching death.
He wanted to teach them through the Law and the Prophets
that the promised Christ had first to suffer
and so come to the glory of his resurrection.

The note of hope and the reality of sharing in the resurrection
of Christ even during Lent are important correctives to an
understanding of the spirituality of Lent which so often concen-
trates only on passion and suffering. Paradoxically, it is through
the glory revealed in Christ that we have the confidence and
hope necessary to face the reality of evil, temptation and sin in
our own lives.

That Lent leads to initiation and the renewal of baptismal
promises is most clearly demonstrated in the liturgies of the
Third, Fourth, and Fifth Sundays of Lent in the "A" cycle of the
lectionary. On these days the community of the faithful welcomes the catechumens for the liturgy of the word during which
they are prayed for and noted in the prayers of the liturgy.[28] The
Gospel passages for these Sundays are the traditional texts from
the Gospel of John which have been used in the Church's liturgy
to refer to the initiation that will occur at the end of Lent. The
texts include the conversation between Jesus and the Samaritan
woman (Jn 4:5–42, symbol of water), the cure of the man born
blind (Jn 9:1–41, symbol of light), and the raising of Lazarus (Jn
11:1–45, symbol of life). That these lead to Easter is clear from
the references throughout these texts to faith and the fact that at
the Easter Vigil the initiation liturgy uses the symbolism of light
and water to accomplish the baptism itself. As is stated in the
preface of the Fifth Sunday of Lent:

As a man like us, Jesus wept for Lazarus his friend.
As the eternal God, he raised Lazarus from the dead.
In his love for us all
Christ gives us the sacraments
to lift us up to everlasting life.

Clearly the liturgy of Lent leads to the Liturgy of the three days
in the sense that these communal celebrations articulate and

give shape to the spirituality of the Christian Church which at this time of year casts aside those things that stand in the way of professing faith freely and fully at Easter.

This is indicated even more concretely for the already initiated in the "C" cycle of Sunday readings for Lent. After the First and Second Sundays of the season which deal (in all three cycles) with the temptation and transfiguration of Christ, the rest of the Sundays speak clearly about the need for repentance and reconciliation. On the Third Sunday of Lent the Gospel is from Luke (13:1–9) which speaks about the fig tree as an image and example of the need for repentance. On the Fourth Sunday the familiar text of Luke (15:1–3, 11–32) about the prodigal son is proclaimed with its emphasis on reconciliation. And on the Fifth Sunday of Lent the Gospel is from John (8:1–11), recounting the incident of the woman caught in adultery and the fact that no one was without sin to condemn her. This is a clear reference to the ever present and overarching forgiveness of God to all people.

The reconciliation accomplished in Christ by his paschal triumph is offered in the sacrament of reconciliation and also understood to be part of what is effected in the liturgy of the three days.[29] The liturgies of these three Lenten Sundays are invitations to continue what was begun on Ash Wednesday: communal reflection on divesting ourselves of what hinders from growing in the life of God in grace. As we pray in the Lenten prefaces:

> Each year you give us this . . . season
> when we prepare to celebrate the paschal mystery
> with mind and heart renewed.
> You give us a spirit of loving reverence for you, our Father,
> and of willing service to our neighbor.
> As we recall the great events that gave us new life in Christ,
> you bring the image of your Son to perfection within us.
>
> (Preface, Lent I)

Just as Christ obediently accepted death for our salvation (Phil 2:6–11, the second reading on Passion Sunday) so we too must freely accept the humiliation that comes from acknowledging weakness and sin. But with the sure hope that comes from our faith, shared in a deep and true way during Lent, we celebrate liturgy with a commitment that is ever stronger and lives which are more deeply imbued with the life of Christ. In faith and hope we pray:

> Though he was sinless, he suffered willingly for sinners.
> Though innocent, he accepted death to save the guilty.
> By his dying he has destroyed our sins.
> By his rising he has raised us up to holiness of life.
>
> (Preface, Passion Sunday)

Once again, the pattern established in Christ is shared by the faithful who celebrate these sacred mysteries, and who live what they celebrate.

The Fifty Days—*The General Norms* for the Liturgical Year and the Calendar state:

> The fifty days from Easter Sunday to Pentecost are celebrated in joyful exultation as one feast day, or better as one "great Sunday." ... The period of fifty sacred days ends on Pentecost Sunday. ... On the fortieth day after Easter the Ascension is celebrated. ... The weekdays after the Ascension until the Saturday before Pentecost inclusive are a preparation for the coming of the Holy Spirit. (nos. 22, 23, 25, 26)

During the "fifty days" the Sundays are called Sundays *of* Easter (as opposed to *after* Easter) and the end of the season is Pentecost (as opposed to the solemnity of the Ascension as had been the conventional understanding). While in popular piety the custom of celebrating Eucharist daily during Lent is greatly emphasized, it should be recalled that it is the season of Easter which is really the time for Eucharist. These days were the first occasions when the newly initiated received the Eucharist; hence, one of the terms associated with this season is "the paschal Communion." As the Rite of Christian Initiation of Adults becomes more fully implemented in pastoral practice the

Easter season may well grow toward reassuming its former status as a special time for the celebration of and reflection on Eucharist.

The Scripture readings for this time are from Acts and the Gospel of John (both on weekdays and Sundays) with the addition of semi-continuous readings from 1 Peter, 1 John and Revelation on Sundays. The absence of any reading from the Old Testament is significant in that the very selection of New Testament texts only indicates that Easter is truly the inauguration of the new covenant in Christ.[30]

This eucharistic emphasis is clearly seen in some of the prayers used in this season: "Father of love,/watch over your Church/and bring us to the glory of the resurrection/promised by this Easter sacrament" (prayer after Communion, Easter Sunday). The eschatological hope promised in Easter is also referred to in these prayers, especially toward the end of the season.

> God our Father,
> make us joyful in the ascension
>   of your Son Jesus Christ.
> May we follow him into the new creation,
> for his ascension is our glory and our hope.
> (Opening Prayer, Solemnity of the Ascension)

The celebration of the Eucharist and the eschatological glory of Christ are combined on Ascension Thursday as they were on Easter itself:

> Father,
> in this eucharist
> we touch the divine life you give to the world.
> Help us to follow Christ with love
> to eternal life where he is Lord for ever and ever.
> (Prayer After Communion)

> You believe that Jesus has taken his seat in majesty
> at the right hand of the Father.

May you have the joy of experiencing
that he is also with you to the end of time,
according to his promise.

(Solemn Blessing)

Christ, the mediator . . .
[the] judge of the world and Lord of all,
has passed beyond our sight,
not to abandon us but to be our hope.
Christ is the beginning, the head of the Church;
where he has gone, we hope to follow.

(Preface, Ascension I)

Once again, the emphasis in liturgical celebration is our present participation in the paschal mystery of Christ who is now gloriously risen from the dead. The season of Easter ends with the commemoration of the coming of the Spirit on the apostles, and as the Father's gift to the Church. What is celebrated in faith liturgically is now to be accomplished in the Church through mutual service. The task to be accomplished in the times between the resurrection of Jesus and the coming of the kingdom is to "live on in [his] love" and share his life with others. The solemnity of Pentecost brings this mission emphasis of resurrection faith into sharp focus. The Scripture texts of the Vigil Mass, for example, emphasize the uniqueness of the Spirit and the power of God dwelling in the Church as a result of the Spirit we call "Holy."

During this Vigil the gathered community listens to the account of the building of the tower of Babel (Gen 11:1–9) with the understanding that where humankind brought division, conflict and many languages, the Spirit brings clarity: "The Holy Spirit made known to all peoples the one true God, and created from . . . many languages . . . one voice to profess one faith" (Pentecost Preface). By the power of the Spirit, the vision of "dry bones" (Ez 37:1–14) is transcended by a new spirit of life and vitality. Seeing visions and dreaming dreams (Jl 3:1–5) is now possible in the Church by the enlivening presence of the Spirit, and it is the intercession and inspiration of the Spirit that helps us in our weakness, especially when we do not know how to pray (Rom 8:22–27). On Pentecost Sunday itself the event of the coming of the Spirit in tongues of fire with all hearing the word in their native language (Acts 2:1–11) is recalled. Where once humans plotted and tried to accomplish great things with the result that confusion reigned (Babel), now through the Spirit clarity and vision will be evident. An even more direct emphasis on mission occurs on this feast in the reading from Paul about many gifts from the one Spirit to build up and be for the good of the body, the Church (1 Cor 12:3–7, 12–13). The Gospel text speaks about mission and service where the Gospel of John (20:19–23) is used to remind contemporary congregations that "as the Father sent me so I send you" all because of the life of the Spirit in the Church. That the endowment of the Spirit is intrinsically connected to the paschal mystery is evident in the preface of the day: "Today you sent the Holy Spirit on those marked out to be your children by sharing the life of your only Son, and so you brought the paschal mystery to its completion."

The holiness we share as Christians comes from the one we call "Holy," and the mission which we share comes from the power and endowment which comes from that same Spirit. The solemn blessing summarizes and concretizes this emphasis when it states:

> This day the Father of light
> has enlightened the minds of the disciples
> by the outpouring of the Holy Spirit.
> May he bless you
> and give you the gifts of the Spirit forever. ℟.Amen.

> May that fire which hovered over the disciples
> as tongues of flame
> burn out all evil from your hearts
> and make them glow with pure light. ℟. Amen.

> God inspired speech in different tongues
> to proclaim one faith.

May he strengthen your faith
and fulfill your hope of seeing him face to face. ℟. Amen.

The tourist's view of time and the chronological approach to the Church year find little credence and support in the liturgy of the Easter season. From the blessing of ashes ("May they keep this Lenten season in preparation for the joy of Easter") through the celebration of the triduum itself ("By hearing his word and celebrating his mysteries, then we may be confident that we shall share his victory over death and live with him forever in God") to the solemnity of Pentecost ("and fulfill your hope of seeing him face to face") it is an eschatological notion that is stressed. What occurs in the liturgy is a present share and participation in the mystery of Christ which we will one day share in its fullness. The liturgy is where and how we meet the risen Lord in this world until we meet him in the kingdom forever.

THE INCARNATION CELEBRATIONS

Christmas—The *General Norms* for the Liturgical Year and the Calendar state:

> Next to the yearly celebration of the paschal mystery, the Church holds most sacred the memorial of Christ's birth and early manifestations. This is the purpose of the Christmas season.
>
> The Christmas season runs from evening prayer I of Christmas until the Sunday after Epiphany or after 6 January, inclusive.
>
> The Sunday falling after 6 January is the feast of the Baptism of the Lord. (nos. 32, 33, 38)

Just as the paschal celebrations are fixed in terms of the seasonal, cosmic changes in the universe, so it can be asserted that the choosing of the time for the commemoration of the incarnation of Christ is determined because of cosmic elements (although these are clearly different in terms of the position of the sun, as opposed to the moon at Easter, and a fixed date rather than the movable Sunday at Easter).[31] The commemoration of the coming among us of the Son of God was placed at the end of December from the fourth century because this was the time when the "birthday of the sun" was commemorated in primitive religions. Custom revered this time as "the day on which the shortening of the hours of daylight was reversed and the sun again began its ascendancy over darkness."[32]

What we celebrate liturgically at Christmas is not just the birth of Jesus, but the fact that "the Word became flesh and dwelt among us" (Jn 1:14). Part of the imagery used to emphasize this dwelling of God with us is reflected in the rising sun over the darkness that precedes; "the light shines in darkness and the darkness has not overcome it" (Jn 1:5). Christmas is about the interchange and irrevocable union between humanity and divinity established in Christ symbolically emphasized in the light/darkness motif evident in the liturgies on this day:

> Father,
> you make this holy night radiant
> with the splendor of Jesus Christ
>   our light.
> We welcome him as Lord, the true
>   light of the world.
>
> (Opening Prayer, Mass at Midnight)

> The Son of God scattered the darkness of
>   this world, and filled this holy night
>   with his glory.
> May the God of infinite goodness scatter
> the darkness of sin and brighten your
>   hearts with holiness.
>
> (Solemn Blessing, Christmas)

In addition to this emphasis on our sharing in the divine nature through the incarnation of Christ, the liturgy of Christmas also emphasizes what is the center of all liturgy: that our commemoration is of the paschal mystery as well as of the incarnation. At the liturgy we celebrate Eucharist to commemorate the incarnation at Christmas, and it is through the Eucharist that we share in the redemption won for us in Christ. Reflection on and the celebration of the incarnation mystery leads to reflection on the accomplishment of redemption realized in the liturgy. When Christians gather for Christmas liturgy they do not observe the incarnation of Christ from the outside. Rather, they share in the fullness of the mystery of the incarnation. Liturgically this includes his dying and rising as well. To cut off the incarnation from the paschal mystery would be to allow the chronological and dramatic aspects of the liturgical year to triumph. As it is celebrated, the liturgy makes us participants in the whole of Christ's life, death and resurrection. Hence, emphasis is also given in the liturgical prayers and readings on the title of Jesus as "Savior" because he will "save his people from their sins" (Mt 1:21).

> Father,
> the child born today is the Savior of the world.
> He made us your children.
> May he welcome us into your kingdom. . . .
> (Prayer After Communion, Christmas Day)

> God our Father,
> every year we rejoice
> as we look forward to this feast of our salvation.
> May we welcome Christ as our Redeemer
> and meet him with confidence when
> he comes to be our judge.
> (Opening Prayer, Vigil Mass of Christmas)

As is stated explicitly in the prayer over the gifts at the Vigil Mass:

> Lord,
> as we keep tonight the vigil of Christmas,
> may we celebrate this eucharist
> with greater joy than ever

> since it marks the beginning of our
>   redemption.

Despite the fact that many customs surrounding Christmas tend to emphasize the historicization of this feast, for example in the Christmas crèche, the liturgy once again orients us to the deeper realization of what is commemorated at Christmas: the Word becoming flesh and our sharing in divine life through Christ.

Advent—The *General Norms* for the Liturgical Year and the Calendar state:

> Advent has a twofold character: as a season to prepare for Christmas when Christ's first coming to us is remembered; as a season when that remembrance directs the mind and heart to await Christ's Second Coming at the end of time. Advent is thus a period for devout and joyful expectation. (no. 39)

While some conventional approaches to Advent would have us think only about the commemoration of the birth of Christ, the liturgy orients our attention to the second coming of Christ (especially in the first days of the season). Such an obvious eschatological orientation moves the overly historical and chronological understanding of Advent into the background. This is particularly helpful in underscoring the participation and commemoration aspects of all liturgical seasons. We do not put on blinders at the start of Advent and pretend as though the incarnation has not occurred. Rather, what we do is to evaluate the ways in which we have or have not been faithful to the Gospel he preached and the redemption he has accomplished. The notion of judgment at the second coming begins even before Advent starts (two weeks before on the Thirty-Third Sunday of the year) suggesting that there is an expectation mood within the liturgy as "ordinary time" ends and Advent begins. This unity of theme should offer reflection on ways in which the word and salvation accomplished in Christ are truly realities in our lives. This is all a far cry from preparing only for

the arrival of Jesus as a child in a manger bed at Christmas.
Because we are a people "between the times" we need to give
Advent its correct emphasis and due. We are a people between
the already and the not yet, between memory and fulfillment,
between Bethlehem and the second coming. Advent offers an
in-between time to pause, to reflect, to be still and to be quiet
before the power and majesty of God made visible in Christ. As
we pray in Advent:

> God of power and mercy,
> open our hearts in welcome.
> Remove the things that hinder us
>   from receiving Christ with joy,
> so that we may share his wisdom
> and become one with him
> when he comes in glory.
>
> (Opening Prayer, Second Sunday of Advent)

> When he humbled himself to come among us as a man,
> he fulfilled the plan you formed long ago
> and opened for us the way to salvation.
> Now we watch for the day,
> hoping that the salvation promised us will be ours
> when Christ our Lord will come again in his glory.
>
> (Preface, Advent I)

As the Advent season comes to a close the liturgy presents the
example of Mary as one who performed God's will willingly and
fully. On the Fourth Sunday of Advent we pray that like Mary we
too might put our lives at the service of Christ and his kingdom:

> Father, all-powerful God,
> your eternal Word took flesh on our earth
> when the Virgin Mary placed her life
> at the service of your plan.
> Lift our minds in watchful hope
> to hear the voice which announces his glory
> and open our minds to receive the Spirit
> who prepares us for his coming.
>
> (Alternative Opening Prayer)

But even on this day, the redemption that was able to be accomplished because of the incarnation is not forgotten:

> Lord,
> fill our hearts with your love,
> and as you revealed to us by an angel
> the coming of your Son as man,
> so lead us through his suffering and death
> to the glory of his resurrection.
>
> (Opening Prayer)

Advent is a time of quiet and restrained joy, a time of confidence and hope in the coming of Christ, and of self-evaluation and judgment as to the ways we have been faithful to the kingdom he inaugurated by his human birth.

Christmas Season—With the Christmas season extending to the commemoration of the baptism of the Lord we realize that through the liturgy we do not observe the events of the first days of the life of Christ so much as we enter into the inauguration of his mission at the epiphany and at his baptism. The ramifications of the event of the incarnation are at stake in the celebration of all Christmas liturgy. On the Sunday after Christmas, the feast of the Holy Family, the context of the incarnation mystery is to be remembered lest this day become a feast in honor of our human families. The preface to be used this day is from those of Christmas, a clear indication of how the context is to be set by Christmas itself. The commemoration of January 1 as the Solemnity of Mary Mother of God reiterates the theology of this season liturgically by noting the redemption:

> God our Father,
> we celebrate at this season
> the beginning of our salvation.
> On this feast of Mary, the Mother of God,
> we ask that our salvation
> will be brought to its fulfillment.
>
> (Prayer Over the Gifts)

On the solemnity of the Epiphany the fullness of the incarnation is recalled and its purpose is reiterated:

> God has called you out of darkness,
> into his wonderful light.
> May you experience his kindness and blessings,
> and be strong in faith, in hope, and in love. ℟. Amen.
>
> Because you are followers of Christ,
> who appeared on this day as a light shining in the darkness,
> may he make you a light to all your sisters and brothers.
> ℟. Amen.
>
> The wise men followed the star,
> and found Christ who is light from light.
> May you too find the Lord
> when your pilgrimage is ended. ℟. Amen.
>
> (Solemn Blessing, Epiphany)

That the incarnation celebration requires a mission dimension is evident in a subtle way throughout the season in the liturgical prayers. Yet on the feast of the Baptism of our Lord this mission and witness emphasis takes on greater significance.[33] Just as Christ was baptized to inaugurate his earthly ministry, so we have been baptized (and who renew our baptismal vows at the Eucharist) continue the work of his ministry on earth.

> Almighty, eternal God,
> when the Spirit descended upon Jesus
> at his baptism in the Jordan,
> you revealed him as your own beloved Son.
> Keep us, your children born of water and the Spirit,
> faithful to our calling.
>
> (Opening Prayer)
>
> Your Spirit was seen as a dove,
> revealing Jesus as your servant,
> and anointing him with joy as the Christ,

sent to bring to the poor
the good news of salvation.

(Preface, Baptism of the Lord)

The season of Christmas offers us a time to share as fully as we can in the mystery of God's love made manifest in the birth and mission of Christ. Just as the word became flesh so that through the eyes of faith we might see God made visible, so too, in the incarnation celebrations, we are to witness to the enduring power of this word so that others might see in us the visible reality of God-with-us, the Emmanuel.

Indeed, a proper understanding and appreciation of the liturgical year can help us to enter into what is celebrated in the liturgy and what feasts and seasons are all about.

Reflecting the journey of the Redeemer (which is as well that of his Church), the cycle of yearly festivals bears what memory has preserved towards the central Paschal Mystery, and from that, empowered by the Spirit, hope reaches out to the end. And in that end is our beginning.[34]

The means for this to be accomplished is the yearly round of feasts and seasons (cyclical time) which are used to commemorate what was done once-for-all in Christ as we look for his second coming (linear time). The liturgy does not take us out of the chronological time of our lives and present histories so much as it aims at disclosing in moments of sacred time what is perennially available for us in Christ. In and through liturgy we participate in and truly share in the resurrection—a reality won because of Christ's obedient life and death. What we bring to liturgy are the humiliations and disobediences of our lives so that in Christ they may be transformed and healed once more. The setting for all this to be accomplished is the liturgy; the liturgical year is what offers this to us for our sharing and indentification year after year.

NOTES

1. See Part Two, Chapter Six, section on "Liturgical Memorial."

2. A. Nocent, *The Liturgical Year*, Vol. One, pp. 16–17.

3. See Part Two, Chapter Six, section on "Participation Through Liturgy."

4. See Part Two, Chapter Seven, section on "Participation Through Ritual."

5. While the notion of a "Church year" has a certain conventional precedent and popularity, it must be asserted that the notion of the "liturgical year" with the gathering together of feasts and seasons is a preferable way of describing what is at stake here. The notion of a "Church year" could lead to the unfounded assumption that the year is clearly divisible into equal sections and parts. The liturgical year is made up of the merging of pre-existing feasts and seasons into an annual cycle for celebration.

6. See, among others, L. Mitchell, *The Meaning of Ritual* and Mircea Eliade, *Cosmos and History. The Myth of the Eternal Return* (New York: Harper Torchbooks, 1959).

7. Thomas Talley, "A Christian Heortology," in *The Times of Celebration*, Concilium, 142, (New York: Seabury, 1981) pp. 14–15.

8. In some writing on the subject of the biblical notion of time, "cyclical" and "linear" time are set in opposition. The intent here is to nuance this approach by showing how liturgical celebration depends on both understandings of time.

9. See Part Two, Chapter Seven, section on "Rhythm of Liturgical Ritual" for a description of daily and weekly ritual observances.

10. M. Eliade, *Cosmos and History*, p. 104.

11. Just as the intent of joining cyclical and linear notions of time is to nuance some conventional understandings, so too this section is intended to join what are more usually separated in descriptions of liturgy.

12. Joseph Martos, *Doors to the Sacred* (Garden City: Doubleday, 1981) pp. 17–18.

13. Marianne Micks, *The Future Present,* p. 45.

14. See Part Two, Chapter Six, sections on "Participation Through Liturgy" and "To 'Bless' God."

15. Milton J. Crumm, "Our Approach to the Church Year: Chronological or Eschatological?" *Worship* 51 (January 1977) 24.

16. *Ibid.*

17. *Ibid.,* 24–25.

18. Adrien Nocent, "Liturgical Catechesis of the Christian Year," *Worship* 51 (November 1977) 497–498.

19. Pope Paul VI, *Motu Proprio* on the Calendar, *Sacramentary* p. 61.

20. See Patrick Regan, "The Three Days and the Forty Days," *Worship* 54 (January 1980) 2–18, and Gabe Huck, *The Three Days* (Chicago: Liturgy Training Publications, 1981).

21. Taken from the decree *Maxima Redemptionis nostrae mysteria,* cited in G. Braso, *Liturgy and Spirituality,* p. 23.

22. Anscar Chupungco, "Liturgical Feasts and the Seasons of the Year," *The Times of Celebration,* p. 32.

23. This brief reflection on the Easter Vigil is not to suggest that it is not without structural flaws. See, among others, Seamus Ryan, "The Easter Vigil: An Alternative Model?" *The Furrow* 25 (May 1974) 239–245.

24. See Part Two, Chapter Six, section on "To 'Bless' God" quoting Exodus 15.

25. See Part Two, Chapter Six, section on "To 'Bless' God" quoting the blessing prayer text.

26. *RCIA,* no. 4: "The initiation of catechumens takes place step by step in the midst of the community of the faithful. Together with the catechumens, the faithful reflect upon the value of the paschal mystery, renew their own conversion, and by their example lead the catechumens to obey the Holy Spirit more generously."

27. "Lord, Who Throughout These Forty Days," *Worship* II, no. 171.

28. See *Sacramentary,* pp. 826–829 for the prayers for the scrutinies held on the Third, Fourth and Fifth Sundays of Lent. See *RCIA,* nos. 154–180.

29. The liturgy of Holy Thursday was traditionally associated with the reconciliation of penitents who had been enrolled in an "order of penitents" during Lent. The process and structure paralleled in some ways that of adult initiation.

30. *Lectionary for Mass, Introduction,* no. 100, p. 39.

31. A. Chupungco, "Liturgical Feasts and the Seasons of the Year," pp. 31–33.

32. Thomas Talley, "A Christian Heortology," p. 18.

33. See Part Three, Chapter Twelve, section on "The Justice of God and the Mission of Christ."

34. Thomas Talley, "A Christian Heortology," p. 18.

Chapter Nine
TRINITARIAN PRAYER

To speak of the content of liturgical prayer is to speak about ways of addressing and "naming" God. From the revelation of God to Moses in the Book of Exodus through the collection of songprayers in the Book of Psalms in the Old Testament, to the full manifestation of the "name" of God in Jesus Christ in the New Testament, biblical authors have been engaged in the necessary but difficult task of finding the correct, or at least the most appropriate names for God. The liturgy addresses God and asks that God intercede on behalf of the community. It offers many images and likenesses for God, among which are those that comprise the Trinity: "three Persons equal in majesty, undivided in splendor, yet one Lord, one God" (Preface of the Holy Trinity).

It is the purpose of this chapter to explore the structure and content of liturgical prayer as it invokes the many names and images of God. It concerns the relationship of biblical revelation and liturgical texts ("naming God"), the specific invocation of the Trinity in liturgical prayer, the pre-eminence given to Christ as mediator in the liturgy, the role of the Spirit in the experience of liturgical prayer, and some comments on what should be borne in mind when composing prayers for the liturgy.

NAMING GOD

When we speak of "naming God" in the liturgy we are speaking about a task that is somewhat different from using names for God in theological discourse. To name God in liturgy is to call on God in the experience of "encounter, confrontation, recognition, [which] is full of the awed sense of the other."[1]

> Liturgy is not the business of taking the terms of theology and trying to make them concrete, memorable, and vivid in popular worship. Rather, liturgical terms tend to be pretheological, preconceptual. They stem from immediate grasp, immediate presentation of that which theology is all about.[2]

One way of stating the issue is that liturgical language is direct, it addresses God in the context of faith experienced by communities which gather to encounter God through the language and forms of worship. Theology, on the other hand, speaks about God, seeks to explore the meaning of the reality of God in concepts and terms that attempt to make the mystery of God understandable (but never manageable or without mystery). The language of liturgy, therefore, can be said to form part of the foundation for the language of theology.[3]

The relationship between revealed (biblical) notions of God and the act of naming God in liturgy is clear in that the terms and concepts used in common prayer are most usually derived from the Bible. The liturgical texts draw inspiration and guidance from the many images and likenesses of God revealed in the Scriptures. In addition, the names used in the liturgy reflect the relationship established between God and redeemed humanity, a relationship forged by the initiative of God and the response of the community. Closely allied with this understanding of our relationship with this named God in worship is the notion that liturgical speaking of God is often accomplished in images that speak of transformation or of the possibility of our being transformed in and through the God named, worshiped and adored in liturgy.

The origin and author of all transformation, of the possibility of changed states of being (in relationship with each other and with the divine) is God, who through Christ has changed our human lives and the way we view and experience all of life itself.

> Christianity is a redemptive faith. It does not accept what is. The present order is a flawed, alienated order to which something must happen. The gospel says that the decisive thing that needs to happen has happened. Transformation images contrast an old condition with a new.

> The Christian community is meant to be a community of the transformed. Its struggle—in language and in life—is to make the new apprehensible, to find ways of holding before itself and the world something that eye has not seen, nor ear heard, nor has entered the human heart.[4]

At liturgy we acknowledge and thank God for life and love in and through Christ. We pray that this sanctifying power and grace be made real and new in the present, that we might deepen our experience of this redemptive love on earth as we seek to come to know it fully in the kingdom. We name God, we remember all that God has done and continues to do, and we beseech this same God to act to transform us and our world as has already happened in Christ. (The context for this prayer is apparent in the structure of the "blessing prayer" noted above.[5]) The God who transformed all creation is besought to transform our lives in the here and now. In the act of naming God we use image and metaphor freely and fully.

> It is instructive to see how the psalms apply metaphors to the name of God. In the Psalter there are over forty nouns used as epithets for God. Some are impersonal objects: shade, shield, refuge, rock, tower, song, fortress. Others are abstract nouns: hope, glory, strength. God is said to be a hiding place, to be an avenger. King, rock and refuge are the three most common metaphors. It is thus good biblical tradition to be free and rich with metaphors in descriptions of God, some of which are as mundane as cup and tower and light.[6]

The images, metaphors and names for God found in some of the classic psalms from the liturgy of the hours are instructive. In Psalm 141 (Sunday Evening Prayer I) we pray:

I have called to you, Lord; hasten to help me!
To you, Lord, my eyes are turned:
in you I take refuge; save my soul!

In Psalm 63 (Sunday Morning Prayer I) we pray:

O God, you are my God, for you I long;
for you my soul is thirsting.
My body pines for you
like a dry, weary land without water.

On you I muse through the night
for you have been my help;
in the shadow of your wings I rejoice.
My soul clings to you:
your right hand holds me fast.

In Psalm 4 (Sunday Night Prayer) we pray:

When I call, answer me, O God of justice;
from anguish you released me; have mercy and hear me!

It is the Lord who grants favors to those whom he loves;
the Lord hears me whenever I call him.

Let the light of your face shine on us, O Lord.
You have put into my heart a greater joy
than they have from abundance of corn and new wine.
I will lie down in peace and sleep comes at once
for you alone, Lord, make me dwell in safety.

The God of relationship is addressed clearly through these
texts: "my" Lord, "my" God; and from the world and all it
offers including "abundance of food and drink" (Ps 4) it is the
Lord whose power, love and providence offers us the greatest
joy. The God prayed to is the God revealed in the Scriptures as
the God of relationship and transformation. He is not addressed
in the abstract or in the language of speculative theology.
    The God addressed in New Testament canticles is a God

made real through the person of Jesus. The face put on God through Christ offers us many new images and metaphors for God:

> Jesus did not deem equality with God
> something to be grasped at.
> . . . being born in the likeness of men.
> God highly exalted him
> and bestowed on him the name
> above every other name.
> So that at Jesus' name
> every knee must bend
> in the heavens, on the earth,
> and under the earth,
> and every tongue proclaim
> to the glory of God the Father:
> Jesus Christ is Lord! (Phil 2:6–11)
>
> (Saturday Evening Prayer I)

> Praised be the God and Father
> of our Lord Jesus Christ
> who has bestowed on us in Christ
> every spiritual blessing.
>
> God has given us the wisdom
> to understand fully the mystery,
> the plan he was pleased
> to decree in Christ. (Eph 1:3)
>
> (Monday Evening Prayer)

> Worthy is the Lamb that was slain
> to receive power and riches,
> wisdom and strength,
> honor and glory and praise. (Rev 4:11)
>
> (Tuesday Evening Prayer)

The God named and prayed to is a God of relationship who transforms all of life and all love. In Christ, God is addressed and simultaneously acclaimed as redeemer, mediator, creator and reconciler. He descends from heaven to earth, he dies, is made alive again and is exalted, enthroned over all cosmic powers.[7] The prayers offered to God in Christ are spoken in images and metaphors which describe the person, mission and present sustaining love of Christ. They image the God of transformation and redemption. The God of biblical revelation and liturgical prayer (as derived from the Scriptures) is "God for us," the God who reveals many images and examples of salvation and transformation in the history we call salvation. From the revelation of the name of God in the Book of Exodus, the naming involves the conviction on our part that this is a God who acts and sustains: "I shall be there as who I ám shall I be there."[8] The God of the Scriptures is a God who is present and in being present is active. As the fullness of the mystery of God, Jesus reveals the *name* of God. "Father . . . I have made your name known to those you gave me out of the world" (Jn 17:6); "To them I have revealed your name, and I will continue to reveal it so that your love for me may live in them, and I may live in them" (Jn 17:26).

In liturgical usage the biblical names for God dominate. The primary biblical names for God—*Deus, Domine,* and *Pater*—are most often used with the adjective "almighty" (and ever-living) God, Lord and Father. "The vast majority of liturgical prayers address God by his biblically revealed names, some prayers and the ordinary hymns use biblical epithets like King and Lamb, proper hymns become more metaphorical, and private prayers can be excessively poetic."[9] The name "Lord" is the one most commonly used in liturgical texts, with "Father, all-powerful and ever-living God" the classical introduction to the eucharistic prayer (*Domine, sancte Pater, omnipotens aeternae Deus*). In proper prefaces, the rest of the eucharistic prayer, and in liturgical hymns biblical metaphors appear: Redeemer, Word, Lamb, Most High, King.[10] Examples of "naming God" at the beginning of the prayers in liturgy include: Father,[11] Lord, almighty Father, Merciful Father, God our Father, Almighty and ever-living God, and Father in heaven (opening prayers), God of mercy, Lord, Father, God our Father, and Lord our God (prayer over the gifts), and Lord God, God our Father, and Father of love and mercy (prayer after Communion). It is often the case that in the sacramental rituals the naming of God at the beginning of prayers involves some aspect of God's power and might invoked in the sacrament: God the Father of mercies (penance, absolution formula), Almighty and merciful God (penance, prayer of thanksgiving), Lord God, loving Father, you bring healing to the sick (anointing of the sick, blessing of oil), and Lord our Redeemer (anointing of the sick, final prayer).

The naming of God at liturgy relies heavily on the biblical evidence of God's self-revelation through Jesus, and the usage often combines metaphors and descriptions with titles of God. The variety provided in biblical sources is reflected in the variety used in liturgical language. Clearly, just as no single name or metaphor or attribute used to acclaim God was sufficient for the authors of the Scriptures, so no single name for God covers the field of liturgical usage and practice. The variety expressed biblically inspires the variety evidenced in liturgical practice. But always in liturgical practice the naming of God is an act of acclamation and an invitation to direct encounter with God in prayer.

INVOCATION OF THE TRINITY

The joining together of names for God into the explicit invocation of the Trinity is the result of the evolution of both theology and the liturgy. While the earliest evidence for both seems to suggest that naming God and naming Christ were the first evidences involving God language, it was not long afterward that invocation of the three persons in God became common in Christian worship. But in clear contrast to what is often assumed about theological reflection and speculation about the Trinity, that this is a dry and wholly academic approach to God (with the understanding that this need not necessarily be the case), clearly in the liturgy it is the dynamic and active images of the triune God which dominate. The selection of Scripture passages for Trinity Sunday reveal the biblical data about the God Christians have come to worship as triune: the revelation of God as Lord to Moses (Ex 34:8), God's deep love released in sending his Son as Lord (Jn 3:16) whose sacrifice established and accomplished redemption and justification (Rom 5:1). The Spirit of truth is promised to guide the Church to all truth (Jn 16:13) especially as it seeks to live in accord with the wisdom of God (Prov 8:22); it is reliance on this same Spirit that helps us in our weakness, inspires our prayer (Rom 8:15) and aids us in accomplishing the mission of teaching and evangelizing all nations in the name of Father, Son and Spirit (Mt 28:19–20).[12] This dynamism and presence of God with us is noted in the prayers carefully phrased and chosen for use at the liturgy this day:

> Father,
> you sent your Word to bring us truth
> and your Spirit to make us holy.
> Through them we come to know
> the mystery of your life.
> Help us to worship you, one God
> in three Persons,
> by proclaiming and living our faith
> in you.
>
> (Opening Prayer)

That the invocation of the Trinity is an important part of the liturgy is seen in the classical conclusion to many liturgical prayers: "We ask this through our Lord Jesus Christ your Son, who lives and reigns with you and the Holy Spirit, one God, for ever and ever."[13] What is contained here is the acclamation of Christ as mediator and the implication that it is through Christ's instrumentality that we come to know the Father. The role of the Spirit operative here is actually twofold: it is the very person of God's Spirit united with the other persons to be God, and it is in the communion established between God and the Church (effected by the Spirit) that we are granted access to God in the liturgy. The same dynamism and power of God active in the Scriptures is evidenced here in this formula for concluding liturgical prayer.

In addition, some liturgies begin with an invocation of the Trinity in words and with a sign of the cross to accompany it. This wedding of text and gesture reminds us that the liturgy is not just words and texts; it is rather, and in fact more appropriately, gestural speech and symbolic action.[14] Hence, the merging of invoking the Trinity and the sign of the paschal mystery of Christ is itself significant. In liturgical art this merging of Trinity and paschal mystery is often pictured in images of the crucified Christ with God the Father and the Holy Spirit pictured above (or alongside) Christ. The "right hand of the Lord has struck with power" is used in Christian liturgy to refer to God's striking out sin and death through Christ; we experience this triumph in and through the liturgy which is often begun "In the name of the Father and of the Son and of the Holy Spirit."[15] We invoke the power of God as we begin the liturgy, which power and might is operative in gathering the community together and is active throughout the experience of common liturgical prayer.

That the power and presence of the Trinity is the basis of our sacramental celebrations is clear in the rite of baptism because initiation occurs through the invocation of Father, Son and Spirit. The minister baptizes only because of the active presence of the Trinity operative in this moment of encounter and grace. While in the Roman rite the direct statement "I baptize you" is used, a former and more traditional usage sheds greater light on the minister's role at baptism and at all liturgical prayer. This traditional formula states: "[Name] is baptized in the name of the Father, and of the Son, and of the Holy Spirit."[16] The use of the passive voice is deliberate because it invokes and expresses what is always occurring in sacraments— the power and activity of the Trinity. It is God who does the baptizing through the instrumentality of the minister and community. The gathered community provides the context for the liturgy and the minister acts both in the person of Christ and in the person of the Church.[17] But over all it is God who is active— Father, Son and Spirit—hence the invocation of the Trinity.

In the rite of penance it is the Trinity that is invoked in the formula for absolution,[18] which invocation is accompanied with the sign of the cross and/or the imposition of hands.[19] Once again it is the association of invoking the Trinity and the sign of the cross to accompany it that offers us the union of text and gesture in the liturgy. After couples profess their marriage vows they offer each other blessed rings, and as they place it on the other's finger (again words and gesture) they state "[Name], take this ring as a sign of my love and fidelity. In the name of the Father, and of the Son and of the Holy Spirit."

That invoking the names of God, Father, Son and Spirit seems to be important in all liturgy (not just sacraments) is seen in the fact that fairly early in the evolution of the liturgy of the hours the (Old Testament) psalms were ended with the doxology. In addition the *Benedictus* and *Magnificat* were also concluded with the doxology—an explicit Trinitarian reference. (These latter were accompanied with the sign of the cross to begin the canticle and the posture of standing since these New Testament canticles were specifically Christian additions to the Jewish liturgy of the word from which the hours evolved.[20]) The present text of the doxology, however, is a later development, and one which loses something of the dynamism and richness evident in the original: "Glory to the Father, through the Son, in the Holy Spirit."[21] The dynamism of the worship of the present community offered through Christ to the Father is more clearly stated here than in "Glory be to the Father and to the Son . . ." In addition, the notion of "unity in the Spirit" referring to the unity of the community (noted above with regard to the conclusion to the opening prayer at the Eucharist) is evident in the earlier usage but is not found in the more developed form "and to the Holy Spirit." Yet, what does perdure in both forms is the emphasis on God in three persons rather than the images of God either from the Old Testament (psalms and Old Testament canticles) or from an unthematized use of the New Testament (Father and Christ specifically).

In addition to the explicit invocation of the Trinity to begin and end liturgical prayers is the usage whereby a more subtle reference to the Trinity is apparent. In the prayer used for blessing water at baptism we pray:

> Father,
> look now with love upon your Church
> and unseal for it the fountain of baptism.
> By the power of the Spirit

give to the water of this font
the grace of your Son.

(as the celebrant touches the water with his hand he prays)
We ask you, Father, with your Son
to send the Holy Spirit upon the water of this font.
                    (Rite of Christian Initiation of Adults)[22]

Once again, it is interesting to note the close association of word and gesture: of invoking the Trinity and touching the water. In the rite of baptism for children the text of the exorcism states:

Almighty and ever-living God,
you sent your only Son into the world
to cast out the power of Satan, spirit of evil,
to rescue [us] from the kingdom of darkness,
and bring [us] into the splendor of your kingdom of light.
We pray for these children:
set them free from original sin,
make them temples of your glory,
and send your Holy Spirit to dwell within them.
                    (Rite of Baptism for Several Children)

In the rite of anointing of the sick the following thanksgiving prayer (invoking the Trinity) is used when the oil has already been blessed:

Praise to you, God, the almighty Father.
You sent your Son to live among us
and bring us salvation.

℟. Blessed be God who heals us in Christ.

Praise to you, God, the only-begotten Son.
You humbled yourself to share in our humanity
and you heal our infirmities. ℟.

Praise to you, God, the Holy Spirit, the Consoler.
Your unfailing power gives us strength
in our bodily weakness. ℟.

God of mercy,
ease the sufferings and comfort the weakness of your servant N.,
whom the Church anoints with this holy oil.
We ask this through Christ our Lord.
℟. Amen.

It is clear that in liturgical prayer the three persons in God are invoked in order that worshipers might enter into an experience of their life at liturgy. Whether as explicit as the sign of the cross and naming the three persons together or more subtle in naming the Trinity in different parts of the prayer, it is most often the case that liturgical prayer relies on the power and presence of the Trinity:

Father, all-powerful and ever living God,
we do well always and everywhere to give you thanks.
We joyfully proclaim our faith
in the mystery of your Godhead.
You have revealed your glory
as the glory also of your Son
and of the Holy Spirit:
three Persons equal in majesty,
undivided in splendor,
yet one Lord, one God,
ever to be adored in your everlasting glory.

(Preface, Holy Trinity)

CHRIST AS MEDIATOR

Just as there is a close connection between the invocation of the Trinity and the sign of the cross in liturgical practice, so also there is a close connection between the invocation of the persons in God and the mediatorship of Christ in liturgical prayer. In his ground-breaking and important study on *The Place of Christ in Liturgical Prayer*,[23] Joseph Jungmann established the traditional pattern of prayer addressed to the Father and mediated through Christ.[24] This re-emphasis on Christ as mediator is evidenced in the name of Pius XII's encyclical *Mediator Dei*, a document that was most significant in the liturgical movement

in this century. That the paschal mystery is central to an understanding of liturgical prayer is an essential underpinning for the
celebration of and appreciation of what happens at liturgy. The
fact that this was not well understood or emphasized is clear
from the private devotions which people used to pray during the
liturgy. Many were addressed to Mary and other saints asking
their intercession with Christ. The notion of "all to Jesus
through Mary" was very common. Christ was so distant that
faith communities needed more approachable channels for
grace and sanctification. There were times in the history of the
liturgy when the cult of the saints came to overshadow (in
popular devotion) the notion of Christ as center and mediator of
the new covenant.

The doxology at the end of the eucharistic prayer (at least
from the middle of the second century onward)[25] was a prime
example of how important the mediation of Christ was:
"Through him, with him, in him, in the unity of the Holy Spirit,
all glory and honor is yours, almighty Father, for ever and ever.
Amen." The restoration of this doxology to a place of emphasis
requiring the community's response evidences a restoration of
the importance of the place of Christ's mediatorship in liturgical
prayer.

In addition to this central text there is the conclusion to
other prayers of the liturgy: "Grant this in the name of Jesus the
Lord" and "Grant this through Christ our Lord."[26] (By custom
this is the more usual way to conclude liturgical prayer, the
invocation of the Trinity being saved for the opening prayer
alone.)

The mediatorship of Christ is clear from the text and structure of the eucharistic prayers, beginning with the traditional
Roman canon. After the preface acclamation the prayer begins:
"We come to you, Father, with praise and thanksgiving, through
Jesus Christ your Son./ Through him we ask you . . ." The other
eucharistic prayers follow this precedent and foundation by
stating: "Father, it is our duty and our salvation,/ always and
everywhere/to give you thanks/through your beloved Son, Jesus
Christ" (Preface, Second Eucharistic Prayer). In the section
following the *Sanctus* the third eucharistic prayer states: "Father,

you are holy indeed,/ and all creation rightly gives you praise./ All life, all holiness comes from you/ through your Son, Jesus Christ our Lord,/ by the working of the Holy Spirit." In the words of the fourth eucharistic prayer: "Father, you so loved the world/that in the fullness of time you sent your only Son to be our Savior." In addition, the memorial prayers (after the words of institution) speak of the centrality of Christ's death and resurrection in God's plan for our salvation, redemption and sanctification.

In the prayer for the consecration of chrism (from the liturgy of Holy Thursday morning) we pray:

> And so, Father, we ask you to bless this oil you have created.
> Fill it with the power of your Holy Spirit
> through Christ your Son.
> It is from him that chrism takes its name.

In the prayer for blessing the oil used at the liturgy of anointing of the sick it states:

> Lord God, loving Father,
> you bring healing to the sick
> through your Son Jesus Christ.
> Father, may this oil be blessed for our use
> in the name of our Lord Jesus Christ
> who lives and reigns with you for ever and ever.

Hence, the important place of Christ in liturgical prayer should be underscored and emphasized when understanding the important place of the Trinity in the liturgy. The Lord Jesus Christ is the one who reveals to us who God is and it is through Christ that we worship the Father. Jesus is the name of God, the fullness of the revelation of God. As we pray in the acclamation in the eucharistic prayer: "Blessed is he who comes in the name of the Lord. Hosannah in the highest." Jesus does come as the *name* of the Lord God; and as Lord God he himself continues as mediator for us with the Father. All liturgical prayer is through, with and in him.

THE HOLY SPIRIT

It is often (correctly) asserted that Western liturgy and theology when compared with that of the Eastern tradition is weak on emphasizing the role of the Holy Spirit in the life and worship of the Church. It is for this reason most especially that the traditional and newly-restored evidences of the role of the Spirit in liturgical prayer are all the more important and significant. The notion of the Christian community as the place where the Spirit of God dwells is as traditional as the New Testament foundations about charisms in the Church as a result of the action of the Spirit and as classical as the understanding of liturgical prayer wherein the "unity of the Holy Spirit" is experienced in the worshiping community, the Church at prayer. One of the most dominant motifs of the epiclesis prayer is precisely how the Spirit is asked to work in the community at liturgy—to unify what can so often be divided, the Church of God on earth. The unity sought for is asked of the Holy Spirit.

The recent revision of the liturgy in the Roman Catholic Church has been careful in restoring the role of the Holy Spirit to a place of prominence as the source of all our prayer and of our attempts to grow in holiness. The traditional understanding of the Spirit as the person of God who makes holy and unites is clearly exemplified in the new eucharistic prayers in the liturgy. Once again it is clear that the heritage of the East is stronger on the role of the Spirit in blessing and uniting the community as the Church of God. The role of the Spirit in blessing is so central to the Eastern understanding of liturgy that it is understood to consecrate bread and wine in the same way that conventional Western interpretations regard the words of institution in the eucharistic prayer as consecratory.[27] Interestingly, the emphasis on the epiclesis as consecratory would coincide with the understanding of the important active role of the Spirit in the liturgy. This is to suggest that the text spoken by the presider "May your Spirit come" is a proper invocation. God is asked to *send* the Spirit; the coming of the Spirit is not induced or produced by our efforts. As always, what we do by inviting the power of God to operate in the liturgy is to beseech God and to pray. Hence, the subjunctive is a helpful caution against some understandings which would be too imperative and demanding (of God!). This notion of transformation of the elements is certainly a welcome addition to and expansion of our conventional understanding of "consecration." The texts of the eucharistic prayers themselves attest to the important role the Spirit plays in blessing bread and wine and in unifying the community:[28]

> Let your Spirit come upon these gifts to make them holy,
> so that they may become for us
> the body and blood of our Lord, Jesus Christ. . . .
>
> May all of us who share in the body and blood of Christ
> be brought together in unity by the Holy Spirit.
>
> (Eucharistic Prayer II)[29]

The third and fourth eucharistic prayers offer fuller texts:

> We ask you to make [these gifts] holy by the power of your
>   Spirit,
> that they may become the body and blood
> of your Son, our Lord Jesus Christ,
> at whose command we celebrate this eucharist. . . .
>
> Grant that we, who are nourished by his body and blood,
> may be filled with his Holy Spirit,
> and become one body, one spirit in Christ.
>
> (Eucharistic Prayer III)
>
> Father, may this Holy Spirit sanctify these offerings.
> Let them become the body and blood of Jesus Christ our Lord
> as we celebrate the great mystery
> which he left us as an everlasting covenant. . . .
>
> Lord, look upon this sacrifice which you have given to your
>   Church;
> and by your Holy Spirit, gather all who share this bread and
>   wine
> into the one body of Christ, a living sacrifice of praise.
>
> (Eucharistic Prayer IV)

Two other examples of the epiclesis in the eucharistic prayers now in use in the Roman rite are from those for children and for reconciliation:

God our Father,
we now ask you
to send your Holy Spirit
to change these gifts of bread and wine
into the body and blood
of Jesus Christ, our Lord. . . .

Lord our God,
listen to our prayer.
Send the Holy Spirit
to all of us who share in this meal.
May this Spirit bring us closer together
in the family of the Church,
with N., our pope,
N., our bishop,
all other bishops,
and all who serve your people.
                    (Eucharistic Prayer for Masses with Children II)

Look with kindness on your people
gathered here before you:
send forth the power of your Spirit
so that these gifts may become for us
the body and blood of your beloved Son, Jesus the Christ,
in whom we have become your sons and daughters.

Father,
look with love
on those you have called
to share in the one sacrifice of Christ.
By the power of your Holy Spirit
make them one body,
healed of all division.
                    (Eucharistic Prayer for Masses of Reconciliation I)

While some have argued that the use of a "split epiclesis" (that is, separating blessing and unifying functions) in the new eucharistic prayers makes for a cumbersome separation of roles for the Spirit into two sections of the prayer,[30] nonetheless, it must be affirmed that the defect of the Roman canon with no explicit invocation of the Spirit has been clearly corrected in the re-formed eucharistic liturgy. The role of the Spirit in the eucharistic liturgy is clearly expressed and underscored.

In the consecratory prayer for chrism, the role of the Spirit is explicitated and the effect of baptism in water and the Holy Spirit is looked to in this prayer of blessing:

> Make this chrism a sign of life and salvation
> for those who are to be born again in the waters of baptism.
> Wash away the evil they have inherited from sinful Adam,
> and when they are anointed with this holy oil
> make them temples of your glory,
> radiant with the goodness of life
> that has its source in you.
> Through this sign of chrism
> grant them royal, priestly, and prophetic honor,
> and clothe them with incorruption.
> Let this be indeed the chrism of salvation
> for those who will be born again of water and the Holy Spirit.
> May they come to share eternal life in the glory of your
>   kingdom.[31]

The role of the Spirit in the sacrament of the anointing of the sick is made explicit in the text of the prayer used to bless the oil used for the anointing:

> Lord God, loving Father,
> you bring healing to the sick
> through your Son Jesus Christ.
> Hear us as we pray to you in faith,
> and send the Holy Spirit, [our] Helper and Friend,
> upon this oil, which nature has provided
> to serve the needs of [all].
> May your blessing
> come upon all who are anointed with this oil,
> that they may be freed from pain and illness
> and made well again in body, mind, and soul.

After the anointing of the sick, the liturgy adds a prayer which asks that the Lord Jesus, "by the power of the Holy Spirit," ease the sufferings of the sick, make them well again in mind and body, grant them full health and so be restored to service in the Lord.[32]

The God invoked in the Christian liturgy and the God prayed to in common prayer is the triune God. The role of the Spirit we call "holy" is to make us grow in the very holiness of God; the liturgy is an important and privileged time for sharing in this life with God through the Holy Spirit.

CREATIVITY IN LITURGICAL PRAYER

The issue of what constitutes appropriate liturgical language is a topic that is of great concern in the Church today as a result of the translations of the revised rites now in use in the Christian churches.[33] Without wanting to either oversimplify this complex issue or to demean its importance by giving it scant attention, it would be important to note that appropriate liturgical language in our day ought to be solemn and inspiring, as well as personal and familiar.

> Yet, liturgy does require a heightened speech. . . .The word requires words of affective power and literate range in being sung and prayed. . . .What is said to God and about God is bound intimately to how it is said. In this sense the "aesthetics" of language is necessarily involved in our work on liturgical texts and their living utterance.[34]

> Liturgy which is insufficiently personal or spontaneous in an era which values personhood may well need to recover this dimension of its life. But liturgy which seeks only to be personal, intimate, and spontaneous leaves untouched another range of essential values. . . .[35]

Certainly the task of offering appropriate liturgical translation requires an understanding of the many images of God which are inherent in liturgical prayer. It also offers us the occasion to reflect on the biblical images of God on which liturgical prayer and naming God is based. The poetry, imagery and metaphor intrinsic to biblical revelation and liturgical usage ought not to be flattened out or bleached in translation.[36]

Besides the question of translation, the model of liturgy we now employ invites the composition of prayers and statements within the liturgical experience which are not already composed: invocations at the penitential rite at Mass, intercessory prayers at sacraments and the liturgy of the hours, etc. These offer opportunities for fresh composition and expression. Like the translations of liturgical texts, these deserve the depth of meaning afforded in the rich symbolism and metaphor apparent in liturgical texts themselves. With regard to spontaneity within the liturgy Clarence Rivers remarks:

> Don't be fooled. Spontaneity takes a great deal of practice. Spontaneity is an illusion. A great deal of exercise is required before an expression can appear spontaneous.[37]

This is not to suggest that spontaneity is not to be encouraged; rather it is an invitation to understand that spontaneity does not mean saying or doing just anything; within the liturgy spontaneity has limits precisely because liturgy as a ritual has self-imposed limits.

One of the self-imposed limits which the liturgy has concerns how language is oriented. If the liturgy is made to serve a particular theme or purpose, then the language of liturgy itself can become strained.[38]

> When the language of worship is made to serve the predominant aim of "conversion," for example, a strain is placed upon the whole language of praise and doxology. Similarly, when the language of worship is primarily didactic or instructional, the whole of liturgical utterance is impoverished.[39]

These observations on correct and useful liturgical language are meant to illustrate what is helpful when composing liturgical prayers, and what are pitfalls to watch out for when naming God in worship. The use of scriptural foundations and images for composing prayers is an important first source. Another fact to bear in mind is how freely liturgical language uses the metaphors about God revealed in the Bible. When these are used in worship there is often a wealth of theology and spirituality inherent in the very naming of God. Hence being aware of the variety involved in the various liturgical seasons can help direct and inspire the kind of names for God used at liturgy. This is to suggest that during Advent the more triumphant names ("Mighty God," "Judge," and "God of power and might") would be appropriately emphasized. At Christmas these names could be retained alongside "Son of God," "Son of Mary," and "Prince of Peace." Giving some attention to the seasons of the liturgical year can help keep liturgical language varied and fresh. A glance at the sample invocations for the penitential rite at Mass reveals the following: Lord Jesus, Mighty God, Prince of Peace, Word made flesh, Splendor of the Father, Way to the Father, and the Good Shepherd. And these are only names for Jesus!

From the moment Christians are baptized to the time when they are called from this life to dwell with God forever, they use images and likenesses, names and titles to speak of God. They are initiated by the triune God, Father, Son, and Spirit, are reconciled with the community in penance by the invocation of this same trinity, and when they celebrate Eucharist they begin and end with the gesture of the cross and the naming of the Triune God. The God in whom we believe is a God who has promised in the Old Testament to be there "as who I am shall I be there" and who promises in the New Testament to be present where two or three are gathered in his name. All of this is accomplished through the power of the Spirit of God dwelling in his Church. Christian liturgy is essentially Trinitarian, as is Christian theology and the Christian life. It is the activity and dynamism of the three persons in God that enables us to pray and work until we see God face-to-face.

Praised be the God and Father of our Lord Jesus Christ, who has bestowed on us in Christ every spiritual blessing in the heavens! In him we were chosen; for in the decree of God, who administers everything according to his will and counsel, we were predestined to praise his glory by being the first to hope in Christ. In him you too were chosen; when you heard the glad tidings of salvation, the word of truth, and believed it, you were sealed with the Holy Spirit who had been promised. He is the pledge of our inheritance, the first payment against the full redemption of a people God has made his own, to praise his glory. (Eph 1:3, 11–14)

NOTES

1. Daniel B. Stevick, "The Language of Prayer," *Worship* 52 (November 1978) 557.

2. *Ibid.*

3. "The first meaning of 'orthodoxy' was also right praise (*orthodoxia*) in the liturgy and it is only in the secondary derived sense that it came to mean right teaching" (from Gerard Lukken, "The Unique Expression of Faith in the Liturgy," in *Liturgical Experience of Faith,* Concilium 82 (New York: Herder and Herder, 1973) p. 19. He goes on to address some implications of this for ecumenical progress: "In the midst of the heated theological discussion and the struggle to reassert the *orthodoxia secunda,* will the Church find the courage to be converted to the primacy of *theologia* and *orthodoxia prima*? A conversion to authentic liturgical practice might, after all, be the right way of bringing and keeping Christians together in *one* Church. The *communio* of all believers with the one Lord and with each other is experienced and expressed in a unique way in the liturgy and we should not underestimate the ecumenical significance of this" (pp. 20–21).

4. D. Stevick, "The Language of Prayer," 548–549.

5. See Part Two, Chapter Six, section on "To 'Bless' God."

6. Gail Ramshaw Schmidt, "Lutheran Liturgical Prayer and God as Mother," *Worship* 52 (November 1978) 530. See also G. Schmidt, "De Divinis Nominibus: The Gender of God," *Worship* 56 (March 1982) 117–131.

244 LITURGY, PRAYER AND SPIRITUALITY

7. Bruce Vawter, "The Development of the Expression of Faith in the Worshipping Community: In The New Testament," in Concilium 82, *Liturgical Experience of Faith*, p. 24.

8. John Courtney Murray, *The Problem of God* (New Haven: Yale University Press, 1964) p. 10.

9. G. R. Schmidt, "Lutheran Liturgical Prayer," 523.

10. *Ibid.*, 523–524.

11. On the subject of God as Mother see, G. R. Schmidt, "Lutheran Liturgical Prayer," 533, 540–541.

12. The readings for the solemnity of the Holy Trinity, on the Sunday after Pentecost are: Year A: Ex 34:4–6, 8–9, 2 Cor 13:11–13, Jn 3:16–18; Year B: Dt 4:32–34, 39–40, Rom 8:14–17, Mt 28:16–20; Year C: Prov 8:22–31, Rom 5:1–5, Jn 16:12–15.

13. See, *General Instruction of the Roman Missal*, no. 32.

14. See Part Two, Chapter Seven, quote of Nathan Mitchell at the beginning of the section on "Participation Through Ritual."

15. There was some debate about the appropriateness of using the sign of the cross to begin the liturgy of the Eucharist. Some argued that it should not be placed here, with preference given to the greeting of the assembly, especially since the first option provided in the sacramentary is the text from 2 Corinthians 13:13: "The grace of our Lord Jesus Christ and the love of God and the fellowship of the Holy Spirit be with you all."

16. See, among others, Edward Yarnold, *The Awe Inspiring Rites of Initiation* (Slough: St. Paul Publications, 1972) pp. 26–27.

17. See Edward J. Kilmartin, *Church, Eucharist and Priesthood* A Theological Commentary on the Mystery and Worship of the Most Holy Eucharist (New York/Ramsey: Paulist Press, 1981) pp. 37–39.

18. See Part Two, Chapter Four, cited in the section on "Communal Celebration of Rites."

19. James Dallen, "The Imposition of Hands in Penance: A Study in Liturgical History," *Worship* 51 (May 1977) 224–247.

20. The rationale for standing to "welcome the new covenant in Christ" at the canticle of Mary during evening prayer in the reform is less compelling because of the inclusion of the canticles about Christ in the structure of the hour. However, something of the traditional understanding is still kept since the New Testament canticles follow two (Old Testament) psalms.

21. Some would suggest that this changed because of the stress on the theology of the Trinity. Something of the same issue is at stake in the shifting of the (greeting) text from 2 Corinthians 13:13 in the

anaphora of James; see *Prex Eucharistica* edited by A. Hanggi and I. Pahl (Fribourg: University Press, 1968) pp. 244–245.

22. *RCIA*, no. 215; the rubrics state: "The celebrant touches the water with his right hand and continues."

23. Joseph Jungmann, *The Place of Christ in Liturgical Prayer*, trans. A. Peeler (Staten Island: Alba House, 1965). The original is 1925.

24. This insight, while still helpful and valid, has not gone unchallenged. The work of K. Gamber, among others, is significant on this question.

25. The text of Justin's *Apology* states: "When the prayers and eucharist are finished all the people present give their assent with an 'Amen!' 'Amen' in Hebrew means 'So be it'!" (See L. Deiss, *Springtime*, p. 92.)

26. See *General Instruction of the Roman Missal*, no. 32.

27. The controversy over the moment of consecration has valid theological underpinnings. However, it must be asserted that too much emphasis on this topic could easily shift the emphasis from the entirety of the blessing prayer of the Eucharist to individual elements within which consecration takes predominance.

28. On this see C. Vagaggini, *The Canon of the Mass and Liturgical Reform*, pp. 100–101.

29. Because the source for this prayer is the eucharistic prayer found in the *Apostolic Tradition* of Hippolytus, and this original has been used by other Christian churches in their reform of the eucharistic prayer, it would be interesting to compare this text with, for example, that found in the *Lutheran Book of Worship*. Some suggest that the Roman Catholic form of the prayer is defective in some ways by comparison. See *Lutheran Book of Worship, Minister's Desk Edition* (Minneapolis: Augsburg, 1978) p. 226.

30. See Aidan Kavanagh, "Thoughts on the New Eucharistic Prayers," 4 and 9. See also Richard Albertine, "Problem of the (Double) Epiclesis in the New Roman Eucharistic Prayers," *Ephemerides Liturgicae* 91 (1977) 193–202 for a very helpful summary of the tradition on this point and a critique of the structure of the three new eucharistic prayers.

31. See *Rite of Consecrating Chrism*, in *The Rites*, no. 25, pp. 524–525.

32. See *Rite of Anointing of the Sick*, no. 77 for full text.

33. See, among others, Daniel Stevick, *Language in Worship—Reflections on a Crisis* (New York: Seabury, 1970) and the November 1978 issue of *Worship*.

34. Don Saliers, "Language in the Liturgy: Where Angels Fear To Tread," *Worship* 52 (November 1978) 486.

35. D. Stevick, *Language in Worship*, p. 175.

36. One particular case is the ICEL translation of the opening prayer for the First Sunday of Advent. The biblical imagery of the "right hand" and being called from this life to the kingdom is hardly retained here. In addition, the sense of this translation is that our efforts at doing good need divine assistance; our efforts are, rather, divine in inspiration and performance.

37. Quoted in L. Mitchell, *The Meaning of Ritual*, p. 136.

38. It is for this reason that some have objected to the officially-approved eucharistic prayers for reconciliation. To make a eucharistic prayer "theme"-oriented can tend to mitigate against its being a unified prayer of blessing. The *berakah* praise and blessing prayer should remain the dominant motif in this prayer.

39. D. Saliers, "Language in the Liturgy," 486–487.

Part Three:

IMPLICATIONS FOR LITURGICAL SPIRITUALITY

Chapter Ten
LITURGY: AN EXPERIENCE OF PRAYER

One of the stated aims of the liturgical reform initiated at the Second Vatican Council was the "full, conscious, and active participation in liturgical celebrations . . . demanded by the very nature of the liturgy."[1] In delineating the elements of liturgical prayer (in Part Two) one assumption which runs through them is that these "elements" are meant to be experienced in a celebration of the liturgy which is prayerful so that physical, intellectual and emotive participation in the liturgy can lead to and itself be a true identification and participation in the life which is ours in and through Christ. Therefore, we now turn to one of the needs implied in delineating the "elements of liturgical prayer"—how it might become a vehicle for prayer-filled and active participation, the kind demanded "by the very nature of the liturgy." In this way the gap that has existed between the doing of liturgy and what has fostered spiritual growth[2] might be bridged with the liturgy once again taking its rightful place in the spirituality of the Church.[3]

THE REFORMED LITURGY

That the liturgy is intended to be a nurturing center for the prayer and spirituality of the Christian community is clear from the very first paragraphs of the *General Instruction on the Roman Missal:*

> Therefore, it is of the greatest importance that the celebration of the Mass, the Lord's Supper, be so arranged that the ministers and the faithful who take their own proper part in it may more fully receive its good effects. (no. 2)

> The celebration of the eucharist, like the entire liturgy, in-
> volves the use of outward signs that foster, strengthen, and
> express faith. There must be the utmost care therefore to
> choose and to make wise use of those forms and elements
> provided by the Church that, in view of the circumstances of
> the people and the place, will best foster active and full
> participation and serve the spiritual well-being of the faithful.
> (no. 5)

To help implement the reforms in the liturgy initiated by the
Council and as envisioned in the reformed rites themselves, the
bishops of the United States constituted a committee of their
own on the liturgy. To assist in the implementation process this
committee has published a number of statements, articles and
pamphlets to help in fostering the liturgical renewal inherent in
the reformed liturgical rites.[4] Among those which have had
significant impact on the implementation of liturgy in America
are music, *Music in Catholic Worship* and *Liturgical Music Today*,
and the environment for worship, *Environment and Art in Catholic
Worship*. That these efforts are oriented ultimately to fostering
the spirituality of Christians and to making the liturgy an experience of prayer is implicit in what is called the pastoral judgment
about the music to be used at liturgy: "Does it help this assembly to pray?"[5]

   What is underscored repeatedly in the statements from the
Bishops' Committee on the Liturgy is that the revised liturgy
cannot be implemented once and for all; rather, the statements
point to the on-going work of liturgical implementation whereby
communities are able to grow in faith and love by the means
offered in liturgy. Clearly, for the liturgy to be experienced as
the "prayer of the Church" far more is required than a one-time
reworking of liturgical rites. The following text from the Liturgy
Constitution points to the total reform of the liturgy (in rite and
in appreciating the rites) called for at Vatican II:

> But in order that the sacred liturgy may produce its full
> effect, it is necessary that the faithful come to it with proper
> dispositions, that their thoughts match their words, and that
> they cooperate with divine grace lest they receive it in vain (cf

2 Cor 6:1). Pastors of souls must therefore realize that, when the liturgy is celebrated, more is required than the mere observance of the laws governing valid and licit celebration. It is their duty also to ensure that the faithful take part knowingly, actively, and fruitfully. (no. 11)

Liturgical Celebration—One of the phrases often used in the reformed liturgy to describe what occurs in liturgy is "celebration." The *Oxford Illustrated Dictionary* states that to celebrate means "[to] perform (religious ceremony, etc.) publicly and duly, [to] officiate at the eucharist; [to] observe, honour (festival, event) with rites, festivities, etc." It means "to make famous, to extol, to publish abroad" and "to speak well of another."

The focus of liturgical celebration is God. It is the thanks, praise, honor and acknowledgement offered to God, Father, Son and Spirit as source of all, the beginning and end of all that has been and ever will be. Hence, Christian celebration is a public ritual of acclamation, thanksgiving, and remembering. It is true "celebration" in this full and rich sense. It is not simply merry-making or fostering good feelings. The good news proclaimed and enacted deserves festivity and joy-filled celebration, but the kind that has God as its center and the paschal mystery as the means through which we enter into the mystery of the God we worship. Christian celebration is meant to be an experience of prayer in the presence of God.

As the document *Music in Catholic Worship* puts it:

We are celebrating when we involve ourselves meaningfully in the thoughts, words, songs, and gestures of the worshiping community—when everything we do is wholehearted and authentic for us—when we mean the words and want to do what is done. (no. 3)

Celebrations need not fail, even on a particular Sunday when our feelings do not match the invitation of Christ and his Church to worship. Faith does not always permeate our feelings. But the signs and symbols of worship can give bodily expression to faith as we celebrate. Our own faith is stimulated. We become one with others whose faith is similarly expressed. We rise above our feelings to respond to God in prayer. (no. 5)

Faith grows when it is well expressed in celebration. Good celebrations foster and nourish faith. Poor celebrations weaken and destroy faith. (no. 6)

That the liturgy implies an appropriate understanding and experience of celebration is clear. But what is also clear is that the kind of celebration envisioned is not meant to be that of emotionalism or forced feelings of joy and enthusiasm. Appropriate liturgical celebration includes doing what is humanly attractive in liturgy and joining in an experience of prayer that is satisfying. To foster an experience of prayer at liturgy that is unencumbered and clear is to work toward the aim of the Council which speaks about the norms for the reform of the liturgy in this way:

The rites should be distinguished by a noble simplicity; they should be short, clear, and unencumbered by useless repetitions; they should be within the people's powers of comprehension, and normally should not require much explanation. (no. 34)

In fostering the implementation of the liturgy on a local level, Archbishop James Hickey (then bishop of the diocese of Cleveland) issued a pastoral letter in which he urged that the liturgy take priority in pastoral ministry and that good celebrations foster the spiritual growth of the Christian people. He makes the analogy between good liturgy and good drama to make his point that liturgy needs careful planning and celebration:[6]

The liturgy, like good drama, seeks to involve the congregation in a deep experience of the meaning of life's joys and sorrows. The goal of the liturgical experience, however, is more than the experience of personal involvement that takes place in the theater. The liturgy grows out of and nurtures the identity of the faith community. This is why one of the goals of the liturgy is to stimulate and sustain a deep and interior religious conversion of the hearts of the participants. This conversion is more than the "good feeling" one might have after a play, for this conversion is the work of the Spirit of Christ. Through him the living waters of Baptism overflow into every aspect of our personal and communal lives.[7]

To state that a good celebration of liturgy is a constant goal is to underscore the important part played by liturgy and sacraments in the on-going conversion and spiritual lives of Christians. Liturgical celebration is meant to foster and sustain the faith lives of those who participate in it. One means used to achieve this goal is the collaborative effort at planning and celebrating liturgy.

Liturgical Planning—Since the reformed liturgy is predicated on the use of options and flexibility built into its ritual structure,[8] the documents of reform envision some means whereby liturgies are planned and celebrated. While, in the pre-conciliar liturgy, rehearsals were held before major ceremonies and the master of ceremonies was largely responsible for the correct execution of the liturgy, the revised rites ask for another kind of preparation and celebration. The task of liturgy planning is to insure that the community is able to "take part knowingly, actively, and fruitfully" in the reformed liturgical rites. Since there are a variety of options in the revised liturgy and since liturgical communities vary with regard to background and training in the liturgy, the task of planning becomes all the more important in order that liturgy be a fitting act of community prayer in response to the proclamation of the love of God in Christ.

Music in Catholic Worship envisions that the planning team involve the presider, those who have special roles in the liturgy, and members of the assembly:

It should include those with the knowledge and artistic skills needed in celebration—men and women trained in music, poetry, and art, and knowledge in current resources in these areas—men and women sensitive to the present day thirst of so many riches of scriptures, theology and prayer. It is always

> good to include some members of the congregation who have not taken special roles in the celebration so that honest evaluations can be made. (no. 12)

Planning obviously leads to communicating with those who will minister at the celebration (who may not be present for the planning) so that they are aware of the options and adaptations in the liturgy. This insures that the liturgical ministries can be carried out carefully, fully, and confidently by the ministers themselves without having to rely on a master of ceremonies for directions and guidance during the celebration (which itself can be distracting and a hindrance to the kind of unencumbered liturgical celebration envisioned in the revised rites). While the following statement refers to the presider,[9] its meaning ought to be applied to all who minister at liturgy:

> No other single factor affects the liturgy as much as the attitude, style, and bearing of the celebrant: his sincere faith and warmth as he welcomes the worshiping community; his human naturalness combined with dignity and seriousness as he breaks the Bread of Word and Eucharist. (no. 21)

The *General Instruction on the Roman Missal* stresses the importance of planning and effective celebration when it states:

> This purpose will best be accomplished if, after due regard for the nature and circumstances of each assembly, the celebration is planned in such a way that it brings about in the faithful a participation in body and spirit that is conscious, active, full, and motivated by faith, hope, and charity. The Church desires this kind of participation, the nature of the celebration demands it, and for the Christian people it is a right and duty they have by reason of their baptism. (no. 3)

One of the challenges in liturgical planning and celebration is to strike a balance between tradition and creativity. Just as there is no single model of liturgy envisioned in the reform of the liturgy, so there is a need to abide by the structure and rites of the liturgy so that adaptation and creativity might serve participation, not hinder it by being excessive.[10]

PLANNING: PRINCIPLES AND PRACTICE

1. *Primacy of Scripture Readings*—"The sacred scriptures ought to be the source and inspiration of sound planning for it is of the very nature of celebration that the people hear the saving words and works of the Lord and then respond in meaningful signs, gestures, music and symbols" (*Music in Catholic Worship*, no. 11). Therefore, Scripture study and reflection is an essential component of liturgy planning. A correct interpretation of the scriptural texts to be used at the liturgy and a consideration of the implications of these texts for the given liturgical community is the essential first step in planning.[11]

2. *Particular Occasion and Assembly*—Liturgy planning should evidence an appreciation of the occasion and the assembly which celebrates the liturgy. The difference between a Sunday Eucharist and a daily Eucharist, between festal and ferial days, between a liturgy with a relatively homogeneous community and one with a wide variety of participants, should be taken into consideration. A principle of "progressive solemnity" should emerge whereby special feasts are duly emphasized and celebrated. Lesser feasts are still be be planned and celebrated well, but the task here is to make them less elaborate by comparison. "Solemnity, however, depends less on the ornateness of song and magnificence of ceremonial than on worthy religious celebration" (*Music in Catholic Worship*, no. 19).

3. *Balance and Proportion*—There is a basic liturgical integrity to be respected in the rites themselves. For example, in the eucharistic liturgy there is the liturgy of the word and the liturgy of the Eucharist. To overemphasize one at the expense of the other is pastorally harmful. The liturgy of the Eucharist is made up of the table of God's word and of Christ's body; word and Eucharist form one act of worship. These should receive due emphasis, and in receiving emphasis should reveal that the other rites at the Eucharist are secondary: entrance, presentation of gifts, dismissal (*Music in Catholic Worship*, no. 43)

4. *Place Within a Liturgical Season*—Each celebration of the liturgy is framed within a liturgical season. In addition, with regard to planning Eucharist it is important to note that part of the influence of the season is that the Scriptures read on a particular day are often parts of the larger semi-continuous readings in the lectionary. In planning a particular celebration an overview of the whole season and the unity of proclaiming a given scriptural book should be respected. Hence, planning for a particular Sunday in Advent, for example, requires an understanding of the unity of the season. Or, determining the shape of the celebration of Christmas liturgy will help determine the progression of the Advent liturgy toward it and its unfolding through Epiphany to the Baptism of the Lord.

5. *Appropriation of Traditional Symbols*—Every celebration of the liturgy involves the use of symbols: the sacred word, water, oil, bread and wine. Planning should include a consideration of ways to vary the procession with the sacred word, for example, and how to maximize the symbolic action which takes place in liturgy. Maximizing the use of central symbols in liturgy (as opposed to extraneous things added onto the liturgy) can help insure the clear and direct involvement of the community in the symbolic action of common prayer.

6. *Selection of Liturgical Texts*—Each liturgical celebration includes many options for the prayer texts to be used at the celebration. For example, at the eucharistic liturgy the following are to be selected from the *sacramentary:* introductory rite, preface, eucharistic prayer, and final blessing. On Sundays the opening prayer is selected from the two provided, and on weekdays in ordinary time it and the prayer over the gifts and the prayer after Communion may be chosen from the weekday Mass, the Mass of an optional memorial, the Mass of a saint listed in the martyrology, a Mass for various occasions, or a votive Mass (*General Instruction on the Roman Missal,* no. 316). These prayers might well be selected in line with the Scripture texts of the day and/or the liturgical season being celebrated. Care and attention to the selection of such prayer texts can help in fostering a unified celebration of the liturgy.

7. *Composition of Introductions and Invitations*—Each liturgy

contains references to adaptations by the ministers of texts offered in the sacramentary. The phrase "in these or similar words" refers to times when a presider can forsake the printed introduction to the liturgy or to a part of the liturgy and use another that is more appropriate and especially composed for a given liturgy. For an example drawn from liturgical seasons the texts for the introduction to the liturgy of Passion (Palm) Sunday and the readings on the Easter Vigil indicate that variety and composition is welcomed. When these texts are altered to suit a particular liturgical gathering they can also aid in sustaining the attention and participation of a particular liturgical assembly.

8. *Music in the Liturgy*—With the advent of the reformed liturgy the former strictures on music have been removed. There is an almost limitless variety of options of what might be sung in the liturgy. Hence, the principle of progressive solemnity comes into play here. For example:

> With regard to the Liturgy of the Hours, formerly a sung office meant a service in which everything was sung. Today the elements which lend themselves to singing . . . should be sung in accordance with the relative solemnity of the celebration. This principle likewise applies to the music sung in all other liturgical celebrations (*Liturgical Music Today,* no. 13).

With regard to Eucharist the order of importance concerning the parts of the liturgy to be sung are the acclamations (which should be sung), processional songs, responsorial psalms, ordinary chants and supplementary songs (see *Music in Catholic Worship,* nos. 53–74).

To foster the experience of prayer which is inherent in the reformed liturgy requires continual care in planning and in celebration. Both celebration and planning are meant to lead worshiping communities of faith to participate fully in the mysteries being celebrated and hence in the very mystery of God.

> We find today a vital interest in the Mass as prayer and here lies the principle of synthesis. When everyone with one accord strives to make the Mass a prayer, a sharing and celebra-

258 LITURGY, PRAYER AND SPIRITUALITY

tion of Faith, then there will be unity—many styles of music, a broad choice of instruments, a wide variety of forms of cele-bration, but a single purpose: that all may proclaim and share faith in prayer and that Christ may grow among us.[12]

THE EXPERIENCE OF LITURGY

In the documents on implementation from the Bishops' Committee on the Liturgy great attention has been given to the liturgy as an experience of prayer that is multi-layered in the sense that it involves many forms of communication and means of expression. *Environment and Art in Catholic Worship* states:

> ... liturgy has its own structure, rhythm and pace: a gather-ing, a building up, a climax, and a descent to dismissal. It alternates between persons and groups of persons, between sound and silence, speech and song, movement and stillness, proclamation and reflection, word and action (no. 25).

The liturgy uses words and actions to make contact with God, to respond to his assured presence, and to offer worshipers a means whereby communities of faith can grow and deepen their experience of God. "While our words and art forms cannot contain or confine God, they can, like the world itself, be icons, avenues of approach, numinous presences, ways of touching without totally grasping or seizing" (*Environment and Art,* no. 2). Hence, the forms of liturgy should be respected for what they are, the means through which God is disclosed and encountered in the community of faith. The forms of worship are composed of things which reflect all means of human communication and involve whole persons who celebrate through them. In a most important statement from *Environment and Art* it states:

> Like the covenant itself, the liturgical celebrations of the faith community (Church) involve the whole person. They are not purely religious or merely rational and intellectual exercises, but also human faculties: body, mind, senses, imagination, emotions, memory. Attention to these is one of the urgent needs of contemporary "liturgical renewal"(no. 5).

To celebrate the liturgy means to do the action or perform the sign in such a way that its full meaning and impact shine forth in clear and compelling fashion. Since these signs are vehicles of communication and instruments of faith, they must be simple and comprehensible. Since they are directed to fellow human beings, they must be humanly attractive. They must be meaningful and appealing to the body of worshippers or they will fail to stir up faith and people will fail to worship the Father (*Music in Catholic Worship*, no. 7).

Hence, when exploring the experience of the liturgy (especially in the light of the elements of liturgical prayer explored above) it is important to explore the implications of the fact that liturgy is composed of parts which are verbal, visual, musical, and gestural and that the liturgical act also involves silence and listening.

Verbal—That the liturgy involves the proclamation of the word of God as an essential element of liturgical prayer has been argued above.[13] The clear proclamation of the Scriptures by lectors, the deacon, and (in some cases) the presider is an assumption in the revised liturgy. In terms of the environment for worship this emphasis is demonstrated by the fact that the lectern is given great prominence in the arrangement of the place for worship. "The dignity of the Word of God demands that the church have a suitable place for announcing its message so that the attention of the people will be easily directed to that place during the liturgy of the word" (*General Instruction*, no. 272). The lectern is the place where the Scriptures are proclaimed, and it is a suitable place from which to preach the homily and announce the intentions of the prayer of the faithful. "Like the altar, it should be beautifully designed, constructed of fine materials, and proportioned carefully and simply for its function. The ambo represents the dignity and uniqueness of the Word of God and of reflection on that Word" (*Environment and Art*, no. 74). The documents (both *General Instruction* and *Environment and Art*) clearly state that it is not suitable for the commentator, cantor or choirmaster to use this lectern. A very simple lectern, "in no way competing or conflicting with the main ambo," can be used by other ministers for announcements, singing, etc.

In addition to the important place of the ambo, the documents on the implementation of the liturgy speak about the texts to be used for the proclamation of the word. In preferred usage two books are used: the lectionary and the Gospel book. The *General Instruction* states that the Gospel book is distinct from the other book with the readings (no. 79), that it may be carried in procession by the deacon (no. 128), that it receives marks of respect in the celebration of the liturgy such as reverence by kissing and incensation (no. 35, 131, 232), and that the deacon or a concelebrant normally should proclaim the Gospel (no. 131, 34). The Gospel book may be carried in procession; this is especially helpful in more solemn celebrations in order to give due emphasis to the proclamation of the word. With regard to the size and shape of the book itself:

> Any book which is used by an officiating minister in a liturgical celebration should be of a large (public, noble) size, good paper, strong design, handsome typography and binding. The Book of the Gospels or lectionary ... is central and should be handled in a special way....The use of pamphlets and leaflets detracts from the visual integrity of the total liturgical action (*Environment and Art,* no. 91).

What is stated here about the ambo and books for the proclamation of the word at Eucharist should be kept in mind when planning and celebrating the liturgy of the hours and the other sacraments as well. The experience of liturgy is meant to include reverencing the word of God in effective announcement and in the handling of the texts themselves.

In addition to the proclamation of the Scriptures, the liturgy involves speaking and praying in other words—presidential prayers, acclamations and responses. These texts, whether done by presider or by assembly and presider ought to be done carefully and reverently. For effective celebration it is important that nothing hinder the clear and understandable proclamation of these texts, especially the presidential prayers which are

offered in the name of the whole assembly. Both the proclamation of the Sacred Scriptures and the presidential prayers ought
to be understood as part of the dialogue of liturgy, for these
invite the response of the community at their conclusion and the
attention of the assembly as they are spoken. The *General Instruction* states that "the readings should be listened to with respect
. . ." (no. 9), that "all should listen to the eucharistic prayer in
silent reverence and share in it by making the acclamations" (no.
55), and that the "presidential prayers should be spoken in a
loud and clear voice so that everyone present can hear and pay
attention" (no. 12). Hence, listening as well as responding to
texts is a form of liturgical participation.

One way in which the proclaimed word and the presidential
prayers can achieve prominence in the celebration of liturgy is
for presiders and celebrating community to differentiate clearly
between these texts and others which are intended to be said
quietly (that is, to oneself) during the liturgy. For example, the
prayers said at the presentation of the bread and wine are not
necessarily to be spoken aloud (and it is distinctly preferable
that they not be).[14] The sacramentary directs that the priest hold
the bread and say the prayer "quietly." If there is no song to
accompany the action, the priest "may" say these words, "in an
audible voice" and the people "may" respond. Clearly, these
directions differ very much from those about the preface and
eucharistic prayer where text and acclamations are to be done in
a significant manner with enthusiasm and forthrightness.[15] Another instance of where words can get in the way of the clarity
and directness of the liturgy is in the priest's "private preparation" for Communion. What is indicated clearly here is that the
texts are for the priest alone; no one else should hear them,
especially because this is a time when the community itself
should prepare for the reception of Communion (*General Instruction*, no. 56f).

Another way for the proclaimed word to assume its place of
prominence in the celebration is for any introductory comments
before the readings (as well as throughout the rest of the liturgy) to be extremely brief. When these comments are inflated in
length, the readings which follow can be perceived to be unnec-

essary or at least to be overly long because they have been introduced too elaborately. In order for the liturgy as a verbal experience to be appreciated in its fullest extent it would be important to allow the texts to speak for themselves and not to allow the liturgy to become an experience that is too wordy.

Visual—While the liturgy has always included and emphasized the use of symbols in worship, what is intended as part of the reformed liturgy is a certain maximizing of symbolic usage in liturgy today. "As our symbols tended in practice to be shriveled up and petrify, they became much more manageable and efficient. They still 'caused' and were still 'efficacious' even though they had often ceased to signify in the richest, fullest sense" (*Environment and Art,* no. 14). In light of the traditional usage of symbols, and their petrification over the recent centuries, it is important to underscore that "renewal requires the opening up of our symbols, especially the fundamental ones of bread and wine, water, oil, the laying on of hands, until we can experience all of them as authentic and appreciate their symbolic value" (*Environment and Art,* no. 15). One example of this symbolic emphasis and usage is seen in the place of the ambo for the liturgy of the word and the books which are used for proclamation.

In addition, the very "environment" for liturgy speaks to the importance of symbol and symbolic usage in worship today.

There are elements in the environment . . . which contribute to the overall experience, e.g., the seating arrangement, the placement of liturgical centers of action, temporary decoration, light, acoustics, spaciousness, etc. The environment is appropriate when it is beautiful, when it is hospitable, when it clearly invites and needs an assembly of people to complete it.

Furthermore, it is appropriate when it brings people close together so that they can see and hear the entire liturgical action, when it helps people feel involved and become involved. Such an environment works with the liturgy, not against it (*Environment and Art,* no. 24).

With regard to liturgical "centers of action" the reform of the rites of Christian initiation call for a place for immersion as well as infusion with water, and the rites (for adults and for children) both speak of immersion as the preferred usage for initiation.[16] In addition, the very fact that communal rites are restored for this sacrament requires that the place for initiation be in a place readily visible for all and accessible for participants. (Whether this is near the front of the assembly or at the entrance to the church does not affect the importance which should be attached to visual clarity and centrality.[17]) When the water for immersion is readily seen, prayed over in the blessing prayer, touched during the praying of this text (as the rubrics require, with repeated touching and swirling of the water to be encouraged) and used as a total bathing for those initiated in the name of the Trinity, then the visual and symbolic aspects of initiation are clearly demonstrated. Allowing central symbols to be central and not to overload them with endless commentary and "explanations" can help in our contemporary restoration of symbolic action and usage.[18] An essential component of the experience of liturgy is the visual clarity and expression that is inherent in common worship.

Music—Beginning with the restoration of chant as a means of fostering community prayer during liturgy in the early years of this century[19] through to the present documents on the implementation of the reformed liturgy, the place of music has been underscored as an important component of the liturgy:

> Among the many signs and symbols used by the Church to celebrate its faith, music is of preeminent importance. As sacred song united to the words it forms an integral part of solemn liturgy. Yet the function of music is ministerial; it must serve and never dominate. Music should assist the assembled believers to express and share the gift of faith that is within them and to nourish and strengthen their interior commitment of faith. . . .
>
> In addition to expressing texts, music can also unveil a dimension of meaning and feeling, a communication of ideas and intuitions which words alone cannot yield. This dimen-

sion is integral to the human personality and to growth in faith. It cannot be ignored if the signs of worship are to speak to the whole person . . .

(*Music in Catholic Worship,* nos. 23–24).[20]

As has frequently been observed, this century has seen the evolution of the association of liturgy and music to an emphasis on liturgical music (that is, music appropriate to the liturgy when music is used), to the present stage where what is assumed is musical liturgy (that is, appropriate music always used at liturgy which of its nature demands music).[21] Or as the recent statement *Liturgical Music Today* states: "These guidelines concern the Church's liturgy, which is inherently musical" (no. 5).

As a rule of thumb, what is underscored in the documents of implementation is that distinct preference is given to music which enhances and underscores the texts of the liturgy itself rather than music that adds to or is extraneous to the rite itself. This is to suggest that the four-hymn structure for planning and celebrating liturgy is no longer operative, for what this approach does is to emphasize what ought not to be emphasized in the Eucharist: the presentation of the gifts and the preparation of the altar (the former "offertory") and the recessional. What is far more important is to sing the acclamations within the eucharistic prayer as well as the music intrinsic to the liturgy of the word: the responsorial psalm and Gospel acclamation. As a general principle "in all liturgical celebrations proper use should be made of the musical elements within the liturgy of the word, i.e., responsorial psalm, gospel acclamation, and sometimes an acclamation after the homily . . ." (*Liturgical Music Today,* no. 7).[22]

Three judgments are offered for the appropriateness of music in the liturgy:

The liturgical judgment: Is the music's text, form, placement and style congruent with the nature of the liturgy? The musical judgment: Is the music technically, aesthetically and expressively good irrespective of musical idiom or style? The pastoral judgment: Will it help this assembly to pray?[23]

It is because of the importance which music should have in the liturgy that the original document of implementation (*Music in Catholic Worship* (1972) has been supplemented with *Liturgical Music Today* (1982) which contains recommendations and guidelines for music in the liturgy of the hours and in sacraments other than Eucharist.[24] Because music is an important means whereby the assembly participates in liturgy it is stated that "the liturgy prefers song to instrumental music" (no. 56): "As a general norm [recorded music should] never be used within the liturgy to replace the congregation, the choir, the organist, or other instrumentalists" (no. 60). Recorded music "may never become a substitute for the community's song . . . as in the case of the responsorial psalm after a reading from Scripture or during the optional hymn of praise after Communion" (no. 61). What these statements serve to do is to emphasize the importance of participation by the assembly through music. It is not sufficient that the liturgy have musical elements; what is envisioned is the full participation of the whole assembly in the liturgy, and one of the means is singing music that is appropriate for the liturgy.

Gesture—That the liturgy is made up of a series of postures is the most obvious example of the use of gesture in worship.[25] Communities stand, sit, bow, kneel and sign themselves during any act of liturgy. In addition, especially in a sacramental action such as initiation and the anointing of the sick, the liturgy uses the symbols of water and oil in the liturgy where symbol and gesture are joined together. Also, there is the aspect of gesture operative in liturgy when ministers process at the beginning and ending of the liturgy, when participants process to the table of the Lord to share in the Eucharist, or process to the baptismal font for initiation, etc. The act of processing itself during the liturgy underscores the importance of gesture in liturgy. When we celebrate liturgy we do so with our whole bodies, our whole selves. As enfleshed human beings we walk and gesture in liturgy as we do in any other act of human movement and communication.

An example of the importance of the combination of symbol, gesture and music in the liturgy of the Eucharist occurs in the rites preparing for and of Communion. With regard to the bread and wine used at Eucharist, the *General Instruction on the Roman Missal* states:

> The nature of the sign demands that the material for the eucharistic celebration truly have the appearance of food. Accordingly, even though unleavened and baked in the traditional shape, the eucharistic bread, should be made in such a way that in a Mass with a congregation the priest is able actually to break the host into parts and distribute them to at least some of the faithful. (When, however, the number of communicants is large or other pastoral needs require it, small hosts are in no way ruled out.) The action of the breaking of the bread, the simple term for the eucharist in apostolic times, will more clearly bring out the force and meaning of the sign of the unity of all in the one bread and of their charity, since the one bread is being distributed among the members of one family. (no. 283)

> The wine for the eucharist must be from the fruit of the vine (see Lk 22:18), natural and pure, that is not mixed with any foreign substance. (no. 284)

With regard to visual clarity for these symbols the use of one large plate for the bread and a large flagon for the wine is recommended so that "one bread, one cup" might be realized visually. Placing the one plate and the one flagon and the chalice on the altar at the preparation of the gifts leaves this rite with the simplicity and directness envisioned in the rite of the Eucharist. The elimination of many chalices and ciboria can help emphasize the visual clarity which should mark the liturgy.[26]

In addition to this directness in symbol at this point, the liturgy emphasizes the use of gesture to emphasize the breaking of bread and sharing of the cup in preparation for Communion. The bread-breaking and wine-pouring signify that "we who are many are made one body in the one bread which is Christ" (1 Cor 10:17).[27] During this action the Lamb of God is sung, and it may be repeated as often as necessary to accompany the gestures with the bread and wine in preparation for their being shared in Communion. *Liturgical Music Today* combines the visual, gestural and musical components of the Eucharist when it states:

> The Lamb of God achieves greater significance at Masses when a larger sized eucharistic bread is broken for distribution and, when communion is given under both kinds, chalices must be filled. The litany is prolonged to accompany this action of breaking and pouring. In this case one should not hesitate to add tropes to the litany so that the prayerfulness of the rite may be enriched (no. 20).

This series of gestures culminates in the procession of the assembly to join in sharing the eucharistic bread and wine. Just as music accompanied the breaking of the bread and pouring of the wine, so too at this point of the liturgy the assembly joins in song as it processes to receive the Eucharist. This song begins while the priest receives the eucharistic species. The purpose of this song is to express "the union of the communicants who join their voices in a single song . . . and [make] the communion procession an act of brotherhood" (*General Instruction,* no. 56, i).

> In the eucharist, bread and wine are basic: their visual and other sensory impact, how they are handled, how they are broken and poured out, how shared. . . . But because we are accustomed to a symbolic minimalism with respect to all sacraments, we tend to think that we have to bring in all sorts of entirely new elements to save this wretched rite. We make our problems more complex than they are. If we attended to the bread and wine we would discover that the rite is powerful indeed.[28]

What is important to emphasize here is that what can be understood as individual parts of the liturgy—symbol, gesture, and music—are presented together in the manner in which they are usually experienced in the liturgy. Recent attention has been (appropriately) given to symbolic action as opposed to symbols alone, and to musical liturgy as opposed to music at liturgy. The integration of these components is assumed in liturgy and should form the perspective within which we view and understand communal prayer. As an experience, liturgy involves the unity of words, symbols, gestures and song. Careful planning and celebration can foster an experience of prayer at liturgy that brings together and respects its component parts.

Silence—In addition to understanding liturgy as a series of actions which involve the community at prayer, a most important component of all liturgical prayer is silent, reflective prayer. In the Foreword to the American edition of the sacramentary it states:

> The proper use of periods of silent prayer and reflection will help to render the celebration less mechanical and impersonal and lend a more prayerful spirit to the liturgical rite. Just as there should be no celebration without song, so too there should be no celebration without periods for silent prayer and reflection.[29]

This instruction is important to reiterate especially because liturgical prayer can sometimes seem to be a series of things to do, see and hear with little time for reflective silent prayer during the liturgy itself. The tradition of prayer before and after the liturgy grew all the stronger when periods for silence came to be all but eliminated from the liturgy.[30]

During the liturgy of the Eucharist the sacramentary states that there should be silence before the blessing of water or the penitential rite during the introductory rites, before the opening prayer, after the readings and homily, and after Communion. These regular and customary times for silent prayer offer the assembly the opportunity to reflect on what is occurring in the liturgy and to appropriate what is proclaimed and enacted in the rites. The importance of silence for all liturgical celebrations is noted clearly in the *General Instruction on the Liturgy of the Hours* where it speaks about "sacred silence."

> It is a general principle that care should be taken in liturgical services to see that "at the proper times all observe a reverent silence." An opportunity for silence should therefore be provided in the celebration of the liturgy of the hours. (no. 201)

> In order to receive in our hearts the full sound of the voice of the Holy Spirit and to unite our personal prayer more closely with the word of God and the public voice of the Church, it is permissible, as occasion offers and prudence suggests, to have an interval of silence. (no. 202)

What is clearly stated in the directives on the Eucharist and the liturgy of the hours should also be reflected in other sacramental celebrations. A liturgy without times for silence can distract from the prayerful rhythm that includes silence as an integral part of the experience of liturgy. One of the essential components of the action of liturgy is reflective silent prayer. As Marianne Micks observes:

> The words of Christian worship have ever acknowledged their own limit. Like all true symbols, they contain within themselves denial of their own adequacy. Before the command to be still and know God, all sounds are harsh. In response to the great pronouncement "The Lord is in his holy temple," worshipers have sought at all times to keep silence before him.[31]

Because of the relative absence of silence in our world and our daily lives it is all the more important for the liturgy to be structured and celebrated in such a way that meeting the divine in Christ can occur in listening as well as speaking, in silent prayer as well as in the speech of gesture.

VARIETY OF LITURGIES

It is not infrequently the case that we refer to Eucharist as "the liturgy" and in a sense this is a traditional understanding of Eucharist (especially in some Eastern usages). Clearly in the Roman Catholic tradition, especially from the time of the Reformation, pride of place and emphasis went to the celebration of Eucharist even when congregations were largely passive as they watched the ritual performed by those in the sanctuary and often settled for watching the elevation rather than share in receiving the eucharistic bread and wine.[32] The undoubted center of liturgical prayer was the Mass even though in pre-conciliar usage it was often not the prayers *of* the Mass that mattered but rather prayers offered individually while Mass was going on.[33] Since the reform of the liturgy active participation in the rites of Eucharist has become a norm.

However, there is a sense in which the Eucharist may be said to be too central to the liturgical prayer of Christians. When "liturgy" is identified with "Eucharist" then there may be a fundamental misunderstanding of the variety which should be experienced in liturgical prayer. The clear intent of the implementation of the liturgy of the hours and the sacraments is to restore them to communal celebration for all Christians. That the liturgy of the hours is now intended for daily communal celebration is clear from the *General Instruction:*

> The liturgy of the hours, like other liturgical services, is not a private matter but belongs to the whole Body of the Church, whose life it both expresses and affects. This liturgy stands out most strikingly as an ecclesial celebration when, through the bishop surrounded by his priests and ministers, the local Church celebrates it. For "in the local Church the one, holy, catholic, and apostolic Church is truly present and at work." Such a celebration is therefore most earnestly recommended. (no. 20)

> Wherever possible the more important hours should be celebrated in common at the church [in parishes]. (no. 21)

Tradition reveals that the daily prayer of the Christian Church has always regarded morning and evening prayer as the two main non-eucharistic forms of liturgical prayer. While the document restoring this prayer allows for the joining of an hour of prayer with the Eucharist, the question of regular non-eucharistic forms of liturgy should be raised pastorally to see to what extent the liturgy of the hours on its own might provide the variety of liturgical celebration envisioned and inherent in the present reformed rites.

In addition, the question of the communal celebration of

sacraments should be raised to determine how well these are celebrated apart from the Eucharist. That the sacraments should form part of the Church's liturgical prayer apart from the Eucharist is envisioned in the rites themselves where caution is given about the all too frequent association and joining of other sacraments to Eucharist. For example, the rite of baptism for children states that a communal rite on Sunday is meant to be the usual way baptism is celebrated. Even though this can be done at Mass, the General Instruction states that "this should not be done too often" (no. 9). This would seem to suggest what is implied in the reform of the liturgy as a whole, that a wide variety of liturgical services should be celebrated, not just Eucharist. What can happen when sacraments are regularly joined to the Eucharist is that the Eucharist itself becomes an afterthought that is eclipsed by the preceding rite.

Another sacrament which is emphasized as a communal liturgy is that of penance. With three of the four forms of the celebration predicated on communal celebration (two sacramental and one non-sacramental) what is clear is that this should become a regular liturgy on its own without being joined to Eucharist. In pastoral practice sometimes the liturgy of penance is joined to the Eucharist with the unfortunate result that the conventional assumption of having to be freed from all sin in order to celebrate Eucharist is not challenged and appears to be operative still. What is a more traditional understanding of Eucharist is that this liturgy itself forgives sins, save for the serious sins of murder, apostasy, adultery, etc. That the Eucharist is for the forgiveness of lesser sins is clear in the text of the eucharistic prayer ("so that sins may be forgiven"), the placement of the Lord's prayer before Communion ("forgive us our trespasses as we forgive those who trespass against us"), the invocation of the Lamb of God ("who takes away the sins of the world"), and the purgative effect of the liturgy of the word concretized in the quiet prayer of the deacon after proclaiming the Gospel ("may the words of the Gospel wipe away our sins").[34] This is not to suggest that there is little need for penance; on the contrary, it is to suggest that regular communal celebrations of this sacrament can foster appropriate attitudes toward forgiveness, penance and reconciliation as celebrated and accomplished apart from the liturgy of the Eucharist.[35]

In these years after the initial reform of the liturgy it is not surprising to find ourselves emphasizing the Eucharist at the relative expense of other liturgical rites because of historical and spiritual reasons. In fact, this situation is one of the reasons why the Bishops' Committee on the Liturgy drafted *Liturgical Music Today*.[36] To speak of the experience of liturgy is to raise the question of the variety of liturgies which are offered on a regular basis: initiation, penance, anointing, hours, as well as Eucharist. Careful planning and celebration can help not only in the quality of liturgy experienced by the celebrating community but also in the variety of liturgy celebrated. To rethink our assumptions about what is "liturgy" (more than Eucharist) and to provide for the rich variety of liturgical celebrations intended in the reform of the liturgy can help make the experience of liturgical prayer more varied and more effectively that which meets the many needs of the Christian community.

What Christians do when they engage in the celebration of liturgy is to proclaim and enact the mystery of God incarnate in Jesus: "This is what we proclaim to you: what was from the beginning, what we have heard, what we have seen with our eyes, what we have looked upon and our hands have touched— we speak of the word of life" (1 Jn 1:1). We do this in the unity of actions, gestures and words which make up the Christian liturgy. Careful planning and celebration of the variety of Christian liturgy can help restore liturgy to its rightful place as the privileged experience and expression of the faith of the Church. What the implementation document *Environment and Art in Catholic Worship* states with regard to the setting for liturgy might well be extended to include all that we have discussed in this chapter on why quality celebration and experiences of liturgy are so important.

When the Christian community gathers to celebrate its faith and vision, it gathers to celebrate what is most personally theirs and most nobly human and truly Church. The actions of the assembly witness the great deeds God has done; they confirm an age-old covenant. With such vision and depth of the assembly can the environment be anything less than a vehicle to meet the Lord and to encounter one another? The challenge of our environment is the final challenge of Christ: We must make ready until he returns in glory (no. 107).

NOTES

1. See *Constitution on the Sacred Liturgy,* no. 14. The understanding of "active participation" is not the same as that argued above regarding participation (Part Two, Chapter Three); however, it is through such active involvement in liturgy that "participation" in the paschal mystery occurs.

2. See, for example, the statements of A. Chupungco, *Towards a Filipino Liturgy,* pp. 78–85, and the thesis of the work by Josef Jungmann, *Christian Prayer Through the Centuries,* trans. John Coyne (New York/Ramsey: Paulist Press, 1978).

3. See, among other statements, *Constitution on the Sacred Liturgy* nos. 16–17; Instruction on *Liturgical Formation in Seminaries* (Rome, 1979) nos. 1–42.

4. Among these are the *Newsletter* of the Bishops' Committee, the series of *Study Texts,* and the *Liturgy Documentary Series.* An example of another liturgically related document to come from other committees of the NCCB is the recent statement on the homily in the Sunday assembly, *Fulfilled in Your Hearing* from the Committee on Priestly Life and Ministry.

5. Taken from *Liturgical Music Today* (Washington: Bishops' Committee on the Liturgy 1982) no. 29.

6. James A. Hickey, *Let Us Give Thanks to the Lord Our God* (Cleveland, 1980) p. 13. The nuances given here about the difference between liturgy and drama as well as the insight that can be gained from the analogy are stated clearly here.

7. *Ibid.,* p. 14.

8. See Part Two, Chapter Seven, entitled "A Patterned Experience of Prayer."

9. The insight of Robert Hovda in *Strong, Loving and Wise* (Washington: The Liturgical Conference, 1976) is adopted here: "The term 'presider' is used . . . because it is more accurate than the common 'celebrating' and 'celebrant' in specifying the particular function in question. All initiated believers are celebrants in liturgy" (p. viii).

10. Recall what was said above regarding tradition and creativity in Part Two, Chapter Seven, section on "Creativity and Option."

11. With regard to the contribution which homily services can make to planning, *Fulfilled in Your Hearing* states: "The primary help that a good homily service will offer is to make available to the preacher recent exegetical work on the specific texts that appear in the lectionary and to indicate some ways in which the biblical word can be heard in the present as God's Word to his people. They can never replace the homilist's own prayer, study and work" (pp. 22–23).

12. *Music in Catholic Worship,* no. 84.

13. See Part Two, Chapter Five, "Proclamation of the Word of God."

14. See, among others, Ralph Keifer, "Preparation of the Altar and the Gifts or Offertory?" *Worship* 48 (1974) 596–600.

15. "The acclamations are shouts of joy which arise from the whole assembly as forceful and meaningful assents to God's Word and Action. They are important because they make some of the most significant moments of the Mass (gospel, eucharistic prayer, Lord's Prayer) stand out. It is of their nature that they be rhythmically strong, melodically appealing, and affirmative. The people should know the acclamations by heart in order to sing them spontaneously. Some variety is recommended and even imperative. The challenge to the composer and people alike is one of variety without confusion" (from *Music in Catholic Worship,* no. 53).

16. See *RCIA* no. 220 and *Rite of Baptism for Children* no. 60. See also Aidan Kavanagh, *The Shape of Baptism* (New York: Pueblo Publishing Co., 1978) pp. 136–138.

17. "The place of the font, whether it is an area near the main entrance of the liturgical space or one in the midst of the congregation, should facilitate full congregational participation, regularly in the Easter Vigil. If the baptismal space is in a gathering place or entry way, it can have living, moving water for immersion. When a portable font is used, it should be placed for maximum visibility and audibility, without

crowding or obscuring the altar, ambo and chair" (*Environment and Art in Catholic Worship*, no. 77).

18. The insight of Robert Hovda on planning and celebration that allows central symbols to be central rather than giving in to the temptation of emphasizing complexity ("the lure of the complex") is well taken (see *Strong, Loving and Wise*, p. 34).

19. See Pope Pius X, Instruction on Sacred Music (1903), in *Papal Legislation on Sacred Music* (Collegeville: The Liturgical Press, 1979) pp. 223–232, especially at 224–225. The Instruction begins with the statement: "Sacred music, being an integral part of the liturgy . . ."

20. See also *Environment and Art in Catholic Worship*, no. 6.

21. See John Gallen, "Musical Liturgy Is on the Way," *Pastoral Music* 2 (June–July 1978) 11.

22. "While metrical psalmody may be employed fruitfully in the Church's liturgy (for instance, when a hymn is part of one of the rites), introduction of this musical form into the psalmody of the Liturgy of the Hours profoundly affects and alters the praying of the psalms as a ritual. Thus, metrical psalms should not be used as substitutes either for the responsorial psalm in a liturgy of the word of one of the rites or for the psalms in the Liturgy of the Hours" (*Liturgical Music Today* no. 40).

23. *Liturgical Music Today* no. 29. See also, *Music in Catholic Worship* nos. 30–38, 26–29, 39–41.

24. *Liturgical Music Today*, nos. 9–10, 22–45.

25. *General Instruction of the Roman Missal* nos. 20–22.

26. See *General Instruction of the Roman Missal* no. 293 and *Environment and Art in Catholic Worship*, no. 96.

27. *General Instruction of the Roman Missal*, no. 56 c. See also, *It Is Your Own Mystery. A Guide to the Communion Rite* (Washington: The Liturgical Conference, 1977).

28. Robert Hovda, *Strong, Loving and Wise*, p. 34.

29. "Foreword," *Sacramentary*, p. 13.

30. One of the reasons that contributed to the lack of periods for silence within the liturgy of the Eucharist was the abuse of the overlong delay at the elevation of host and chalice. The elevation at Mass substituted for the people's reception of the sacred species; hence to delay at this point in the liturgy did meet a felt need in spirituality at the time. To correct this abuse priests were instructed not to delay during the Mass. See Nathan Mitchell, *Cult and Controversy The Worship of the Eucharist Outside of Mass* (New York: Pueblo Publishing Co., 1982) pp. 47–49, 129–184.

31. Marianne Micks, *The Future Present,* p. 70.

32. This is often called "ocular Communion." See Nathan Mitchell, *Cult and Controversy,* pp. 129–163; and Robert Taft, "The Frequency of the Eucharist Throughout History," in *Can We Always Celebrate the Eucharist?* Concilium Vol. 152 (New York: Seabury, 1982) pp. 13–24.

33. See Louis Bouyer, *Liturgical Piety* p. 2.

34. See John J. Quinn, "The Lord's Supper and the Foregiveness of Sins," *Worship* 42 (May 1968) 281–290.

35. See, among others, Nathan Mitchell, ed., *The Rite of Penance: Commentaries.* Background and Directions. Vol. Three (Washington: The Liturgical Conference, 1978) and Ladislas Orsy, *The Evolving Church and the Sacrament of Penance* (Denville: Dimension Books, 1978).

36. See *Liturgical Music Today,* no. 3, and this chapter on "The Reformed Liturgy," and "The Experience of Liturgy."

Chapter Eleven
LITURGY AND THE LIFE OF FAITH

One of the clear implications of describing the elements of liturgical prayer involves indicating how these elements relate to other aspects of our lives. Specifically, it involves relating how liturgy is lived out in the witness we give to Gospel values outside liturgical settings, and how liturgical prayer relates to and influences other forms of personal prayer. It is the genius and uniqueness of the liturgy that it demands and supports other action and prayer. If liturgy is allowed to become self-contained and self-serving it can lose this outward direction (witness) and this other dimension (personal prayer). The most traditional understanding of Christian worship is that it itself is a privileged experience of relating to God in the midst of the assembly of believers which experience influences and grounds how we come to serve and know God through witness, reflection and prayer. The place where this occurs is not just in the cult, it is in our *lives* of faith.

LITURGY AND THE SPIRITUAL LIFE

It was noted above that spirituality may be described as

the experience of our relationship with God in faith, and the ways in which we live out that faith. Spirituality involves our coming to know God, our response to God, and the prayer and work we perform in faith. For Christians spirituality occurs in and among the community of the church, the community formed by hearing and responding to the same call and invitation from God.[1]

Clearly a part of spirituality is liturgy. Hearing and responding to the initiative of God in Christ is part of the action involved in worship. Yet, in addition, the liturgy can be regarded as an important locus that discloses the presence of God to us which presence is available and operative throughout all of our lives. Liturgy does not take us out of the world so that we can find an absent God; rather it is an experience within our world of this revealing God who has transformed all life in and through the incarnation and redeeming death of Jesus. Hence, in an incarnational approach to spirituality the place of liturgy is significant as that which focuses our experience of God and as that which forges an important juncture between what is experienced in prayer and what is lived out in the rest of our lives.[2]

From the perspective of describing what is meant by liturgical spirituality we can say that while liturgy is disclosive and a significant juncture in the Christian's life it is by no means coterminous with "spirituality." To join in liturgy only, or to plan, celebrate and minister at liturgy is not sufficient for Christian liturgical spirituality. What is required is that we live out what is implied in common worship and to make important connections between this prayer and other forms of prayer.

It is interesting to note the cultic terminology used by St. Paul when he addresses the church at Rome: "And so, brothers, I beg you through the mercy of God to offer your bodies as a living sacrifice holy and acceptable to God, your spiritual worship" (Rom 12:1). True Christian life involves a continual identification with God in service as well as in liturgy. The use of cultic terminology here is very significant:

> Since the apostle (according to Rom. 12:1f.) transfers the true service of God to everyday life, liturgy must on no account remove us from this real, everyday world. The church is not the church at all without the counterpart of the world, even in its worship, and thus ceases to be pleasing to God. Paul allows Christian worship especially to be the manifestation of a deep, even if highly-charged, solidarity between church and world. For if its liturgy is what it should be, worship expresses the fact that the whole world is called with us to the liberty of the children of God. . . .[3]

What is required is that our whole selves, our whole persons, every dimension and capacity of our lives be transformed and offered in free and willing service to God.[4] That this exhortation is fully consonant with Paul's theology is noted by Käsemann:

> When, in a deliberate paradox and moved by an anti-cultic tendency, Paul demands the sacrifice of our bodies as our spiritual worship (Rom. 12:1 and 1 Cor. 6:20), this is not done by chance. According to Rom. 6:12 ff. [which text follows upon vs. 3–11 used at the Easter Vigil, and is classically used to refer to Christian initiation] the new obedience to be offered in the body is the mark of Christian status, being the fruit of baptism and the anticipation of the bodily resurrection of the dead. . . .[5]

"Hence true Christian ritual is the opposite of magic rituals, which concentrate on the working of *things*. Christian ritual is *personalistic:* the purpose of eucharist is not to change bread and wine, but to change you and me."[6] St. Paul is clear in his instruction to the feeble church at Corinth on this point. The reason that their assemblies were not correct was not that their ritual was defective; it was that their lives did not express what Eucharist means—unity in faith and love. The prayer to "strengthen in faith and love your pilgrim church on earth" in our eucharistic prayer today reflects the intention of liturgy in general.

> Nothing is clearer in the New Testament, especially in St. Paul, than this fact: the true cult of the Christian is interior; it is the life of self-oblation in charity; a life, like Christ's, that is lived in loving service—in short, a life of self-giving. Paul tells the Corinthians (1 Cor. 11:17–34) that their eucharist is in fact no eucharist at all because the mystery of communion— i.e. unity in Christ—which eucharist expresses was not lived in their lives.[7]

A correct understanding and use of liturgy involves more than cultic prescriptions; it involves the prescription to live in all of life what is celebrated in the cult.

That this anti-cultic critique is built into the Christian liturgy itself is exemplified in the scriptural texts chosen for use and proclamation at the beginning of Lent. This is particularly significant, for every time the Christian community assembles to begin the "forty days" it is reminded that what is needed is the conversion of heart, not just the offering of sacrifice. The text from the prophet Joel from the first reading at Eucharist on Ash Wednesday begins with the words:

> Even now, says the LORD,
> > return to me with your whole heart,
> > with fasting, and weeping and mourning;
> Rend your hearts, not your garments
> > and return to the Lord your God.   (2:12–13)

The Gospel for this day from Matthew (6:1–6, 16–18) speaks directly to the penitential practices which have traditionally characterized this season: almsgiving, prayer and fasting. The admonitions "not to let your left hand know what your right hand is doing" when giving alms, to "go to your room, close your door, and pray to your Father in private"[8] instead of behaving like hypocrites "who love to stand and pray in synagogues or on street corners in order to be noticed," or "to groom your hair and wash your face" when fasting are clearly directed to proper motivation when undertaking these and other practices during Lent.

In addition to these readings the liturgy offers the prophet's critique from Isaiah about sacrifices in the eucharistic liturgy for Friday after Ash Wednesday. The prophet instructs us:

> Lo, on your fast day you carry out your own pursuits
> > and drive all your laborers.
> Yes, your fast ends in quarreling and fighting,
> > striking with wicked claw.
> Would that today you might fast
> > so as to make your voice heard on high!
> Is this the manner of fasting I wish,
> > of keeping a day of penance:

That a man bow his head like a reed,
    and lie in sackcloth and ashes?
Do you call this a fast, a day acceptable
    to the LORD?
This, rather, is the fasting that I wish:
    releasing those bound unjustly,
    untying the thongs of the yoke;
Setting free the oppressed,
  breaking every yoke;
Sharing your bread with the hungry,
    sheltering the oppressed and the homeless;
Clothing the naked when you see them,
    and not turning your back on your own.   (Is 58:3–7)[9]

The clear proclamation of these texts on days that traditionally require fasting and abstinence for Christians is compelling and may be unsettling. Religious rituals and practices of self-discipline do not satisfy alone. These do not necessarily imply that one is living a spiritual life. The responsorial psalm on each of these days (Psalm 51) points up even more directly what is intended in such practices (especially because it is used throughout the season of Lent):

A clean heart create for me, O God,
    and a steadfast spirit renew within me.
Cast me not off from your presence,
    and your holy spirit take not from me.
Give me back the joy of your salvation,
    and a willing spirit sustain in me.   (vv. 12–14)

O Lord, open my lips,
    and my mouth shall proclaim your praise.
For you are not pleased with sacrifices;
    should I offer a holocaust, you would not
    accept it.
My sacrifice, O God, is a contrite spirit;
    a heart contrite and humbled, O God, you
    will not spurn.   (vv. 17–19)[10]

That there is the tradition of a prophetic and evangelical critique against the misuse of liturgy in the canonical Scriptures is significant; but the fact that these texts which represent this tradition are included in liturgical proclamation and emphasized at the beginning of Lent is all the more significant. It is assumed that what is proclaimed and enacted in the liturgy of Eucharist will lead to lives lived in witness to this mystery. What these texts do in the liturgy of the word is to challenge communities to live what they celebrate and to realize that the liturgy acts on and influences persons throughout their lives, not just things at times of celebration. Things can be managed and manipulated to serve many purposes; the liturgy is meant to challenge and direct our whole lives to greater fidelity in following the Lord. Hence, the need for an annual "forty days of Lent." As Taft states with regard to the hours:

> The Liturgy of the Hours . . . is a sanctification of the day by turning to God at its beginning and end to do what all liturgy always does: to celebrate and manifest in ritual moments what is and must be the constant stance of our every minute of the day: our priestly offering, in Christ, of self, to the praise and glory of the Father in thanks for His saving gift in Christ.[11]

THE DYNAMIC OF LITURGY

That the liturgy holds a central and significant place in the spirituality of the Church is noted in the very first paragraph of the Liturgy Constitution of Vatican II. Since this was the first document promulgated by the Council fathers their comments are particularly significant in that they address the place of liturgy in the life of the Church as well as the goal of the Council:

> It is the goal of this most sacred Council to intensify the daily growth of Catholics in Christian living; to make more responsive to the requirements of our times those Church observances which are open to adaptation; [and] to nurture whatever can contribute to the unity of all who believe in

Christ. . . . Hence the Council has special reason for judging
it a duty to provide for the renewal and fostering of the
liturgy (no. 1).

This broad understanding of the aims of the Council and their
conjunction with the liturgy offers a clear example of the wide
understanding of the appropriate context for and understanding
of liturgy in the life of the Church. This wide understanding is
substantiated in *Music in Catholic Worship* in its introductory
paragraphs:

> We are Christians because through the Christian community
> we have met Jesus Christ, heard his word in invitation, and
> responded to him in faith. We gather at Mass that we may
> hear and express our faith again in this assembly and, by
> expressing it, renew and deepen it. (no. 1)

> We do not come to meet Christ as if he were absent from the
> rest of our lives. We come together to deepen our awareness
> of and commitment to the action of his Spirit in the whole of
> our lives at every moment. We come together to acknowledge
> the love of God poured out among us in the work of the
> Spirit, to stand in awe and praise. (no. 2)

By intention of conciliar decree and this document on liturgical
implementation the liturgy is given a significant place in the
Church's life not only for the experience of common prayer, but
because of what is understood by the celebration of the liturgy.
Everyday life is the context for Christian celebration, and part of
the dynamic of celebration involves understanding this intrinsic
relationship. It is not liturgy for the sake of the cult, it is liturgy
celebrated for the sake of those celebrating, that they, in union
with the whole Church, might continue to become what they
already are, faithful worshipers in Spirit and in truth. It is this
rich and full understanding of the liturgy that should be operative in giving worship its proper place in the Christian life.

This understanding was clearly operative in the composition of the Rite of Christian Initiation of Adults. Unlike most
other liturgical rites reformed since the Council, the Rite of

Christian Initiation of Adults underwent a period of experimentation and evaluation in catechetical centers in Africa, France
and Japan. This was done in order to avoid the publication of a
"desk rite." This was especially important for adult initiation
because so much of the tradition and foundation on which it is
based is from the patristic era, and the wholesale imposition of
these liturgical forms without testing and evaluation could well
have led to a careful and "correct" ritual, but one that did not
meet the actual needs of the Church in the twentieth century.[12]
One general criticism that came from these experimental centers and which influenced the final drafting of the rite of adult
initiation was that the proposed catechumenal structure and
accompanying liturgical ceremonies led to the *rite* of initiation
but did not necessarily initiate one to the Christian *life*. This
keen insight was elaborated on further:

> The catechumenate is not to be reduced to the realization of
> its steps; it should also lead the convert toward the new life
> possessed by the one who has been baptized and should
> express the life of a community which is beginning to in-
> crease. In other words, from this encounter issued a request
> that the catechumenal liturgy not only mirror great liturgical
> knowledge and beautiful imagination, but also solid pastoral
> experience.[13]

The net result of this experimentation and evaluation is a rite
that is eminently flexible in length, structure and content de-
pending on the felt pastoral needs of the given Church community. It is values of the catechumenate (whatever its precise
form) as a communal process of conversion, profession of faith
and initiation into the life of Christ lived in community, that is
repeatedly stressed in the General Instruction:

> The initiation of catechumens is a gradual process that takes
> place within the community of the faithful. Together with the
> catechumens, the faithful reflect upon the value of the pas-
> chal mystery, renew their own conversion, and by their exam-
> ple lead the catechumens to obey the Holy Spirit more
> generously. (no. 4)

The phrase "fellow-journeyers"[14] is used to describe the situation of the already-initiated as they grow in their faith profession and life commitment to the Lord along with inquirers and candidates:

> Familiar with living the Christian way of life and helped by the example and support of sponsors and godparents and the whole community of the faithful, the catechumens will learn to pray to God more easily, to witness to the faith . . . [and] to exercise charity toward neighbors to the point of self-renunciation.[15]

> Since the Church's life is apostolic, catechumens should also learn how to work actively with others to spread the Gospel and build up the Church by the testimony of their lives and the profession of their faith.[16]

The dynamic operative in the process of the catechumenate and in the rites leading to and of initiation point to the dynamic that is operative in all liturgy—that rite and ceremony come from the context of living the Christian life and lead to a return to a deeper commitment and conversion to the Lord. What is celebrated in rite and ritual signifies what is operative in the rest of the lives of those who celebrate—a conversion to the Gospel's values and way of living that can be called truly Christian. These high expectations for the newly-initiated are the same for the already-baptized. The *rite* of adult initiation must necessarily reflect a commitment to the Christian *life*.

The sacrament of on-going conversion and the renewal of the covenant of baptism is the Eucharist.[17] In being just that, a renewal of conversion, the Eucharist relates to the lives of those who worship. The dismissal "Go in peace to love and serve the Lord" explicitates what is inherent in the rite. The particularly expressive words of the eucharistic prayers state:

> And that we might live no longer for ourselves but for him,
> he sent the Holy Spirit from you, Father,
> as his first gift to those who believe,

to complete his work on earth
and bring us the fullness of grace.

(Eucharistic Prayer IV)

Keep us all
in communion of mind and heart
with N., our pope, and N., our bishop.
Help us to work together
for the coming of your kingdom
until at last we stand in your presence
to share the life of the saints. . . .

(Eucharistic Prayer of Reconciliation I)

It is also in the prayers after Communion that the life relation of the liturgy is underscored: "In the prayer after communion the priest petitions for the effects of the mystery just celebrated, and by their acclamation, Amen, the people make the prayer their own."[18] Most often these prayers refer to the present celebration of Eucharist, the future glory to be shared in the kingdom of heaven, and the living out of the Eucharist in our lives. The texts of the prayers after Communion for the Advent Sundays state:

Father,
may our communion
teach us to love heaven.
May its promise and hope
guide our way on earth.

(First Sunday of Advent)

Father,
you give us food from heaven.
By our sharing in this mystery,
teach us to judge wisely the things of earth
and to love the things of heaven.

(Second Sunday of Advent)

God of mercy,
may this eucharist bring us your divine help,

free us from our sins
and prepare us for the birthday of our Savior. . . .

(Third Sunday of Advent)

Lord,
in this sacrament
we receive the promise of salvation;
as Christmas draws near
make us grow in faith and love
to celebrate the coming of Christ
    our Savior,
who is Lord for ever and ever.

(Fourth Sunday of Advent)[19]

The second reading of the Christmas Mass at midnight from Titus (2:11–14) is reflected in the prayer after Communion of this liturgy:

God our Father,
we rejoice in the birth of our Savior.
May we share his life completely
by living as he has taught.

The final prayer of the feast of the Baptism of the Lord reflects the readings of the day and the intended effects of the Eucharist:

Lord,
you feed us with bread from heaven.
May we hear your Son with faith
and become your children in name and in fact.

These examples of Church documents, liturgical rites, and prayer texts serve to illustrate what is inherent in the dynamic of the liturgy. The community that gathers for worship comes together for common prayer, reflection, and sharing in the paschal mystery of Jesus so that it might be sent forth again to live what is celebrated. The liturgical assembly is not a clique. Nor is the liturgy intended to make us satisfied by the ritual alone. Liturgy should always direct us outward to others and to the rest of our lives. The dynamic of gathering and dispersing reflects what is intended in every liturgy. Liturgy comes from the context of our actual and real lives; after it we return to live out the mysteries celebrated in lives of deeper conversion and love.

LITURGICAL AND CHURCH MINISTRY

The tradition of the Church with regard to the ministries performed at liturgy is that these are best understood from the perspective of the self-understanding of the Church and as they manifest themselves in the community of the Church. The issue centers on the fact that whereas relatively recent convention stressed "priestly power" in sacraments and liturgy, a far more traditional understanding of priesthood (and other ministries) places emphasis on the Church which witnesses to the life of Christ with varying ministries and functions performed for the building up of the body of Christ. A review of some of the liturgical ministries that are operative in the reformed liturgy along with reference to their proper understanding can help illustrate the relationship between liturgical ministries and service rendered outside the specifically liturgical context. Among the plurality of liturgical ministers and ministries there are the roles of presbyter, deacon, lector, acolyte and special minister of the Eucharist.[20]

Presbyter—Recent studies regarding the role of the presbyter as he presides at liturgy indicate clearly that the position of responsibility and ministry of the presbyterate originally derived less from the function of liturgical presidency itself and far more from the position of leadership which these persons assumed in the community. Presidency of community and presidency of Eucharist were complementary manifestations of the charism of leadership. History suggests that the one who was suited to assume the presidency of community also assumed the presidency at liturgy.[21] In addition, contemporary emphases in ordained ministry show that one is called to the ministry of liturgy, preaching and community presidency, with each understood in relation to the others.[22] The very fact that the title "priest" is now frequently replaced by the term "presbyter" demonstrates that the one who presides at liturgy does more than offer sacrifice cultically (a notion associated with the notion "priest" in a rather individualistic sense). To be a presbyter includes notions of being elder, prophet, preacher, and minister to the community.[23] Historically, this most often meant that one was a member of the college of presbyters. The rather individual notions of priesthood that we have inherited evolved from and sometimes derogated from the essentially communal under-standing of this ministry in the Church. As the bishop says in choosing a man for ordination: "We rely on the help of the Lord God and our Savior Jesus Christ, and we choose this man, our brother, for priesthood in the presbyteral order."[24] That Chris-tian witness is intrinsically connected with this ministry is clearly evident in the text of the ordination rite:

> As a co-worker with the order of bishops
> may he be faithful to the ministry
> that he received from you, Lord God,
> and be to others a model of right conduct.
> May he be faithful
> in working with the order of bishops,
> so that the words of the Gospel
> may reach the ends of the earth. . . .[25]

When receiving the gifts presented for the celebration of the Eucharist the bishop admonishes the one ordained:

> Accept from the holy people of God the gifts to
>   be offered to him.
> Know what you are doing, and imitate the mystery
>   you celebrate:
> model your life on the mystery of the Lord's
>   cross.[26]

What is clearly enunciated in the rite of ordination reflects the richness of the recent recovery of this more traditional understanding of the presbyterate. Certainly one important emphasis in this restoration places the ministry of presiding, of preaching and of leadership within the context of service to the community.

Deacon—The close association of diaconal ministry at liturgy with other service performed in the community is clearly underscored in the tradition and in the present rite for ordination. In the prayer of consecration it states:

> Lord,
> send forth upon him the Holy Spirit,
> that he may be strengthened
> by the gift of your sevenfold grace
> to carry out faithfully the work of the ministry.
> May he excel in every virtue:
> in love that is sincere,
> in concern for the sick and the poor,
> in unassuming authority,
> in self-discipline,
> and in holiness of life.
> May his conduct
> exemplify your commandments
> and lead your people
> to imitate his purity of life.
> May he remain strong and steadfast in Christ,
> giving to the world
> the witness of a pure conscience.
> May he in this life imitate your Son,
> who came, not to be served but to serve,
> and one day reign with him in heaven.[27]

The role of the deacon in the community as one who is especially concerned with the charity and teaching is imaged in the liturgy where he assists in the following ways:

> Among ministers, the deacon, whose order has been held in high honor since the early Church, has first place. At Mass he has his own functions: he proclaims the gospel, sometimes preaches God's word, leads the general intercessions, assists the priest, gives communion to the people (in particular, ministering the chalice), and sometimes gives directions re-

garding the assembly's moving, standing, kneeling, or sitting.[28]

The fact that the deacon was and ought to be involved in the charitable work of the community is exemplified in the liturgy where he, who would know who was ill or needed prayers, would be the natural person to announce the intentions of the prayer of the faithful.[29] When the deacon assists the priest in the preparation of the bread and wine at the altar, he exemplifies the role he once played in assisting in the collection of gifts for the poor during the liturgy, some of which would be used at the Eucharist itself. Hence, once again, he would be responsible for liturgical ministry in the wide sense of cult and of life.

The task of the deacon to proclaim the Gospel, and sometimes to preach, reflects his role as teacher and example to the community. In receiving the book of the Gospels during the ordination ceremony the bishop says to the deacon:

> Receive the Gospel of Christ,
> whose herald you now are.
> Believe what you read,
> teach what you believe,
> and practice what you teach.[30]

The cultic role is once more set within the life role of exemplar and model of Gospel values. Whether in speech or in deed the diaconal ministry involves far more than assisting in the celebration of the liturgy. The restoration of this role in the Church today offers limitless possibilities for associating what is lived with what is done in liturgy and vice versa.[31] Robert Hovda remarks:

> Roles cannot be defined in isolation, but only in the context of the church's life. History shows a definite relationship between a decline in Christian appreciation of the bonds that link community work for justice with common prayer and a decline in the deacon's role as a permanent and essential ministry.[32]

Reader—The reader is instituted (not ordained as are presbyters and deacons) to proclaim the Scripture readings except for the Gospel. The reader has a rightful and proper function in the liturgical assembly and is to exercise this role even when ordained ministers are present.[33] Just as in the ordination rites noted above, the rite of installation of readers includes explicit reference to the readers' cultic and wider ministry in the Church:

> You will proclaim that word in the liturgical assembly, instruct children and adults in the faith and prepare them to receive the sacraments worthily. You will bring the message of salvation to those who have not yet received it. Thus with your help men and women will come to know God our Father and his Son Jesus Christ, whom he sent, and so be able to reach eternal life.

> In proclaiming God's word to others, accept it yourselves in obedience to the Holy Spirit. Meditate on it constantly, so that each day you will have a deeper love of the Scriptures, and in all you say and do show forth to the world our Savior, Jesus Christ.[34]

The roles of proclaiming and teaching are seen as correlative in this ministry as they are in the ministry of deacons. With all other liturgical ministers, readers are to exemplify in action the word they proclaim:

> Take this book of holy Scripture
> and be faithful in handing on the word of God,
> so that it may grow strong in the hearts
>   of his people.[35]

Acolyte—The General Instruction on the Roman Missal gives the following description of the role of the acolyte:

> The acolyte is instituted to serve at the altar and to assist the priest and deacon. In particular it is for him to prepare the

altar and the vessels and, as a special minister of the eucharist, to give communion to the faithful. (no. 65)

Just as the institution rite for readers gives more concrete dem-
onstration to the life dimension of their role, so too does the
institution rite for acolytes:

Grant that they may be faithful
in the service of your altar
and in giving to others the bread of life;
may they grow always in faith and love,
and so build up your Church. . . .

Take this vessel with bread (wine)
for the celebration of the eucharist.
Make your life worthy of your service
at the table of the Lord and of his Church.[36]

Some of the assumptions which we almost automatically
make about the role of acolytes ("servers") deserve some reflection whether these ministers are instituted or not. One of the
important aspects of this role is that it be carried out by those
who are acquainted with the structure and flexibility of the
liturgy. The practice of having youngsters serve in this capacity
derives from the original thinking that "acolyte" was among the
"minor orders" leading to priesthood. Hence acolytes served at
the altar before they were ordained deacons and then priests. In
this former practice when seminary candidates were unavailable
other young men took their place. Younger boys would serve at
the liturgy at a rite that rarely changed and whose prayers and
gestures could be memorized. Especially because variety and
flexibility are built into the reformed liturgy[37] and because this
role is not intended to be reserved to young men only, a re-
evaluation of who should minister in this role may well be in
order.[38]

Special Minister of the Eucharist—The most recent of the
liturgical ministries to evolve is that of the special minister of the
Eucharist, and it is notably one that has been implemented very

widely. In the proposed homily for the commissioning of special ministers the ordinary (or his delegate) may say:

> Our brothers and sisters . . . are to be entrusted with administering the eucharist, with taking communion to the sick, and with giving it as viaticum to the dying.

> [Then addressing the ministers]
> In this ministry, you must be examples of Christian living in faith and conduct; you must strive to grow in holiness through this sacrament of unity and love. Remember that, though many, we are one body because we share the one bread and one cup.

> As ministers of holy communion be, therefore, especially observant of the Lord's command to love your neighbor. For when he gave his body as food to his disciples, he said to them: "This is my commandment, that you should love one another as I have loved you."[39]

What is especially significant about the ministry exercised by those so designated is that it frequently involves a regular ministry of bringing Eucharist to the sick and the homebound. The services provided in the ritual for this ministry give ample evidence of the importance of ministering outside the liturgy as well as during it.[40]

This review of the present experience of liturgical roles and ministries confirms the principle with which we began, that liturgical ministries are best understood when they reflect services and functions experienced in the community. "Liturgical ministry" is understood in its wide sense as that which images in the cultic life of the Church what is lived as Church life in service to the Gospel of Jesus.

It should also be noted that these are not necessarily the only non-ordained ministries to be exercised in the Church, for in the apostolic constitution *Ministeria quaedam* Pope Paul VI invites episcopal conferences to request the establishment of ministries other than acolytes and readers for their territories.[41] What is interesting to note is that in establishing other ministries many national episcopal conferences have been slow in instituting any which might appear to be limited to the cult of liturgy only.[42] The pre-conciliar barrier about the individuality of the ordained and the pre-conciliar tentative first steps in the direction of a wide understanding of "lay ministry" have been transcended in the contemporary understanding, appreciation of and assumptions about ministry. The clear relationship of liturgy and the life of faith is here appropriately imaged and exemplified.

LITURGICAL AND PERSONAL PRAYER

In addition to the aspects of the life of faith argued here, there is the important place which personal prayer has in the life of the Christian. The fact that liturgical prayer should not constitute all of a Christian's prayer is stated clearly in the Liturgy Constitution:

> The spiritual life, however, is not confined to participation in the liturgy. The Christian is assuredly called to pray with his brethren, but he must also enter into his chamber to pray to the Father in secret (cf. Mt. 6:6); indeed, according to the teaching of the Apostle Paul, he should pray without ceasing (cf. 1 Th. 5:17) . . . (no. 12).

With the revival of interest in and the experience of the liturgy as an important focal point for Christian prayer it is important to recall that this "summit and source" of the Christian life itself needs a solid base and support. This base comes from an ever-deepening conversion to the Lord and to the values of the Gospel. It also requires the continual support of personal reflective prayer outside the liturgy. When approaches to spirituality are predicated on the demands of the apostolate, and therefore emphasize service and action, the time left for prayer can be limited. It is not infrequently the case that such apostolic "spiritualities" grew up at a time in the Church's life when private, individual prayer was prized above all else as the prayer dimension of one's life. With the recent revival of the liturgy, there can sometimes be a conflict between the liturgical and the personal dimension to prayer. As Thomas Merton observes:

> The early Christian tradition and the spiritual writers of the Middle Ages knew no conflict between "public" and "private" prayer, or between the liturgy and contemplation. This is a modern problem. Or perhaps it would be more accurate to say that it is a pseudo-problem. Liturgy by its very nature tends to prolong itself in individual contemplative prayer, and mental prayer in its turn disposes us for and seeks fulfillment in liturgical worship.[43]

Nathan Mitchell takes up this important insight and speaks about prayer of the heart and the prayer of worship.[44] The two are correlatives for the Christian life, not only because each is needed to foster the spiritual life, but because the inclusion of liturgy (especially in the more apostolic forms of spirituality) can help give direction and perspective to what is used in personal meditation. In this sense, what is inherent in the liturgy is intended to influence how we pray outside the liturgy and how we understand what Christian prayer is in the first place. As Mitchell states boldly:

> For a Christian, then, regular engagement in the ritual repertoire of the community at worship prevents personal prayer and meditation from becoming mere patterns of withdrawal. In his private contemplative prayer the Christian realizes that his identity . . . is forged out of the patterns of common worship. He returns to those patterns in a regular rhythm because they remain the generative source for that grace of prayer he received in baptism. A form of meditation that consistently cuts the Christian loose from the worshiping assembly may have some transcendent or therapeutic value, but is less than fully Christian.[45]

What the pattern and content of liturgical prayer offers is the Church's way of praying in common, and the Church's way of understanding and appreciating the central mysteries of our faith. The balance inherent in the liturgy can offer a guide for the Christian's individual prayer in order that what is expressed and what is inherent in the liturgy might also be reflected in personal prayer. The notions of liturgical prayer as essentially corporate, involving the proclamation of the word, as a real participation in the paschal mystery, through a patterned experience of prayer, done through a year in a cycle of feasts and seasons, and in prayer that is essentially in the name of the Father, Son and Spirit, are essential elements of the liturgy. That these elements should be reflected in our personal prayer would be important in order that contemplative prayer not emphasize one or another element to the detriment of the others. This is to suggest that Christian prayer ought to have the outward dimension toward others which is part of the structure of liturgy. Without this sense (of "corporate work" or corporateness) personal meditation could tend to become so individually oriented that the essentially communal dimension of redemption in the Judaeo-Christian tradition could become lost. In addition, a program of prayer that so emphasizes the life of Christ or prayer in Christ could run the risk of ignoring the significant place of the Holy Spirit in the Christian life. Also, in the light of the thesis of this chapter about the liturgy relating to the life of faith (and not just to itself or other prayer) the aspect of understanding spirituality as that which is reflected and lived throughout all of life is important to factor into any program or approach to personal prayer. Should this not occur, Christianity and the implications of the incarnation mystery would not be well served at all. Just as the liturgy relies on the base of personal prayer for it to be experienced fully and truly lived, so personal prayer needs the experience of the liturgy to keep it from going its own way.

The temptation of institutionalized forms of religious practice (such as the liturgy) is that they can become fossilized and closed in on themselves. That this can happen to the liturgical prayer of the Judaeo-Christian tradition is clear from the first utterances of the prophets' critique of the cult through to our day when these are read annually at the liturgy itself. By its very nature the liturgy is meant to be a coming together to express and deepen faith so that the sending forth at the end of the liturgy can be for the building up of the Church and living lives of Gospel witness in the world. Liturgical ministries, fully understood as those services which reach beyond the cult itself, exemplify what ought to be essential dimensions of this form of spirituality with liturgical prayer an essential component. Both personal and liturgical prayer are meant to serve the on-going and ever deepened conversion to the Lord which liturgy assumes and which it fosters. That prayer leads to life and that life is an essential context for our prayer is an important assumption in the Church's spiritual tradition.

> To say "yes" to God and "no" to man is impossible for the Christian. "If anyone says 'I love God,' and hates his brother, he is a liar" (1 Jn. 4:20). Worship, then, is not a department of life; it is life itself.
>
> And all true Christian Liturgy is a celebration of that reality. Thus the Offices at the beginning and the end of the day [for example] are just ritual moments symbolic of the whole of time. As such they are a proclamation of faith to the world and partake of our mission to witness to Christ and His salvation. They are also a praise and thanksgiving for this gift of salvation in Christ. Lastly, they are our priestly prayer, as God's priestly people, for our needs and those of the entire world. That is what Liturgy means. That is what Vespers means. As a matter of fact, that is what life means.[46]

NOTES

1. See Part One, Chapter One, section on "Spirituality and Liturgy."

2. See Part One, Chapter Three, sections on "Incarnational Spirituality" and "Liturgy and Sacraments."

3. Ernst Käsemann, "The Cry for Liberty in the Worship of the Church," *Perspectives on Paul*, trans. by Margaret Kohl (Philadelphia: Fortress Press, 1971), p. 136.

4. Victor Paul Furnish, *Theology and Ethics in Paul* (N.Y./Nashville: Abingdon, 1968) p. 101.

5. Ernst Käsemann, "On Paul's Anthropology," in *Perspectives*, p. 18.

6. Robert Taft, "Thanksgiving for the Light," 44, citing Joseph Powers.

7. *Ibid.* See also Jerome Murphy O'Connor, "Eucharist and Community in First Corinthians," *Worship* 50 (September 1976) 370–385 and *Worship* 51 (January 1977) 56–69.

8. For a treatment of this text and the context for early Christian worship see Jacques Dupont, "Jesus and Liturgical Prayer," *Worship* 43 (April 1969) 198–213.

9. The actual text at Eucharist is vs. 1–9 and of the reading at Office of Readings is vs. 1–12.

10. The fact that this same psalm contains the invitatory for the daily liturgy of the hours is also significant for this same reason: "O Lord, open my lips."

11. Robert Taft, "Thanksgiving for the Light," 44.

12. This is not to suggest that tradition is unimportant in formulating the reformed rites of the liturgy. It is to suggest that this particular experimental usage may well provide a paradigm for future liturgical implementation and indigenization.

13. Andre Aubry, "Le projet pastoral de l'initiation des Adultes," *Ephemerides Liturgicae* 88 (1974) 176.

14. This phrase is attributed to Regis Duffy. See above, Part Two, Chapter Four, section on "Communal Celebration of Rites."

15. *RCIA* no. 19, 2. This text continues by citing the *Decree on the Missions* of Vatican II: "This transition, which brings with it a progressive change of outlook and morals, should become evident together with its social consequences and should be gradually developed during the time of the catechumenate. Since the Lord in whom he believes is a sign of contradiction, the convert often experiences human divisions and separations, but he also tastes the joy which God gives without measure."

16. *RCIA* no. 19, 4. See also the *Decree on the Missions*, no. 14.

17. That the Eucharist is a renewal of baptism is explicitly noted in the introductory rite of blessing and sprinkling with holy water which is reserved for Sundays alone.

18. *General Instruction of the Roman Missal,* no. 56 k. See also Thomas A. Krosnicki, *Ancient Patterns in Modern Prayer,* Studies in Christian Antiquity, Vol. 19 (Washington: Catholic University of America Press, 1973) pp. 15–16.

19. These prayers are also used on the weekdays of the First and Second Weeks of Advent.

20. The office of episcopacy is not noted here because the intent is to argue from what is the usual experience of most worshipers on a regular basis.

21. See Herve-Marie Legrand, "The Presidency of the Eucharist According to the Ancient Tradition," *Worship* 53 (September 1979) 413–438.

22. David N. Power, *Gifts That Differ:* Lay Ministries Established and Unestablished (New York: Pueblo Publishing Co., 1980) p. 127.

23. For a brief review of the prayers used at ordination in the Western Church and some theological and liturgical perspectives, see H. Boone Porter, *The Ordination Prayers of the Ancient Western Churches* (London: SPCK, 1967); David N. Power, *Ministers of Christ and His Church.* The Theology of the Priesthood, (London: Geoffrey Chapman, 1969) and *The Christian Priest:* Elder and Prophet (London: Sheed and Ward, 1973).

24. *Rite of Ordination of a Priest, The Rites of the Catholic Church* Vol. Two (New York: Pueblo Publishing Co., 1980) no. 13, p. 61.

25. "Prayer of Consecration," Ordination Rite, no. 22, p. 67.

26. "Presentation of the Gifts," Ordination Rite, no. 26, p. 68.

27. *Rite of Ordination of a Deacon, The Rites, Vol. Two,* no. 61, pp. 56–57.

28. *General Instruction of the Roman Missal,* no. 61.

29. See Robert Hovda, "For Deacons," in *Touchstones for Liturgical Ministers,* edited by Virginia Sloyan (Washington: Liturgical Conference and the Federation of Diocesan Liturgical Commissions, 1978) pp. 17–18; see above, Part Two, Chapter Four, section on "Prayer for the Local and Universal Church."

30. "Presentation of the Book of the Gospels," *The Rites, Vol. Two,* no. 24, p. 58.

31. See Robert Hovda, "For All Who Exercise Any Specialized Office of Liturgical Ministry," in *Touchstones,* pp. 13–14 for some practical applications of this relationship.

32. *Ibid.,* p. 17. This statement speaks of the hopes implicit in the restoration of this ministry. That these hopes have been or are being realized is cause for contemporary consideration and evaluation.

33. *General Instruction of the Roman Missal*, no. 66.

34. "Instruction," *Institution of Readers, The Rites Vol. One*, no. 4, p. 741.

35. "Prayer," *Institution of Readers, The Rites Vol. One*, no. 6, pp. 741–42. It should be noted that this rite is rarely used in the American church outside of seminaries because to be instituted as a reader one must be male. On this whole (difficult and often explosive) issue see David N. Power, *Gifts That Differ*, Chapter One, pp. 3–32.

36. "Prayer," *Institution of Acolytes, The Rites Vol. One*, no. 6, pp. 744–45, and "Institution," no. 7, p. 745. See note 35 about those who are so instituted.

37. See Part Two, Chapter Seven, section on "Creativity and Option."

38. G. Thomas Ryan, "For Acolytes," in *Touchstones*, p. 16.

39. *Rite of Commissioning Special Ministers of Holy Communion, The Rites Vol. Two*, no. 2, p. 165.

40. See "The Ordinary Rite of Communion of the Sick," in *Administration of Communion and Viaticum to the Sick by an Extraordinary Minister* (Washington: USCC, 1976) pp. 7–16.

41. See *The Rites Vol. Two*, pp. 7–8.

42. See David N. Power, *Gifts That Differ*, pp. 12–32.

43. Thomas Merton, *Contemplative Prayer* (New York: Herder and Herder, 1969) p. 55.

44. See Part One, Chapter One, section on "Formative Nature of Liturgical Prayer." See also the articles by R. Duffy, A. Kavanagh, C. Kiesling, G. Martinéz, M. Searle and A. van Kaam in "Liturgy as a Formative Experience," in *Studies in Formative Spirituality* 3 (November 1982).

45. Nathan Mitchell, "Useless Prayer," *Christians at Prayer*, p. 20.

46. Robert Taft "Thanksgiving for the Light," 46.

Chapter Twelve
LITURGY AND MISSION

In the opinion of Louis Bouyer, a decisive turning point for the liturgical movement in this century took place in 1909 at the Malines (Belgium) conference on liturgical renewal. This meeting was made notable by the address given by Dom Lambert Beauduin, a monk of Mont Cesar, whose ministry as a parish priest before becoming a monk left an indelible mark on his approach to worship. He maintained that

> the liturgy itself, properly understood, is the fundamental catechesis of Christian doctrine, and that its presentation is the means most capable of stimulating and feeding the highest and purest spiritual life. And he also realized that the liturgy itself, thus understood, is meant to be the well-spring of spiritual vitality and to provide the framework for Christian living, not only for some Christians, but for the whole Christian people in the Church.[1]

The liturgical movement was thus called to be concerned with life as well as the experience of worship, with mission as well as the performance of the cult, with ministry and service before and after common prayer. It was to be a prayer which focuses and discloses the power of God at work in all of life. Properly understood, the "liturgical movement" was and should be concerned with the implications that derive from common celebration of the sacred mysteries: implications that involve action, service and mission.

J. Bryan Hehir notes that during the first half of this century in the American church this integrated approach to the meaning of liturgy was sustained and fostered. Yet he also argues that in the past two decades this interrelationship was separated (in practice if not in theory) and that the significant progress made in the celebration and the appreciation of liturgy occurred apart from parallel (although separate) progress in social action and in the justice demands of the Gospel.[2]

That the liturgy relates to mission and justice issues in our day (and in every age of the Church) is the thesis of this chapter. What is at issue is how and why liturgy relates to the rest of the Christian life in its action dimensions (as opposed to the more reflective dimensions noted above)[3] and what is the proper role of liturgy in them. What is at stake here is a delicately balanced approach to the phenomenon of Christian worship that discloses the relationship of liturgy specifically, as opposed to other forms of prayer, to the task of living as a Christian when the noises of solemn assemblies have died down and the work of Christian living continues. The title "liturgy and mission" has been chosen to indicate from the outset that while "liturgy and justice" is clearly included in this service dimension, justice is not co-terminous with the outward, mission dimension of worship.

RESPONSE TO WORSHIP

That liturgy is related to life has been argued above with regard to the incarnational approach to spirituality.[4] The very fact that we use the things of this earth in our worship (bread, wine, water, oil, incense, art, music, etc.) as the symbols of our communal action in liturgy exemplifies how on this significant level (literally) the things of this earth help us relate to God and how God acts through them to relate to and sanctify us. Rahner cautions against a too facile relating of "liturgy" and "life" where the liturgy is seen to be so contained that the grace received there (but not found elsewhere) gives participants the strength to live the life of God outside worship. This "two different worlds" approach is really a distortion if it becomes such a neat separation between the cult and real life. For

Rahner, real life is in the cult and the cult discloses what life is all about.[5]

The real issue is to see that both the doing of liturgy and the living of life are interrelated, whether in Rahner's or any other's approach. That God is experienced and very present to us in all of life is a principle of spirituality that derives from the incarnation. The question that arises when speaking about the "mission" dimension of liturgy, however, concerns how this mission is carried out, and what constitutes our understanding of "mission." Involvement in service outside the liturgy can quite legitimately take on a variety of forms, because the context for worship differs among communities, and because the needs of individual liturgical communities differ.

For example, among the kinds of communities which gather for liturgy are parishes, schools, religious congregations and monastic communities. To suggest that each is necessarily bound to mission and service is to reiterate what is intrinsic to the understanding of liturgy. But to suggest that all of these are bound to the same *kind* of involvements is to ignore the important place which each kind of liturgical community has in the vitality of the whole Church. A parish community may well be called to a more politically active involvement in dealing with the questions of world hunger and feeding, so clearly articulated in the eucharistic action of eating and drinking from the Lord's fullness and the abundance of this earth. A school community might well focus on the relationship between what is celebrated in school and what is lived at home, among peers, and in witness in the world. The service rendered here might well involve carefully organized "service projects" so that participants come to understand the intrinsic connection between personal prayer in sanctification and service in Christian living. A religious community might well seek to take a more prophetic and public witness as a community on significant issues of our day (for example, nuclear armaments and war) and to see these as essential components of living out their participation in the Church's liturgy. A monastic community, by its very nature, is called to a qualitatively different, though no less real, commitment to mission and service, lest the monastery itself become an enclave from the concerns of the whole world. Yet, it is this qualitatively different response that makes the notion of "mission" a varied aspect in spirituality rather than an aspect that admits of a single definition whose axis is action in the world. For those bound to the monastic enclosure "political" action cannot mean the same thing as it does for the active religious. Yet, the demands of our times about food distribution may well mean that the simple lifestyle of a monastery be re-examined to determine whether it is indeed simple enough. The mission and action parts of life are intrinsically connected with the celebration of liturgy. The ways in which these occur, however, do admit of varying inter-pretations and concrete programs.

In addition to this distinction about the variety of possible responses to liturgy, there is the important emphasis that should be placed on the liturgy as a form of communal prayer in spirituality, as opposed to other forms of prayer. If the liturgy is solely understood as that which inspires, directs, and strength-ens one for action, then it may well be substituted for by other forms of prayer. However, what needs to be remembered throughout is that it is the intrinsic relationship between the liturgy and mission that is argued here and that needs to be articulated. That other forms of personal prayer are important in the fostering of the spiritual life has been argued above.[6] What is at stake here is the important place which liturgy as liturgy has for the mission and service dimensions of the Chris-tian life. By its nature the liturgy flows from the rest of life and flows back into that life. The issue here concerns how the liturgy's content and structure articulate the mission demands of the Christian life. It is not so much that the liturgy energizes for fulfilling a program of action that reflects Christian values, however important this clearly is. The issue centers on how the component elements of liturgical prayer articulate and direct Christian living. This means reflecting on what real life issues are touched and addressed in preaching the word, how prayer for and in a Christian community requires deeds of love and service in that community, and how what is done in sign and symbol (for example, anointing for comfort and eating for suste-nance) leads to lives that offer the healing strength of Christ apart from the liturgy. This intrinsic relationship is stressed in order that what is done in response to the action of common worship is in fact a response to the proclaimed word of God and the enacted word of Christ in sign and symbol. While the inter-relatedness of these things is assumed, it is this inter-relatedness that often needs to be articulated and demonstrated lest the liturgy be turned inward when it is meant to be directed outward, and lest the deeds of service and ministry we perform are cut loose from their generative source in liturgy.

SOCIAL DIMENSIONS OF THE LITURGY

It is important to underscore the fact that while a certain (and much needed) revival of interest in the relationship between liturgy and social justice is occurring,[7] such an inter-relationship has been assumed in the structure and rites of liturgy from the very beginning. Even when the action of the liturgy was far removed from the comprehension and active participation of the community present, there was a certain relationship that still existed between liturgy and social concerns. Nathan Mitchell argues persuasively that the experience of eucharistic congresses often fostered such an understanding, and this is all the more significant because such experiences often were far removed from an experience that fostered full, conscious and active participation in the liturgy. Mitchell states: "Significantly, therefore, the Eucharistic Congresses were not limited to specifically liturgical and devotional issues. They provided a regular international forum for discussing Christian social responsibility in a rapidly developing world."[8] At the 1976 Eucharistic Congress, for example, Mother Teresa of Calcutta and Dom Helder Camara of Brazil spoke of their work with the poor and the latter passionately denounced injustice in third world countries.[9] Hence, it is interesting to note that even when participation in liturgy was all but neglected, the correlatives of common prayer and deeds of justice were still maintained.

What is a significant contribution to this issue in our day is the fact that built in to the liturgical reforms we now experience is a signficant emphasis on how the theology of liturgy and the liturgical rites relate to social concerns.

Christian Initiation—In addition to the emphasis (noted above)[10] on charity toward neighbor to the point of self-renunciation as part of Christian formation, the Rite of Christian Initiation of Adults speaks clearly about the apostolic nature of church membership.[11] In addition, in the period of mystagogia, " . . . the community of the neophytes move forward together, meditating on the Gospel, sharing in the eucharist, and performing works of charity. In this way they understand the paschal mystery more fully and bring it into their lives more and more" (no. 37). What is clearly underscored in the rites of Christian initiation is that the mission and social demands of Christian living are intrinsically connected to the celebration of initiation.

While some commentators have wondered whether already existing church communities offer catechumens a true example of what the practice of the faith really means, especially when it comes to the issues of mission and justice, it is not infrequently the case that it is the catechumens and newly-initiated themselves who encourage Christian communities to greater attentiveness to the mission and outreach demands of the Gospel.

Rite of Penance—From the general instruction on the rite of penance through all the ritual forms for reconciliation, the social dimensions of sin and reconciliation are stressed. Repentance, penance and reconciliation occur in the Church in many ways, among which is the sacrament of penance. But the setting for this and the required context is the community of the Church.[12] In dealing with the issue of sin as an offense against God and against one another, the instruction notes the social dimension very clearly:

> Since every sin is an offense against God that disrupts our friendship with him, "the ultimate purpose of penance is that we should love God deeply and commit ourselves completely to him." Therefore, the sinner who by the grace of a merciful God embraces the way of penance comes back to the Father

who "first loved us" (1 Jn 4:19), to Christ who gave himself up for us, and to the Holy Spirit who has been poured out on us abundantly.

"The hidden and gracious mystery of God unites us all through a supernatural bond: on this basis one person's sin harms the rest even as one person's goodness enriches them." Penance always therefore entails reconciliation with our brothers and sisters who remain harmed by our sins.

In fact, people frequently join together to commit injustice. But it is also true that they help each other in doing penance; freed from sin by the grace of Christ, they become, with all persons of good will, agents of justice and peace in the world. (no. 5)[13]

Godfrey Diekmann comments on the new rite of penance and our contemporary understanding of "private sin."

Never before have so many been aware that "private sin" is a contradiction in terms. This conscious need and stance of reconciliation in broadest terms seems to be more keenly felt by more Christians today than when the practice of multiple "private confessions" was still taken for granted. The "decline" in penance may actually signal a more mature and more responsible approach to the enormous social problems our world faces today.[14]

That the revised rite of penance is predicated on the active role that ought to be played by the Church in the process of forgiveness of sins is underscored when it states:

The whole Church, as a priestly people, acts in different ways in the work of reconciliation that has been entrusted to it by the Lord. Not only does the Church call sinners to repentance by preaching the word of God, but it also intercedes for them and helps penitents with a maternal care and solicitude to acknowledge and confess their sins and to obtain the mercy of God, who alone can forgive sins. Further, the Church becomes itself the instrument of the conversion and absolution of the penitent through the ministry entrusted by Christ to the apostles and their successors. (no. 8)

With regard to the forms of penance, the communal forms demonstrate clearly what is underscored here in theory by the fact that the Lord's prayer is part of the rite ("Forgive us our trespasses as we forgive those who trespass against us") because it aptly illustrates the dynamic of the forgiveness of sins.[15]

Even more dramatic is the statement made in the communal forms of penance which states that "the social aspect of grace and sin, by which the actions of individuals in some degree affect the whole body of the Church"[16] might well be addressed in the homily preached. With regard to the homily at penitential celebrations it notes:

The celebrant may speak about:
- sin, by which we offend God and also Christ's body, the Church, whose members we become in baptism;
- the way we affect each other when we do good or choose evil;
- the social and ecclesial dimension of penance by which individual Christians share in the work of converting the whole community;
- the celebration of Easter as the feast of the Christian community which is renewing itself by the conversion or repentance of each member, so that the Church may become a clearer sign of salvation in the world.[17]

The social dimension of what had conventionally come to be experienced and understood as individual forgiveness of sins is here transcended in favor of the more traditional understanding (both theologically and liturgically) of the dynamic of sin, forgiveness, and reconciliation.

Eucharist—The justice demands of the Gospel are clearly issues that are forged out of the Church's experience of the ministry of Jesus: "to the poor he proclaimed the good news of salvation, to prisoners, freedom, and to those in sorrow, joy" (fourth eucharistic prayer). The call and continual summons to

the Church, that it share in and ever experience anew this
ministry and imitate it in its present life, is indicated in the
eucharistic prayers for reconciliation. These are especially noted
because they were composed initially for the Holy Year of 1975
for renewal and reconciliation:

> [Father] you invite us
> to serve the family of mankind
> by opening our hearts
> to the fullness of your Holy Spirit.   (First Prayer)

> Father, all-powerful and ever-living God,
> we praise and thank you through Jesus Christ our Lord
> for your presence and action in the world.
> In the midst of conflict and division,
> we know it is you
> who turn our minds to thoughts of peace.
> Your Spirit changes our hearts:
> enemies begin to speak to one another,
> those who were estranged join hands in friendship,
> and nations seek the way of peace together.
> Your Spirit is at work
> when understanding puts an end to strife,
> when hatred is quenched by mercy,
> and vengeance gives way to forgiveness.

> God our Father,
> we had wandered far from you,
> but through your Son you have brought us back.
> You gave him up to death
> so that we might turn again to you
> and find our way to one another.
> Therefore we celebrate the reconciliation
> Christ has gained for us.   (Second Prayer)

What is clearly evidenced in these texts drawn from the
present liturgical rites of the Church is that the social dimensions of redemption and mission are indeed stressed and emphasized. Taking particular note of the rite of penance and the
eucharistic prayers for reconciliation, it is important to under-

score the theological and spiritual balance presented here between God's work and our response to that work of
reconciliation.[18] The foundation for spirituality is that we understand the Christian life as a way of living in response to God's
redeeming love in Christ; it is not primarily something we do. It
is God's life in us through baptism that makes all the difference.
Where God is (in us through baptism) there can be no sin;
hence our freedom from the sin we call "original" and our
participation in his (similarly original) justice. As we lead the
spiritual life we do so in response to his forgiveness, his justice
and his peace. It is this foundation that makes the liturgy an
essential component for the Christian involvement in peace and
justice concerns. Guided and strengthened by liturgy, Christians
are to engage in such works; but they are essentially the works of
God.

This approach to mission respects the liturgy for what it
is—an experience of the mission of God to us in Christ and of
the justice Christ came to bring.[19] The works of justice originate
in and derive from Christ. Programs and strategies to accomplish these ends ought to find the liturgy a source of life,
inspiration, and challenge. The proclamation of the word of
God and the enactment of God's kingdom at liturgy demand
their establishment and deepening outside cultic assemblies.
Liturgy, then, is not useful in the sense that it should be used to
support pre-determined strategies or movements. Rather, it is
central in the sense that through it Christians experience again
and again the reconciliation and justice of God's kingdom.

In reflecting on the present state of liturgical participation
and the witness which Christians give to what they say and do at
worship, Regis Duffy observes:

> Worship and sacrament have always formed an important
> part of the Christian heritage. The disturbing question, how-
> ever, persists: why is there so much worship and so little
> commitment? For the Christian, the answer does not lie in
> God's absence but, perhaps, in our own. Worship and sacra-
> ment as symbols are filled with God's presence. But we can
> only symbolize out of our experience. There's the rub. Do we

use the signs of God's presence in worship and sacrament to avoid his presence?

Do our current ecclesiologies talk of discipleship but, in reality, demand only membership? Do our sacraments, as Pascal once remarked, excuse us from the cost of loving?[20]

From the texts we have cited it is clear that the liturgy demands responses and commitments. At issue, then, is the frequent experience of a divorce between what is stated and what is perceived, between what is clear in theory and what is actually done in practice.[21]

In order that the mission dimension of liturgy again be appreciated as constitutive of the experience of worship it would be important, for example, to critique the usual programs for sacramental preparation and celebration.[22] The values seen in the rite for adult initiation and penance should find clear and ample expression in the programs which concern the celebration of other sacraments, especially Eucharist.

The catechesis of the Mass should emphasize that Christians are called on to consecrate themselves, their work, and the fruit thereof to God. It should further stress the relationship between the service of God in the liturgy and the service of humankind in the world.[23]

In addition, the collection of gifts at Eucharist might well be evaluated and freed from an exclusively parochial concern so that what is symbolized in liturgy can be made all the more apparent through the ritual of giving and offering:

The collections at the Eucharist should be interpreted as a symbolic expression of ... consecration to God. The use made of these collections should not be self-serving but should correspond to the wider horizon of the Christian community's social obligations. It should be taken for granted by the community that the normal recipients are God's poor. In this way the community is enabled consciously to actualize the relation between worship and social justice.[24]

In order that the essential relationship between liturgy and mission be maintained it would be helpful to review the structures of (parish/diocesan) committees such as those for social ministry and for liturgy. Where and how these intersect can help toward the unity of approach first envisioned (and assumed) by liturgical pioneers such as Lambert Beauduin. The linking of "liturgy and life" could thus be helped by constant reference between ministry concerns and cultic needs. Each could be seen to be an extension of the life and ministry of Jesus whose mission we share.

THE JUSTICE OF GOD AND THE MISSION OF CHRIST

From the perspective of developing a liturgical spirituality it is important to underscore the formative nature of what is required by way of personal appropriation of liturgical prayer. One example of uniting what is celebrated liturgically with a spirituality that reflects the liturgical seasons is evidenced, for example, in the way we approach the Advent and Christmas seasons. In addition to the incorrect interpretation of the liturgical year which fosters a biographical or chronological approach (noted above),[25] there is the temptation to impose on the liturgy categories of thought and expression that are not there. An overly nostalgic or sentimental approach to viewing the Christmas crèche does not reflect the challenge and full mystery celebrated in this season.

By design, the Advent lectionary presents for our reflection the challenge of the person and preaching of John the Baptizer, the vision and hope afforded by the prophets (especially Isaiah), and the response to God's word and the values of the Gospel enunciated by the Blessed Virgin Mary.[26] What is clear in these texts and rites is that Advent is about the very serious business of our responding to the word of God. It is about our communal living out of what Christ made real in his incarnation, of what ought to be sustaining values for Christians as they lead lives in the light of the incarnation and before Christ's return in glory. The annual assessment of fidelity to the word which is intrinsic to Advent invites the Church to be ever more attentive to the many comings of Christ into our lives: at Christmas, in the ordinariness of everyday life, at the end of our lives, and at the end of time. The babe of Bethlehem cannot be unborn; but precisely because the babe has been born humanity has been irrevocably divinized and reconciled to God. The estrangement inherited from our first parents is overcome once for all by the coming of Christ. Our Advent response is to this event of history, and to the implications which this event points to in terms of a way of living Gospel values.

The season begins with the clear reminder that this world will pass away and that the judgment to be exacted by the Son of Man will concern how faithful we have been to the life and love made flesh in Christ. This clear eschatological emphasis makes real demands on those who celebrate this season as it focuses on exacting a judgment from ourselves on how faith-filled and Gospel-oriented we are as we lead this human life. The focus is fidelity to the deeds of witness and mission, not just words uttered in assemblies for worship. The preaching and personal integrity of John the Baptizer mark the Second and Third Sundays of Advent. The piercing challenge: "Give some indication that you mean to reform" and "Make straight the way of the Lord" orient Christians to the changes in human life that are required of one who follows Christ. Advent is less about the birth of the child Jesus than it is about our communal response to the preaching and teaching of the adult Christ. The preaching of the Baptist sets us up for the full meaning of the incarnation celebrated at Christmas. The Fourth Sunday of the season focuses on the response of Mary to the Lord's word to her: "Blessed is she who trusted that the Lord's words to her would be fulfilled" (Lk 1:45). A similar trusting the word of the Lord and living according to that word should mark the lives of those who at this part of Advent eagerly anticipate Christmas. What the liturgy presents is a clear counter-cultural symbol this last Sunday—Mary, from whose virginal womb would come forth a Messiah-Lord. In fact, it is in the last week of Advent (December 22) that Mary's canticle is offered for proclmation and reflection at the Eucharist. It is not only that Mary submits to the word of

God, she also utters profound proclamation of what it means that God took on human flesh in Christ and thereby changes accustomed ways of living. Now the lowly will be exalted, the hungry will be filled, and the rich will be sent away empty. There is no annunciation or visitation without the profound statement of faith in Gospel values, the *Magnificat*. Mary's canticle is indeed Christian proclamation of the first order, and it is one of the reasons why it is prayed daily at evening prayer in the liturgy of the hours.

By no means is Advent a domesticated, calm or tranquil time. It is meant to be a time of reflection and evaluation about the ways in which we live out what has become real in Jesus: the coming of "the Lord our justice" (Jer 33:16), for whom "justice shall be the band around his waist, and faithfulness a belt upon his hips" (Is 11:10). In addition to presenting Mary as the one who does the will of the Lord and who obeys the word of the angel, so the liturgy reminds us that Jesus also obeyed his Father's will and hence brought salvation for all who believe: "By this 'will' we have been sanctified through the offering of the body of Jesus Christ once for all" (Heb 10:10).

From these illustrations it is clear that the concerns of being responsive to the word of the Lord and living according to the integrity demanded by the Gospel are paramount values in Advent. The warnings of the prophets (including John the Baptist) are not strident denunciations, however, for they also contain essential elements of comfort, quiet joy and forgiveness—all because the source of all life is the source of response, the Lord who will lead us to the kingdom of God. It is the Lord who has accomplished all these things, and it is by the sustaining arm of the Lord that we can live the challenging words we hear in Advent.

> Comfort, give comfort to my people,
>   says your God.
> Speak tenderly to Jerusalem, and proclaim to her
>   that her service is at an end,
>   her guilt is expiated.   (Is 40:1–2)

As Isaiah reminds us, the judgment which God will exact includes his mercy and love:

> Not by appearance shall he judge
>   nor by hearsay shall he decide,
> But he shall judge the poor with justice,
>   and decide aright for the land's afflicted.   (Is 11:3–4)

Advent provides a very appropriate time for reflecting on the ways in which we live out the justice and mercy of God. It is a time when personal prayer and reflection[27] as well as educational programs[28] and the preaching at liturgy can be directed to the pressing needs of justice and peace. In this way, what is prayed liturgically is allowed to influence the rest of our prayer and action. Advent is, indeed, not a time to domesticate the liturgy. This season strikes to the heart of the matter: how well we ourselves experience and appreciate the incarnation, and so live what the coming of God in human flesh is all about.[29]

That the Christmas season is concerned with living out the implications of our being divinized in Christ is clear from the present emphasis given in the liturgy to the solemnity of Epiphany and the feast of the Baptism of Jesus. That the incarnation leads to the mission of Jesus to do his Father's will, to the point of offering his life on the cross, is seen clearly in the readings for the Baptism of the Lord. The prophet Isaiah offers the servant song acclaiming the one who is to establish justice on the earth, who will open the eyes of the blind, bring prisoners out of confinement, and offer light to those in darkness (Is 42:1–4, 6–7). In the Synoptic accounts of the event of the baptism a voice from heaven speaks to confirm: "This is my beloved Son. My favor rests on him." This declaration is particularly significant because later on in the Synoptic tradition it is a voice from heaven that confirms Jesus' identity at the transfiguration, which event ends with the prediction that this Messiah would have to suffer and die in order to enter his glory (Mk 9:9–13). The mission inaugurated in Jesus is commemorated by the Christian community annually so that it too may share in the mystery of God's design, that we should be saved by one like us in all things but sin. Our task is to respond to this mystery by living as those who respond to the favor given us in Christ—the divine life. As Jesus' ministry began at his baptism, so we should understand that our ministries, our lives of Christian service and mission, begin with our baptism into the Christian community.

Clearly, the liturgy of the Advent-Christmas season hardly allows us to domesticate the event of the incarnation by emphasizing reminiscences about the birth of Jesus only. It speaks of the coming of God among us, our being redeemed by Christ's paschal mystery, and our joining in his work and mission. To over-emphasize the birth of Jesus could well make the paschal mystery, so central to redemption, seem to be unconnected to the incarnation. The liturgy does not allow such a separation. Our participation in the Advent-Christmas cycle also points toward and is commemorated through the center of all liturgical participation—the paschal mystery.

> God was in Christ, reconciling the world to himself and it was done through cross and resurrection. The basic grammar of God's dealings with us is that of the paschal mystery, and because this is so it is impossible to speak of Advent and Christmas without Easter perspectives opening at every turn.... Mary's obedient "Fiat" at the Annunciation presages Jesus' "Fiat" as he confronts the passion; his sonship to the Father, present humanly from the moment of his incarnation, has to be worked out in human living until it is made perfect on the cross and revealed in the glory of his resurrection. He inaugurates his vocation as Servant already in the humility of his coming. His human birth is the beginning of that new creation which will be complete in him at his new birth from the dead and shared with us through the gift of his Spirit.[30]

The mission-inaugurating event of Jesus' baptism signals our participation in the work of reconciliation, justice and peace in and through Christ because of our baptism. We are initiated into a community of service and mission as well as to a community of prayer and praise. The Advent-Christmas cycle serves to remind us of what is at the heart of the incarnation mystery—

that in Christ we who are one with God are to share in this mission which he came to accomplish. The fact that it is yet to be completed is a fact of the Christian life. The justice and peace of the Gospel, personified and manifest in Jesus, will be unfulfilled and not totally complete until the kingdom comes finally and fully. It is in the meantime that our participation in liturgy and mission serves the coming of that kingdom. But even then, we make present the kingdom of God only because God has made it present and manifest in Christ. It is less a question of building the kingdom than allowing God to complete its establishment begun in the incarnation.[31] Such is our task when we celebrate our common faith and hear again and again the proclamation of the values of God's kingdom.

A DELICATE BALANCE

The task of delineating and living what may be described as a liturgical spirituality involves a delicate balancing of a number of factors among which include the experience of liturgical prayer and living a life in conformity with what is prayed. By way of paradigm, the evening liturgy of the Lord's Supper on Holy Thursday offers helpful insight about the way one can determine how what is celebrated in liturgy ought to be reflected in the rest of life. In many ways this particular liturgy articulates what is involved and implied in all liturgy—that common worship discloses and evokes the very presence of God and our being made sharers in his life; it is this divine life which is meant to be shared both within and outside the assembly for worship.[32]

What is clearly demonstrated in the liturgy of the evening Mass of the Lord's Supper on Holy Thursday is the understanding that worship and service, liturgy and mission, Church ritual and the reconciliation of peoples are intrinsically connected and can never be separated.

In the mid-1950's and more recently in 1970, the liturgies that comprise Holy Week underwent significant changes. The simplification of Holy Thursday and reorientation of the liturgy to essential rites, signs, gestures and texts was based on many very traditional practices. During the Holy Thursday liturgy in history and in the present reform, the Church underscores the service demanded of those who celebrate Eucharist, the reconciling love of the Father calling the community to unity in him, and the memorial of Christ's passing from death to life eternal. This commemoration is done in sign, gesture, proclamation and prayer. And in reflecting on what we do on Holy Thursday we realize once again who we are as the body of Christ and what is expected of us as those who share in the body of Christ in the Eucharist.[33]

The Washing of Feet—The Gospel proclaimed on Holy Thursday evening is from John 13 (vv 1–15) and it sets up the correlation between table-fellowship and service to each other. At the Last Supper Jesus assumes the role of both leader and servant and he exemplifies this in word and gesture. He leads his disciples in the meal as would be expected of a "Teacher and Lord." But what breaks social custom and pierces to the heart of his mission and their share in his mission is that he humbles himself to wash the feet of those who are his followers. "But if I washed your feet, I who am Teacher and Lord, then you must wash each other's feet. What I just did was to give you an example ..." (Jn 13:14–15). The instruction is clear and the proclamation is firm: to share in the eucharistic meal demands our sharing in the work of serving each other outside such sacred settings. The point of the text is brought out clearly, for the action of washing feet follows the Gospel and homily. It is by word and gesture that the Holy Thursday liturgy affirms the unity of Christ's role as leader and servant and the role of Christians as imitators of him.

The *mandatum* (the Latin term for foot washing, which is the origin of another term for this day, Maundy Thursday) was a common gesture in the early centuries of the Church as an act of hospitality. It was done on Holy Thursday in Jerusalem in the mid-fifth century, in Spain it is found in the seventh century, and in Rome from the seventh century on it was done by the Pope himself, sometimes in two ceremonies: one for clerics and the other for the poor. Even when the Mass for blessing chrism was held on Holy Thursday morning this ceremony was reserved to the evening. In the reform of Holy Week by Pius XII it was

restored as an option after the Gospel. What had occurred
liturgically from the fourteenth century to this revision in 1955
was a greater emphasis given to the reservation of the eucharistic species after the liturgy and less emphasis on the signs,
gestures and texts that were part of the liturgy itself and they
simplify the transfer of the Eucharist. The reforms of the 1950's
and of 1970 help redirect attention to the act of liturgy. The
gesture of foot washing can serve as graphic testimony of the
heart of Holy Thursday: that worship in sacred and solemn
assembly necessarily leads to service in our everyday lives and
that the correlation of these is what the liturgy and theology of
Holy Thursday is all about.

In the liturgy of Holy Thursday the antiphons which accompany this ceremonial foot washing are drawn from the Gospel of
John (chapter 13) and 1 Corinthians (13:13 about allowing faith,
hope and love to endure, "and the greatest of these is love").
Clearly the proclamation of this Gospel and the action of foot
washing combine to give significant witness to the importance of
service to each other and our acts of common worship.

This kind of service and mission is underscored in the
liturgy of the Eucharist that follows. As the gifts of bread and
wine are presented and prepared the liturgy suggests that
"there may be a procession of the faithful with gifts for the
poor." Again the antiphon suggested to accompany this gesture
refers to love and service: "Where charity and love are found,
there is God." Presenting bread and wine for transformation is
paralleled by presenting gifts for the poor in order to demonstrate in sign (and hopefully in reality) the commitment involved
in being a member of the body of Christ. To share in the liturgy
of Holy Thursday means to share in the life and love of Christ in
cultic worship and in Christian service.

Accepting the challenge of what it really means to be a
member of the Church which shares in the eucharistic meal
involves seizing the towel of service to wash the feet of our
brothers and sisters. This means taking seriously the "brothers
and sisters" who gather for worship as well as all who comprise
the family of humankind. No one of us lives in isolation and no
one of us celebrates liturgy in isolation. What makes us more

than a group of individuals, in fact, what makes us members of each other, is our share in the life of Christ in the community of the Church. As one of the Fathers of the Church asked, "If we live in isolation, whose feet will we wash?" We can continue by asking: If we live in isolation, whose burdens will we help bear, or whose crosses will we help carry, or whose brother, or sister, or keeper will we be?

What is proclaimed in word and deed on Holy Thursday is the washing of the feet. And this central part of the Holy Thursday liturgy should be an essential part of every Eucharist we celebrate. Along with blessed bread and shared cups of wine at the Eucharist there is the towel and basin of service. Sharing in the bread of life and sharing lives of service are joined in the liturgy to remind us of what the body of Christ and common worship is all about.

Reconciliation and Unity in Christ—The New Testament reading proclaimed on Holy Thursday evening is from the First Letter to the Corinthians (1 Cor 11:23–26). It concerns the tradition of the Last Supper of Jesus with his disciples and the continuation of the Lord's presence with his Church: "Every time, then, you eat this bread and drink this cup, you proclaim the death of the Lord until he comes" (v 26). Yet what is most helpful in interpreting this reading is to situate it in the context of the verses which precede and follow it in 1 Corinthians (vv 17–34). This section of the Letter speaks about the conduct which the Corinthians were not observing and which should mark those who celebrate Eucharist. Paul is very direct in pointing to the Corinthians' lack of charity and unity, precisely when they would gather for Eucharist. The sign of the Eucharist as the "bread of life" and our "spiritual drink" is to be an enduring sign of unity and reconciliation in Christ.[34]

In most primitive witnesses to the evolution of Holy Thursday it is clear that this day was seen to end the fast of Lent and begin the preparation for initiation at the Easter Vigil. For those who had committed serious sin, Lent (or an even longer period) was a time for doing public penance, and the solemn reconciliation of these penitents was performed on Holy Thursday morning. Just as those to be initiated were to share in the Eucharist for the first time on Holy Saturday night, so those who had sinned seriously were welcomed back to the community on Thursday in order to share in the paschal Communion on Holy Saturday night. (While it was the custom at Rome to reconcile penitents on Thursday, it was done on Good Friday at Milan, evidence that the orientation was to the sharing of Eucharist at the Vigil.) The ceremony of reconciling penitents occurred at Rome through the tenth century. Yet, there are references to reconciliation and unity still apparent in the liturgy for Lent, and some remain in our liturgy today. The Gospel for Friday of the First Week in Lent states: "So, if you are offering your gift at the altar, and there remember that your brother has something against you, leave your gift there before the altar and go first be reconciled to your brother, and then come and offer your gift" (Mt 5:23–24).

Hence, the second reading on Holy Thursday evening takes on greater significance as a link with the Church practice of reconciling penitents and proclaiming the unity in Christ which should characterize the Christian community. There is a fundamental unity and equality in the Church and it is celebrated in Eucharist—our equality in Christ and its basis is baptism. The only dignity, identity and status that Christians can ever lay claim to is the status which comes from being brothers and sisters in baptism. Such a fundamental equality and unity means that we live in such a way that we lord it over no one and see everyone as equals in Christ. All distinctions pass away, for in Christ there is no longer male–female, Jew–Greek, have–have not, instructor–student, pastor–parishioner, guru–disciple. There is one Lord, Jesus the Christ, and our identity comes sharing in the eucharistic bread we break and the community of the body of Christ which we are. In the eucharistic prayer we pray: "See the Victim whose death has reconciled us to yourself. Grant that we who are nourished by his body and blood may be filled with his Holy Spirit and become one body, one spirit in Christ" (Eucharistic Prayer III).

The meaning of such texts is clear. There can be no sacrifice, no sacrament, no liturgy where there is quarreling, suspicion or lack of love. The only acceptable sacrifice is Christ's death and resurrection and we are worthy of offering it when and if we are in harmony with each other in him. At the liturgy we offer each other a sign of the peace of Christ in order to demonstrate our common life with each other because of his life and his enduring love. And that is the source of our unity—that he has called us to himself and made us his sons and daughters in baptism. It is at the Eucharist that this status as fellow believers in the community of the Church is confirmed and made real again. The history of reconciliation on Holy Thursday and the text of 1 Corinthians are significant as they remind us of who we are as members of the body of Christ.

In Memory and Hope—The essence of the Eucharist is remembering, and in remembering to be in the presence of the living Lord.[35] Such is the burden of the first reading for the Holy Thursday evening liturgy taken from the Book of Exodus (12:1–8, 11–14), for it tells the people of Israel how to share in later generations what was accomplished for their forefathers in the Passover event. Just as their forefathers were saved by God's intervention, so later generations were saved by recounting these saving events and by joining in this annual solemn "memorial" of the past deeds of redemption.

The Old Testament ritual called for the use of the blood of lambs slain at this commemoration. It is no surprise, then, that the Christian usage of this Old Testament text emphasizes Christ as the Lamb of God who takes away the sins of the world. As there was one Old Testament Passover, the Lamb slain for our redemption, Christ, is the one perfect New Testament sacrifice. What we Christians do at Eucharist is to recall, remember and make a memorial of the saving events by which Christ has redeemed us from sin and death. On Holy Thursday we pray: "Lord,/make us worthy to celebrate these mysteries./Each time we offer this memorial sacrifice/the work of our redemption is accomplished" (Prayer Over The Gifts).

And yet there is an essential aspect of "memorial" that should not be forgotten. Every celebration in the present of Christ's past deeds of dying and rising is also the means of looking beyond past and present to the future. We long for and pray for the day "when sacraments will cease," when all sacraments, all present liturgy, all contemporary remembrances long to be fulfilled and completed in the kingdom of heaven. On Holy Thursday we pray: "Almighty God,/we receive new life/ from the supper your Son gave us in this world./May we find full contentment/in the meal we hope to share/in your eternal kingdom" (Prayer After Communion).

Because the Church is the community of those who share in the reality of the Eucharist, who share the redemption of Christ in memory and hope, it must necessarily become a community that proclaims redemption for all the world and not just for itself. The sacrifice of Christ is the blood of the new and the everlasting covenant, shed for all for the forgiveness of sins. All liturgy is for the building up of the community of the Church. The reality of the Eucharist is for the forging of real bonds of unity and peace in this world. But this is done in order that the Church be and continually become what it is supposed to be: the community of those who witness in this day and age to the enduring power of Christ's life and love in the world.

The spirituality inherent in the Eucharist of Holy Thursday clearly involves service, reconciliation, and witness. But this outward orientation must necessarily go beyond the boundaries of even a pilgrim model of Church. It must be for the witnessing in the world of what Christ came to accomplish in giving his life as a ransom for all. On Holy Thursday we wash each other's feet and collect gifts for the poor to show that sharing in Eucharist means sharing in the ordinariness of life when solemn ceremonies have ended. On Holy Thursday we are reminded of the fundamental unity and equality we share in Christ and the task that is continually before us to share that status with each other in him. We "remember" the one saving event of Christ's death in order that we may share in this sacrifice in the present and witness to the reality of this redemption until we are called from this life to the kingdom of heaven.

To say "amen" to the eucharistic bread is to say "amen" to the reality of unity in Christ. To say "amen" to the eucharistic "body of Christ" is to say "amen" to the poorest of the poor and to share with them the richness of God's mercy in Christ. To say "amen" to the prayers, gestures and ceremonies of Holy Thursday is to say "amen" to the understanding that worship and service, liturgy and mission, Church ritual and the reconciliation of all peoples are intrinsically connected and can never be separated. This is the liturgy and spirituality of Holy Thursday. It is the theology of Eucharist and Church that is as old as St. Paul's First Letter to the Corinthians and which is as new as the revised rituals for Holy Week. In the words of Augustine: "It is to what you are that you reply 'Amen.' Be a member of the body of Christ, and let your 'Amen' be true."

To engage in acts of Christian worship requires a correlative engagement in responding to worship in witness and mission. A major contribution of the present revision of the liturgy is that this component is emphasized in the rites themselves. That liturgy relates to other, social dimensions of life and to the living of the justice of God by sharing in the mission of Christ is clear. Yet, as is the case for all spirituality, the task remains to see to what extent we live what we celebrate. The setting for this life relation is the stuff of our very human lives and the very world in which we live. But for the Christian, what is celebrated in liturgy and what is to be realized in our world itself will be incomplete and unfinished until the kingdom comes in its fullness in Christ's second coming.[36] In the meantime, it is the Church's prayer, the liturgy, which helps orient our lives—both prayer and mission—around the paschal mystery of Christ whose mission it was to inaugurate the realization of the kingdom of God on this earth. It is for the full realization of the kingdom that we pray at liturgy and serve in our response to communal prayer in mission.

> In that new world where the fullness of your peace will be
>   revealed,
> gather people of every race, language, and way of life

to share in the one eternal banquet
with Jesus Christ the Lord.
                    (Eucharistic Prayer for Masses of Reconciliation II)

Through him,
with him,
in him,
in the unity of the Holy Spirit,
all glory and honor is yours,
almighty Father,
for ever and ever.
℟. Amen.

NOTES

Chapter Twelve

1. Louis Bouyer, *Liturgical Piety*, pp. 59–60.

2. J. Bryan Hehir, "Foreword," in *Liturgy and Social Justice*, pp. 9–10.

3. See Part Three, Chapter Eleven, section on "Liturgical and Personal Prayer."

4. See Part One, Chapter Three "Human Life and Christian Worship."

5. See "Considerations on the Active Role of the Person in the Sacramental Event," pp. 162ff.

6. See Part Three, Chapter Eleven, section on "Liturgical and Personal Prayer."

7. Mark Searle argues persuasively that the justice hoped for in this world is God's justice, not ours. Liturgy celebrates this reality. "The two—justice toward God and justice toward one's fellows—are inseparable, and both reached their consummation in the death and resurrection of Jesus": from "Serving the Lord With Justice," in *Liturgy and Social Justice*, p. 23.

8. Nathan Mitchell, *Cult and Controversy*, p. 320.

9. That these concerns were also reflected in the 1981 Congress of Lourdes is evident in the essays by Helder Camara, Dermot Lane and Eugene Laverdiere (among others). See Sean Swayne, ed., *Eucharist for a Hungry World*, A Selection of Homilies, Addresses and Confer-

ences from the 42nd International Eucharistic Congress, Lourdes, 1981 (Carlow: Irish Institute of Pastoral Liturgy, 1981).

10. See, Part Three, Chapter Eleven, section on "Liturgy and the Spiritual Life," as well as *RCIA* 19, 2 and the *Decree on the Missions* no. 10.

11. *RCIA* no. 19, 4 and the *Decree on the Missions,* no. 14. See Part Three, Chapter Eleven, section on "The Dynamic of Liturgy."

12. *General Instruction, Rite of Penance,* no. 4.

13. The quotations here are from Paul VI, *Paenitemini* and *Indulgentiarum doctrina.*

14. Godfrey Diekmann, "The New Rite of Penance: A Theological Evaluation," in N. Mitchell, ed., *The Rite of Penance: Commentaries. Background and Directions,* pp. 88–89.

15. See G. Diekmann, "Reconciliation Through the Prayer of the Community," in N. Mitchell, ed., *The Rite of Penance,* pp. 40–42.

16. *General Instruction, Rite of Penance,* no. 25.

17. Penitential Celebration for Lent, as found in *Rite of Penance,* Appendix, no. 17.

18. See Part One, Chapter Two, "Liturgy: Communal Response to God."

19. M. Searle comments: "The Kingdom of God is certainly present among us, but it is not to be identified with any particular form of the social order or with any given political system" (in "Serving the Lord with Justice," p. 23).

20. Regis Duffy, *Real Presence.* Worship, Sacraments, and Commitment (San Francisco: Harper and Row, 1982) p. xii.

21. *Ibid.,* p. xiii.

22. See above about the anti-cultic critique within the liturgy itself, Part Three, Chapter Eleven, section on "Liturgy and the Spiritual Life."

23. Edward J. Kilmartin, "The Sacrifice of Thanksgiving and Social Justice," in *Liturgy and Social Justice,* p. 70.

24. *Ibid.,* pp. 70–71. Some have observed that this position, if taken very strictly, would ignore the real needs of local communities to finance important programs of education and outreach which may not immediately affect the poor. While such a critique is valid to an extent, Kilmartin himself is clear in stating what should be the primary orientation. Clearly, this observation offers an important critique to the business-as-usual collection basket passing at Sunday worship.

25. On the defects of viewing the liturgical year chronologically or historically, see Part Two, Chapter Eight, sections on "Liturgical Time"

and "One Mystery of Christ."

26. See *Lectionary For Mass, Introduction,* nos. 93–94, p. 36.

27. See, among others, the important work of Francis X. Meehan, *A Contemporary Social Spirituality* (Maryknoll: Orbis Books, 1982) especially pp. 39–46.

28. See the aid for educators published by Catholic Relief Services, *Prayer and the Struggle Against World Hunger* (Green Bay: Alt Publishers, n.d.). The lesson plans presented here reflect the progress of liturgical seasons. In addition the second part of the booklet offers essays by E. Russell Naughton, Francis X. Meehan, Paul Bernier, and Edward Brady about Eucharist and justice issues.

29. See Part One, Chapter Three, section on "Liturgy and Life," and Part Two, Chapter Eight, "The Incarnation Celebrations."

30. Maria Boulding, *The Coming of God* (London: SPCK, 1982) pp. 184–185.

31. See Part One, Chapter Two, section on "The New Covenant" on the notion of liturgy (and life) as a response to God's call.

32. Much of this is from a larger article by the author, "Ecclesiology as Expressed in Eucharistic Celebration," *New Catholic World* 224 (July/August 1981) 165–168.

33. St. Augustine observes: "Would you understand the body of Christ? Hear the apostle saying to the faithful: 'You are the body and members of Christ.' If, then, you are Christ's body and his members, it is your own mystery which is placed on the Lord's table; it is your own mystery which you receive. It is to what you are that you reply 'Amen.' Be a member of the body of Christ, and let your 'Amen' be true" (Sermon 272).

34. See Part Three, Chapter Eleven, section on "Liturgy and the Spiritual Life."

35. See Part Two, Chapter Six: "Participation in Memory and Hope."

36. *Constitution on the Sacred Liturgy,* no. 8: "In the earthly liturgy, by way of foretaste, we share in that heavenly liturgy which is celebrated in the holy city of Jerusalem toward which we journey as pilgrims, and in which Christ is sitting at the right hand of God, a minister of the sanctuary and of the true tabernacle (cf. Apoc 21:2; Col 3:1; Heb 8:2); we sing a hymn to the Lord's glory with all the warriors of the heavenly army; venerating the memory of the saints, we hope for some part and fellowship with them; we eagerly await the Savior, our Lord Jesus Christ, until he, our life, shall appear and we too will appear with him in glory (cf. Phil 3:20; Col 3:4)."

BIBLIOGRAPHY

Adam, Adolf. *The Liturgical Year.* Its History and Its Meaning After the Reform of the Liturgy. Trans. Matthew O'Connell. New York: Pueblo Publishing Co., 1982.

Bouyer, Louis. *Introduction to Spirituality.* Trans. Mary Perkins Ryan. Collegeville: The Liturgical Press, 1960, pp. 1–55.

———. "Jewish-Christian Liturgies," in Lancelot Sheppard, ed. *True Worship.* Baltimore: Helicon Press, 1963, pp. 29–44.

———. *Liturgical Piety.* Notre Dame: University of Notre Dame Press, 1955, pp. 1–22, 38–56, 243–256.

———. *The Spirituality of the New Testament and the Fathers.* New York: Desclee, 1963.

Boyd, Rena. "The Prayer of the Community," *The Way* 10 (July 1970) 220–229.

Braso, Gabriel. *Liturgy and Spirituality.* Trans. Leonard J. Doyle. Collegeville: The Liturgical Press, 1960, pp. 3–55.

Casel, Odo. *The Mystery of Christian Worship.* Edited by Burkhard Neunheuser. Westminster: Newman Press, 1962, pp. 63–70, 71–93, 97–165.

Chupungco, Anscar. *Cultural Adaptation of the Liturgy.* New York/Ramsey: Paulist Press, 1982.

Collins, Mary. "Spirituality for a Lifetime," *Spirituality Today* 34 (March 1982) pp. 60–69.

Crichton, J. D. "An Historical Sketch of the Roman Liturgy," in *True Worship,* pp. 45–82.

Davies, J. G. *Worship and Mission.* New York: Association Press, 1967.

Dix, Gregory. *The Shape of the Liturgy.* London: Dacre Press, 1945, pp. 303–396.

Duffy, Regis. *Real Presence.* Worship, Sacraments, and Commitment. San Francisco: Harper and Row, 1982.

Duggan, Robert D. "Liturgical Spirituality and Liturgical Reform," *Spiritual Life* 27 (Spring 1981) 46–53.

Dupont, Jacques. "Jesus and Liturgical Prayer," *Worship* 43 (April 1969) 198–213.

Duquoc, Christian, "Theology and Spirituality," in *Concilium 19*. Trans. J. B. Foster, New York: Paulist Press, 1966, pp. 89–99.

Eisenhofer, L., and Lechner, J. *The Liturgy of the Roman Rite*. Trans. A. J. and E. F. Peeler. New York: Herder and Herder, 1961, pp. 166–176.

Eliade, Mircea. *Cosmos and History*. The Myth of the Eternal Return. New York: Harper Torchbooks, 1959.

————. *Patterns in Comparative Religion*. New York: Meridian, 1963.

————. *The Sacred and the Profane*. New York: Harper Torchbooks, 1961.

Empereur, James. "Liturgy and Spirituality," in Malcolm C. Burson, ed., *Worship Points the Way*. New York: Seabury, 1981, pp. 167–180.

Fink, Peter E. "Liturgical Prayer and Spiritual Growth," *Worship* 55 (September 1981) 386–398.

Gelineau, Joseph. *The Liturgy Today and Tomorrow*. Trans. David Livingstone. New York/Ramsey: Paulist Press. 1978.

General Norms on the Liturgical Year.

Hatchett, Marian. *Sanctifying Life, Time and Space*. New York: Seabury Press, 1976.

Hebert, Gabriel. "Worship in the Old Testament," *True Worship*, pp. 14–28.

Holleran, Warren, "Christ's Prayer and Christian Prayer," *Worship* 48 (March 1974) 171–182.

Holmes, Urban T. *A History of Christian Spirituality. An Analytical Introduction*. New York: Seabury Press, 1980.

————. "A Taxonomy of Contemporary Spirituality," in John Gallen, ed., *Christians at Prayer*. Notre Dame: University of Notre Dame Press, 1977, pp. 26–45.

Jungmann, Joseph A. *Christian Prayer Through The Centuries*. Trans. John Coyne. New York/Ramsey: Paulist Press, 1978.

Kavanagh, Aidan, "The Tradition of Judaeo-Christian Worship: Our Debt to Each Other," in Philip Scharper, ed., *Torah and Gospel*. Jewish and Christian Theology in Dialogue. New York: Sheed and Ward, 1966, pp. 47–59.

Larkin, E. E. "Christian Spirituality," *New Catholic Encyclopedia*. Vol. 13. New York: McGraw-Hill, 1967, pp. 598–602.

Leclerq, Jean. *The Love of Learning and the Desire for God*. Trans. Catherine Misrah. New York: Fordham University Press, 1961, pp. 287–308.

———— *Et al. The Spirituality of the Middle Ages.* New York: Seabury 1961.

Leech, Kenneth. *Soul Friend.* A Study of Spirituality. London: Sheldon Press, 1977, pp. 137–167.

Macquarrie, John., *Paths in Spirituality.* New York: Harper and Row, 1972, pp. 10–24.

Maloney, George A., "Prayer and Eastern Christian Spirituality," in *Christians at Prayer,* pp. 100–112.

Mitchell, Nathan, "Useless Prayer," in *Christians At Prayer,* pp. 1–25.

————. "The Spirituality of Christian Worship," *Spirituality Today* 34 (March 1982) 1–18.

Neuman, Matthias. "The Religious Structure of a Spirituality," *American Benedictine Review* 32 (June 1982) 115–148.

Nocent, Adrien. *The Liturgical Year.* Four Volumes. Trans. Matthew O'Connell. Collegeville: Liturgical Press, 1977.

Rahner, Karl. "Dogmatic Notes on 'Ecclesiological Piety,'" *Theological Investigations,* Vol. 4. Baltimore: Helicon Press, 1966. pp. 336–365.

————. "Personal and Sacramental Piety," *Theological Investigations,* Vol. 2, pp. 109–133.

————. "Some Theses on Prayer 'In the Name of the Church'." *Theological Investigations,* Vol. 5, pp. 419–438.

————. "Considerations on the Active Role of the Person in the Sacramental Event," in *Theological Investigations,* XIV, trans. David Bourke. New York: Seabury Press, 1976, pp. 161–184.

————. "The Presence of the Lord in Christian Community at Worship," in *Theological Investigations* X. New York: Herder and Herder, 1973, pp. 71–83.

Searle, Mark, ed. *Liturgy and Social Justice.* Collegeville: Liturgical Press, 1981.

Sheets, J. R. "Personal and Liturgical Prayer," *Worship* 47 (August–September 1973) pp. 405–416.

Skudlarek, William, ed. *The Continuing Quest For God.* Monastic Spirituality in Tradition and Transition. Collegeville: The Liturgical Press, 1982.

Stanley, David. *Faith and Religious Life.* New York/Ramsey: Paulist Press, 1971, pp. 31–55.

Steere, Douglas V. "Solitude and Prayer," *Worship* 55 (March 1981) pp. 120–136.

Stevick, Daniel. "Toward a Phenomenology of Praise," in *Worship*

Points the Way, pp. 151–166.

Sudbrack, Josef. "Spirituality I" *Sacramentum Mundi*, Vol. VI. New York: Herder and Herder, 1970, pp. 148–153.

Swayne, Sean. *Eucharist for a New World.* 42nd International Eucharistic Congress, Lourdes, 1981. Carlow: Irish Institute of Pastoral Liturgy, 1981.

Text of the Roman Calendar.

The Times of Celebration. Concilium 142. New York: Seabury Press, 1981.

Truitt, Gordon E. "Liturgy as a School of Prayer: A Question," *Spiritual Life* 27 (Spring 1981) pp. 3–13.

Vagaggini, Cipriano. *Theological Dimensions of the Liturgy.* Trans. Leonard J. Doyle and W. A. Jurgens. Collegeville: Liturgical Press, 1976, pp. 647–739.

Vandebroucke, Francois, "Spirituality and Spiritualities." Trans. Kathryn Sullivan. *Concilium 9.* New York: Paulist Press, 1965, pp. 45–60.

Van Doren, R. "Liturgical Year in the Roman Rite," *New Catholic Encyclopedia, Vol. 8.* New York: McGraw-Hill, 1967, pp. 915–919. See also Charles Gusmer, "Liturgical Year in the Roman Rite," in *Supplement to the New Catholic Encyclopedia,* pp. 259–260.

Vatican II, *Constitution on the Sacred Liturgy.*

Von Balthasar, Hans Urs, "The Gospel as Norm and Test of All Spirituality," trans. Theodore Westow, in *Spirituality in Church and World, Concilium Vol. 9.* New York; Paulist Press, 1965, pp. 7–23.

"Word of God," in Daniel Rees, *et al. Consider Your Call.* A Theology of Monastic Life Today. London: SPCK, 1978.